CASENOTE® Legal Briefs®

REMEDIES

Keyed to Courses Using

Laycock and Hasen's
Modern American Remedies: Cases and Materials
Sixth Edition and Concise Sixth Edition

Authored by: Publisher's Editorial Staff

ASPEN PUBLISHING

To contact Customer Service, e-mail customer.service@aspenpublishing.com, call 1-800-950-5259, or mail correspondence to:

Aspen Publishing
Attn: Order Department
1 Wall Street
Burlington, MA 01803

1 2 3 4 5 6 7 8 9 0

ISBN 979-8-8861-4359-1

ABOUT ASPEN PUBLISHING

Aspen Publishing is a leading provider of legal education content and digital learning solutions in the United States and globally. Our innovative products and platforms—designed based on best practices in learning science—engage students and enhance outcomes. From textbooks and audiobooks authored by renowned experts to digital platforms and products like LEAF, Connected eBooks, Connected Quizzing, PracticePerfect, and JD-Next, we empower the next generation of legal professionals with innovative, trusted, and accessible resources.

The Aspen Casebook Series, affectionately known as the "red and black" casebooks among law faculty and students, includes hundreds of highly regarded textbooks across more than 80 disciplines. These range from foundational courses like Torts and Contracts to emerging electives such as Sustainability and the Law of Policing. Our study aids, including the popular *Examples & Explanations* series, help law students master complex topics with clarity and confidence.

Aspen's expertise extends to undergraduate education with our Paralegal, Criminal Justice, and Business Law series, offering the same hallmark quality to a broader audience. JD-Next, our groundbreaking online law school prep course and admissions test, provides a realistic preview of law school, equips students with essential skills for academic success, and evaluates their readiness for legal studies.

Aspen Publishing Is Proud to Be a UWorld Company

Since 2003, UWorld has been a global leader in developing high-quality learning tools for students preparing for high-stakes exams. With a commitment to excellence, UWorld has helped millions of students in undergraduate, graduate, and professional programs in fields such as medicine, nursing, finance, and law achieve their academic and career goals.

Founded by Chandra S. Pemmasani, M.D., during his medical residency, UWorld began focusing on medical education and has since expanded into various academic fields, including law. In 2020, UWorld launched its Legal vertical, starting with its comprehensive Multistate Bar Exam (MBE®) Question Bank, followed by the acquisition of Themis Bar Review, which integrated resources to provide a complete bar exam preparation experience. In 2024, UWorld expanded its offerings by acquiring Aspen Publishing, enhancing its suite of legal education products.

Today, UWorld offers an unparalleled range of study materials that blend active learning methods with expert content, ensuring students and educators can access the most effective resources. From bar preparation to law school success, UWorld is committed to supporting the next generation of legal professionals. Learn more at uworld.com.

Format for the Casenote® Legal Brief

Nature of Case: This section identifies the form of action (e.g., breach of contract, negligence, battery), the type of proceeding (e.g., demurrer, appeal from trial court's jury instructions) or the relief sought (e.g., damages, injunction, criminal sanctions).

Palsgraf v. Long Island R.R. Co.

Injured bystander (P) v. Railroad company (D)

N.Y. Ct. App., 248 N.Y. 339, 162 N.E. 99 (1928).

NATURE OF CASE: **Appeal from judgment affirming verdict for plaintiff seeking damages for personal injury.**

FACT SUMMARY: **Helen Palsgraf (P) was injured on R.R.'s (D) train platform when R.R.'s (D) guard helped a passenger aboard a moving train, causing his package to fall on the tracks. The package contained fireworks which exploded, creating a shock that tipped a scale onto Palsgraf (P).**

RULE OF LAW

The risk reasonably to be perceived defines the duty to be obeyed.

FACTS: Helen Palsgraf (P) purchased a ticket to Rockaway Beach from R.R. (D) and was waiting on the train platform. As she waited, two men ran to catch a train that was pulling out from the platform. The first man jumped aboard, but the second man, who appeared as if he might fall, was helped aboard by the guard on the train who had kept the door open so they could jump aboard. A guard on the platform also helped by pushing him onto the train. The man was carrying a package wrapped in newspaper. In the process, the man dropped his package, which fell on the tracks. The package contained fireworks and exploded. The shock of the explosion was apparently of great enough strength to tip over some scales at the other end of the platform, which fell on Palsgraf (P) and injured her. A jury awarded her damages, and R.R. (D) appealed.

ISSUE: Does the risk reasonably to be perceived define the duty to be obeyed?

HOLDING AND DECISION: (Cardozo, C.J.) Yes. The risk reasonably to be perceived defines the duty to be obeyed. If there is no foreseeable hazard to the injured party as the result of a seemingly innocent act, the act does not become a tort because it happened to be a wrong as to another. If the wrong was not willful, the plaintiff must show that the act as to her had such great and apparent possibilities of danger as to entitle her to protection. Negligence in the abstract is not enough upon which to base liability. Negligence is a relative concept, evolving out of the common law doctrine of trespass on the case. To establish liability, the defendant must owe a legal duty of reasonable care to the injured party. A cause of action in tort will lie where harm, though unintended, could have been averted or avoided by observance of such a duty. The scope of the duty is limited by the range of danger that a reasonable person could foresee. In this case, there was nothing to suggest from the appearance of the parcel or otherwise that the parcel contained fireworks. The guard could not reasonably have had any warning of a threat to Palsgraf (P), and R.R. (D) therefore cannot be held liable. Judgment is reversed in favor of R.R. (D).

DISSENT: (Andrews, J.) The concept that there is no negligence unless R.R. (D) owes a legal duty to take care as to Palsgraf (P) herself is too narrow. Everyone owes to the world at large the duty of refraining from those acts that may unreasonably threaten the safety of others. If the guard's action was negligent as to those nearby, it was also negligent as to those outside what might be termed the "danger zone." For Palsgraf (P) to recover, R.R.'s (D) negligence must have been the proximate cause of her injury, a question of fact for the jury.

ANALYSIS

The majority defined the limit of the defendant's liability in terms of the danger that a reasonable person in defendant's situation would have perceived. The dissent argued that the limitation should not be placed on liability, but rather on damages. Judge Andrews suggested that only injuries that would not have happened but for R.R.'s (D) negligence should be compensable. Both the majority and dissent recognized the policy-driven need to limit liability for negligent acts, seeking, in the words of Judge Andrews, to define a framework "that will be practical and in keeping with the general understanding of mankind." The Restatement (Second) of Torts has accepted Judge Cardozo's view.

Quicknotes

FORESEEABILITY A reasonable expectation that change is the probable result of certain acts or omissions.

NEGLIGENCE Conduct falling below the standard of care that a reasonable person would demonstrate under similar conditions.

PROXIMATE CAUSE The natural sequence of events without which an injury would not have been sustained.

Party ID: Quick identification of the relationship between the parties.

Fact Summary: This is included to refresh your memory and can be used as a quick reminder of the facts.

Rule of Law: Summarizes the general principle of law that the case illustrates. It may be used for instant recall of the court's holding and for classroom discussion or home review.

Facts: This section contains all relevant facts of the case, including the contentions of the parties and the lower court holdings. It is written in a logical order to give you a clear understanding of the case. The plaintiff and defendant are identified by their proper names throughout and are always labeled with a (P) or (D).

Issue: The issue is a concise question that brings out the essence of the opinion as it relates to the section of the casebook in which the case appears. Both substantive and procedural issues are included if relevant to the decision.

Concurrence/Dissent: All concurrences and dissents are briefed whenever they are included by the casebook author.

Analysis: This last paragraph gives you a broad understanding of where the case "fits in" with other cases in the section of the book and with the entire course. It is a hornbook-style discussion indicating whether the case is a majority or minority opinion and comparing the principal case with other cases in the casebook. It may also provide analysis from restatements, uniform codes, and law review articles.

Holding and Decision: This section offers a clear and in-depth discussion of the rule of the case and the court's rationale. It is written in easy-to-understand language and answers the issue presented by applying the law to the facts of the case. When relevant, it includes a thorough discussion of the exceptions to the case as listed by the court, any major cites to the other cases on point, and the names of the judges who wrote the decisions.

Quicknotes: Conveniently defines legal terms found in the case.

Note to Students

Aspen Publishing is proud to offer *Casenote® Legal Briefs*—continuing thirty years of publishing America's best-selling legal briefs.

Casenote® Legal Briefs are designed to help you save time when briefing assigned cases. Organized under convenient headings, they show you how to abstract the basic facts and holdings from the text of the actual opinions handed down by the courts. Used as part of a rigorous study regimen, they can help you spend more time analyzing and critiquing points of law than on copying bits and pieces of judicial opinions into your notebook or outline.

Casenote® Legal Briefs should never be used as a substitute for assigned casebook readings. They work best when read as a follow-up to reviewing the underlying opinions themselves. Students who try to avoid reading and digesting the judicial opinions in their casebooks or online sources will end up shortchanging themselves in the long run. The ability to absorb, critique, and restate the dynamic and complex elements of case law decisions is crucial to your success in law school and beyond. It cannot be developed vicariously.

In addition to *Casenote® Legal Briefs*, Aspen Publishing offers the following study aids:

- *Casenote® Legal Briefs*
- *Emanuel Law Outlines®*
- Emanuel® *Law in a Flash Flash Cards*
- Emanuel *CrunchTime® Series*

Each of these series is designed to provide you with easy-to-understand explanations of complex points of law. Each volume offers guidance on the principles of legal analysis and, consulted regularly, will hone your ability to spot relevant issues. We have titles that will help you prepare for class, prepare for your exams, and enhance your general comprehension of the law along the way.

To find out more about our law school tools for success, visit us at *www.AspenPublishing.com* or e-mail us at *customer.service@aspenpublishing.com*. We'll be happy to assist you.

How to Brief a Case

A. Decide on a Format and Stick to It

Structure is essential to a good brief. It enables you to arrange systematically the related parts that are scattered throughout most cases, thus making manageable and understandable what might otherwise seem to be an endless and unfathomable sea of information. There are, of course, an unlimited number of formats that can be utilized. However, it is best to find one that suits your needs and stick to it. Consistency breeds both efficiency and the security that when called upon you will know where to look in your brief for the information you are asked to give.

Any format, as long as it presents the essential elements of a case in an organized fashion, can be used. Experience, however, has led *Casenote® Legal Briefs* to develop and utilize the following format because of its logical flow and universal applicability.

NATURE OF CASE: This is a brief statement of the legal character and procedural status of the case (e.g., "Appeal of a burglary conviction").

There are many different alternatives open to a litigant dissatisfied with a court ruling. The key to determining which one has been used is to discover *who is asking this court for what.*

This first entry in the brief should be kept as *short as possible.* Use the court's terminology if you understand it. But since jurisdictions vary as to the titles of pleadings, the best entry is the one that addresses who wants what in this proceeding, not the one that sounds most like the court's language.

RULE OF LAW: A statement of the general principle of law that the case illustrates (e.g., "An acceptance that varies any term of the offer is considered a rejection and counteroffer").

Determining the rule of law of a case is a procedure similar to determining the issue of the case. Avoid being fooled by red herrings; there may be a few rules of law mentioned in the case excerpt, but usually only one is *the* rule with which the casebook editor is concerned. The techniques used to locate the issue, described below, may also be utilized to find the rule of law. Generally, your best guide is simply the chapter heading. It is a clue to the point the casebook editor seeks to make and should be kept in mind when reading every case in the respective section.

FACTS: A synopsis of only the essential facts of the case, i.e., those bearing upon or leading up to the issue.

The facts entry should be a short statement of the events and transactions that led one party to initiate legal proceedings against another in the first place. While some cases conveniently state the salient facts at the beginning of the decision, in other instances they will have to be culled from hiding places throughout the text, even from concurring and dissenting opinions. Some of the "facts" will often be in dispute and should be so noted. Conflicting evidence may be briefly pointed up. "Hard" facts must be included. Both must be *relevant* in order to be listed in the facts entry. It is impossible to tell what is relevant until the entire case is read, as the ultimate determination of the rights and liabilities of the parties may turn on something buried deep in the opinion.

Generally, the facts entry should not be longer than three to five *short* sentences.

It is often helpful to identify the role played by a party in a given context. For example, in a construction contract case the identification of a party as the "contractor" or "builder" alleviates the need to tell that that party was the one who was supposed to have built the house.

It is always helpful, and a good general practice, to identify the "plaintiff" and the "defendant." This may seem elementary and uncomplicated, but, especially in view of the creative editing practiced by some casebook editors, it is sometimes a difficult or even impossible task. Bear in mind that the *party presently* seeking something from this court may not be the plaintiff, and that sometimes only the cross-claim of a defendant is treated in the excerpt. Confusing or misaligning the parties can ruin your analysis and understanding of the case.

ISSUE: A statement of the general legal question answered by or illustrated in the case. For clarity, the issue is best put in the form of a question capable of a "yes" or "no" answer. In reality, the issue is simply the Rule of Law put in the form of a question (e.g., "May an offer be accepted by performance?").

The major problem presented in discerning what is *the* issue in the case is that an opinion usually purports to raise and answer several questions. However, except for rare cases, only one such question is really the issue in the case. Collateral issues not necessary to the resolution of the matter in controversy are handled by the court by language known as *"obiter dictum"* or merely *"dictum."* While dicta may be included later in the brief, they have no place under the issue heading.

To find the issue, ask *who wants what* and then go on to ask *why did that party succeed or fail in getting it.* Once this is determined, the "why" should be turned into a question.

The complexity of the issues in the cases will vary, but in all cases a single-sentence question should sum up the issue. *In a few cases,* there will be two, or even more rarely, three issues of equal importance to the resolution of the case. Each should be expressed in a single-sentence question.

Since many issues are resolved by a court in coming to a final disposition of a case, the casebook editor will reproduce the portion of the opinion containing the issue or issues most relevant to the area of law under scrutiny. A noted law professor gave this advice: "Close the book; look at the title on the cover." Chances are, if it is Property, you need not concern yourself with whether, for example, the federal government's treatment of the plaintiff's land really raises a federal question sufficient to support jurisdiction on this ground in federal court.

The same rule applies to chapter headings designating sub-areas within the subjects. They tip you off as to what the text is designed to teach. The cases are arranged in a casebook to show a progression or development of the law, so that the preceding cases may also help.

It is also most important to remember to *read the notes and questions* at the end of a case to determine what the editors wanted you to have gleaned from it.

HOLDING AND DECISION: This section should succinctly explain the rationale of the court in arriving at its decision. In capsulizing the "reasoning" of the court, it should always include an application of the general rule or rules of law to the specific facts of the case. Hidden justifications come to light in this entry: the reasons for the state of the law, the public policies, the biases and prejudices, those considerations that influence the justices' thinking and, ultimately, the outcome of the case. At the end, there should be a short indication of the disposition or procedural resolution of the case (e.g., "Decision of the trial court for Mr. Smith (P) reversed").

The foregoing format is designed to help you "digest" the reams of case material with which you will be faced in your law school career. Once mastered by practice, it will place at your fingertips the information the authors of your casebooks have sought to impart to you in case-by-case illustration and analysis.

B. Be as Economical as Possible in Briefing Cases

Once armed with a format that encourages succinctness, it is as important to be economical with regard to the time spent on the actual reading of the case as it is to be economical in the writing of the brief itself. This does not mean "skimming" a case. Rather, it means reading the case with an "eye" trained to recognize into which "section" of your brief a particular passage or line fits and having a system for quickly and precisely marking the case so that the passages fitting any one particular part of the brief can be easily identified and brought together in a concise and accurate manner when the brief is actually written.

It is of no use to simply repeat everything in the opinion of the court; record only enough information to trigger your recollection of what the court said. Nevertheless, an accurate statement of the "law of the case," i.e., the legal principle applied to the facts, is absolutely essential to class preparation and to learning the law under the case method.

To that end, it is important to develop a "shorthand" that you can use to make marginal notations. These notations will tell you at a glance in which section of the brief you will be placing that particular passage or portion of the opinion.

Some students prefer to underline all the salient portions of the opinion (with a pencil or colored underliner marker), making marginal notations as they go along. Others prefer the color-coded method of underlining, utilizing different colors of markers to underline the salient portions of the case, each separate color being used to represent a different section of the brief. For example, blue underlining could be used for passages relating to the rule of law, yellow for those relating to the issue, and green for those relating to the holding and decision, etc. While it has its advocates, the color-coded method can be confusing and time-consuming (all that time spent on changing colored markers). Furthermore, it can interfere with the continuity and concentration many students deem essential to the reading of a case for maximum comprehension. In the end, however, it is a matter of personal preference and style. Just remember, whatever method you use, underlining must be used sparingly or its value is lost.

If you take the marginal notation route, an efficient and easy method is to go along underlining the key portions of the case and placing in the margin alongside them the following "markers" to indicate where a particular passage or line "belongs" in the brief you will write:

N	(NATURE OF CASE)
RL	(RULE OF LAW)
I	(ISSUE)
HL	(HOLDING AND DECISION, relates to the RULE OF LAW behind the decision)
HR	(HOLDING AND DECISION, gives the RATIONALE or reasoning behind the decision)
HA	(HOLDING AND DECISION, applies the general principle(s) of law to the facts of the case to arrive at the decision)

Remember that a particular passage may well contain information necessary to more than one part of your brief, in which case you simply note that in the margin. If you are using the color-coded underlining method instead of marginal notation, simply make asterisks or checks in the margin next to the passage in question in the colors that indicate the additional sections of the brief where it might be utilized.

The economy of utilizing "shorthand" in marking cases for briefing can be maintained in the actual brief writing process itself by utilizing "law student shorthand" within the brief. There are many commonly used words and phrases for which abbreviations can be substituted in your briefs (and in your class notes also). You can develop abbreviations that are personal to you and which will save you a lot of time. A reference list of briefing abbreviations can be found on page x of this book.

C. Use Both the Briefing Process and the Brief as a Learning Tool

Now that you have a format and the tools for briefing cases efficiently, the most important thing is to make the time spent in briefing profitable to you and to make the most advantageous use of the briefs you create. Of course, the briefs are invaluable for classroom reference when you are called upon to explain or analyze a particular case. However, they are also useful in reviewing for exams. A quick glance at the fact summary should bring the case to mind, and a rereading of the rule of law should enable you to go over the underlying legal concept in your mind, how it was applied in that particular case, and how it might apply in other factual settings.

As to the value to be derived from engaging in the briefing process itself, there is an immediate benefit that arises from being forced to sift through the essential facts and reasoning from the court's opinion and to succinctly express them in your own words in your brief. The process ensures that you understand the case and the point that it illustrates, and that means you will be ready to absorb further analysis and information brought forth in class. It also ensures you will have something to say when called upon in class. The briefing process helps develop a mental agility for getting to the *gist* of a case and for identifying, expounding on, and applying the legal concepts and issues found there. The briefing process is the mental process on which you must rely in taking law school examinations; it is also the mental process upon which lawyers rely in serving their clients and in making a living.

Abbreviations for Briefs

acceptance	acp
affirmed	aff
answer	ans
assumption of risk	a/r
attorney	atty
beyond a reasonable doubt	b/r/d
bona fide purchaser	BFP
breach of contract	br/k
cause of action	c/a
common law	c/l
Constitution	Con
constitutional	con
contract	K
contributory negligence	c/n
cross	x
cross-complaint	x/c
cross-examination	x/ex
cruel and unusual punishment	c/u/p
defendant	D
dismissed	dis
double jeopardy	d/j
due process	d/p
equal protection	e/p
equity	eq
evidence	ev
exclude	exc
exclusionary rule	exc/r
felony	f/n
freedom of speech	f/s
good faith	g/f
habeas corpus	h/c
hearsay	hr
husband	H
injunction	inj
in loco parentis	ILP
inter vivos	I/v
joint tenancy	j/t
judgment	judgt
jurisdiction	jur
last clear chance	LCC
long-arm statute	LAS
majority view	maj
meeting of minds	MOM
minority view	min
Miranda rule	Mir/r
Miranda warnings	Mir/w
negligence	neg
notice	ntc
nuisance	nus
obligation	ob
obscene	obs
offer	O
offeree	OE
offeror	OR
ordinance	ord
pain and suffering	p/s
parol evidence	p/e
plaintiff	P
prima facie	p/f
probable cause	p/c
proximate cause	px/c
real property	r/p
reasonable doubt	r/d
reasonable man	r/m
rebuttable presumption	rb/p
remanded	rem
res ipsa loquitur	RIL
respondeat superior	r/s
Restatement	RS
reversed	rev
Rule Against Perpetuities	RAP
search and seizure	s/s
search warrant	s/w
self-defense	s/d
specific performance	s/p
statute	S
statute of frauds	S/F
statute of limitations	S/L
summary judgment	s/j
tenancy at will	t/w
tenancy in common	t/c
tenant	t
third party	TP
third party beneficiary	TPB
transferred intent	TI
unconscionable	uncon
unconstitutional	unconst
undue influence	u/e
Uniform Commercial Code	UCC
unilateral	uni
vendee	VE
vendor	VR
versus	v
void for vagueness	VFV
weight of authority	w/a
weight of the evidence	w/e
wife	W
with	w/
within	w/i
without	w/o
without prejudice	w/o/p
wrongful death	wr/d

Table of Cases

Note: There are no principal cases in Chapter 1 of the Sixth Edition or the Concise Sixth Edition of the casebook.

CHAPTER 2

Paying for Harm: Compensatory Damages

Quick Reference Rules of Law

CHAPTER 2

United States v. Hatahley

Federal government (D) v. Property owner (P)

257 F.2d 920 (10th Cir. 1958)

NATURE OF CASE: Appeal from award of damages for trespass.

FACT SUMMARY: The Government (D) appealed from the district court's calculation of damages for trespass to Hatahley's (P) and other plaintiffs' property.

RULE OF LAW

An award of damages that compensates for the commission of a tort must be based on the principle that the injured party must be restored to the same position the injured party was in had the tort not been committed.

FACTS: The Government (D) tortiously rounded up and sold farm animals owned by Hatahley (P) and other Indians. The district court determined a set amount of damages for each animal and multiplied that amount by the number of animals lost by each plaintiff. It also arrived at a sum for mental distress and awarded each plaintiff an equal amount. The Government (D) appealed, contending the award was arbitrary and not based on substantial evidence.

ISSUE: Must an award of damages that compensates for the commission of a tort be based on the principle that the injured party must be restored to the same position the injured party was in had the tort not been committed?

HOLDING AND DECISION: (Pickett, J.) Yes. An award of damages that compensates for the commission of a tort must be based on the principle that the injured party must be restored to the same position the injured party was in had the tort not been committed. By making a blanket damage determination, the court failed to consider the damages actually incurred by each plaintiff. Each had different levels of economic damage incurred as each had differently valued animals. Also, each suffered a different level of mental distress. Reversed and remanded.

ANALYSIS

This case illustrates the fundamental remedial goal in tort law. Placing a person in the position they would have been in without the tort is often speculative and always inexact. This is especially true where the damages are based on lost profits or mental distress.

Quicknotes

TORT A legal wrong resulting in a breach of duty by the wrongdoer, causing damages as a result of the breach.

TORT DAMAGES Monetary compensation awarded by the court to a party injured as the result of the tortious act of another.

In re September 11th Litigation

Property owner (P) v. Airlines (D)

590 F. Supp. 2d 535 (S.D.N.Y. 2008)

NATURE OF CASE: Ruling on damages recoverable by the plaintiff.

FACT SUMMARY: After September 11, 2001, the owner of the World Trade Center in New York brought a negligence suit against several airlines and airport security companies.

RULE OF LAW

Recovery for property damage is the lesser of the replacement cost or the diminution of the property's market value.

FACTS: In April 2001, Larry Silverstein and his companies, collectively referred to as WTCP (P), purchased 99-year leases for four of the World Trade Center towers. WTCP (P) paid the New York Port Authority $491 million dollars at the closing in July of 2001 and would also pay rental payments to New York over 99 years. The value of those rental payments at the time of the closing was $2.8 billion dollars. After the events of September 11, 2001, WTCP (P) sued several airlines, security companies, and the operator of Boston's Logan Airport in federal court for negligence on the grounds their alleged actions that morning contributed to the terrorist attacks. WTCP (P) seeks $16 billion in replacement costs. The district court issued this intermediate ruling of law on the amount of damages WTCP (P) could recover in the suit.

ISSUE: Is recovery for property damage the lesser of the replacement cost or the diminution of the property's market value?

HOLDING AND DECISION: (Hellerstein, J.) Yes. Recovery for property damage is the lesser of the replacement cost or the diminution of the property's market value. This is the "lesser of two" rule. The New York Court of Appeals recently reaffirmed the rule in a case involving a private home. In that case, the replacement cost of the damaged home was $1,033,000 while the diminution in the property's market value was $480,000. The court ordered a recovery of $480,000. Here, WTCP (P) argues the World Trade Center was a specialty property, exempt from the "lesser of two" rule. A property qualifies for this exception when it is unique, specially built for a specific purpose, and lacks a readily available resale market. Such properties typically include hospitals and churches. The exception does not apply to the World Trade Center. Just five months prior to the attacks, the Port Authority conducted a worldwide bidding process that resulted in a determinable and verifiable value in the marketplace for the property. If WTCP (P) is entitled to recover at all, the value of the diminution of the market value of the property will fully compensate it. In addition, WTCP (P) had contractual obligation to the Port Authority to "rebuild, restore, repair and replace" the towers. It seeks to recover from the defendants the costs of this contractual obligation. The provisions of WTCP (P) contracts with the Port Authority cannot be passed on to the defendants. WTCP's (P) contract obligations to rebuild the towers were not a foreseeable consequence of the defendants' alleged negligence. Lastly, the defendants requested the court rule that the $2.8 billion value of the towers in July of 2001 be deemed the market value of the property. Because property values fluctuate greatly and sometimes quickly, the parties will be able to offer evidence to determine the value of the property in September of 2001.

ANALYSIS

The "lesser of two" rule applied in New York is not followed in many states. In those that do use it, courts allow exceptions if the application of the rule will undercompensate the plaintiff. Most states now use a more flexible approach, allowing courts to award whatever damages fairly compensate the plaintiff given the particular circumstances of each case.

Quicknotes

FORESEEABILITY OF HARM An inquiry into the relatedness of events that contributed to the plaintiff's injury; whether the harm was foreseeable determines whether the tortfeasor's conduct was the proximate cause of the injury.

MARKET VALUE The price of particular property or goods that a buyer would offer and a seller accept in the open market, following full disclosure.

REPLACEMENT VALUE The monetary amount necessary in order to replace property or improvements.

Trinity Church v. John Hancock Mutual Life Insurance Co.

Local church (P) v. Corporation (D)

Mass. Sup. Jud. Ct., 502 N.E.2d 532 (1987)

NATURE OF CASE: Appeal of an award of damages for injury to property.

FACT SUMMARY: Trinity Church's (P) building was damaged during the construction of the nearby John Hancock (D) building, and it sought damages for the structural harm to the church.

RULE OF LAW

Reasonable costs of reconstruction or replacement are allowed as a measure of damages where the diminution of market value of property cannot be determined.

FACTS: Trinity Church (P) was built in 1876 in Boston. It was constructed almost entirely of stone masonry, which cracks over time and cannot be repaired except by reconstruction. By 1968, the church had experienced settlement of four inches, but because the subsidence was fairly uniform, no structural stress or damage had resulted. During construction of the John Hancock (D) Tower Building next to Trinity Church (P) between 1968 and 1972, the foundation of the church was undermined by a failure of the excavation system at the Hancock (D) site. Trinity Church's (P) foundation settled unevenly and produced cracks that affected the structural integrity of the church. Trinity Church (P) sought compensation for the structural damages and quantified the damages based upon the percentage change in the structure in terms of the church's ultimate "takedown" condition, the point at which reconstruction would be necessary. The jury awarded Trinity Church (P) $3.6 million for the structural damage, and John Hancock (D) appealed.

ISSUE: Are reasonable costs of reconstruction or replacement allowed as a measure of damages where the diminution of market value of property cannot be determined?

HOLDING AND DECISION: (Lynch, J.) Yes. Reasonable costs of reconstruction or replacement are allowed as a measure of damages where the diminution of market value of property cannot be determined. The general rule for measuring property damage is diminution in market value but is not a universal test because it does not always afford a correct measure of indemnity. Special purpose properties, such as properties owned by religious organizations, are not subject to the general rule because there is no active market from which the market value may be determined. For special purpose properties, other proofs of value may be used, such as the cost of reproduction, less depreciation, or the cost of restoration or replacement. These costs must meet a test of reasonableness, and the restoration must be necessary in light of the damage inflicted. In certain situations, restoration might be uneconomical and improper if the expenses are disproportionate to the injury. Here, Trinity Church's (P) method of computing structural damages was reasonable because it computed the percentage of damage caused by John Hancock (D) against the ultimate necessity of reconstructing the church. Thus, where sections of the church would require reconstruction at a certain point and John Hancock (D) caused damages representing 50 percent of the total, Trinity Church (P) was awarded half of the total restoration costs. This is appropriate even though Trinity Church (P) does not yet have to restore the church because the remedy reasonably reflects the depreciation caused by John Hancock (D). Affirmed.

DISSENT: (O'Connor, J.) Damages are only appropriate as compensation for actual losses. Here, there is no evidence that Trinity Church (P) has suffered any present loss of use or enjoyment of the church or diminution of its market value. The estimated future restoration costs are simply too speculative.

ANALYSIS

Buildings such as churches pose special problems in these cases because there is truly no market value. There are virtually no other uses for a large church building. Courts generally rule that the value to an owner should exclude sentimental considerations, although it is not clear whether the religious significance of a church should be considered where it must be rebuilt.

Quicknotes

COMPENSATION Payment given in exchange for a service rendered or injury incurred, intended to satisfy the receiving party as an equivalent transfer of value.

DIMINUTION IN VALUE A measure of computing damages pursuant to a breach of contract representing the decrease in the value of the subject matter of the contract as a result of the breach.

Neri v. Retail Marine Corp.

Individual (P) v. Corporation (D)

N.Y. Ct. App., 285 N.E.2d 311 (1972)

NATURE OF CASE: Appeal from award of damages for lost profits.

FACT SUMMARY: Neri (P) contended Retail Marine (D) could not recover lost profits and incidental damages for Neri's (P) failure to purchase a boat he had contracted to buy.

RULE OF LAW

Under the Uniform Commercial Code, the seller of goods rejected by a breaching buyer may recover their lost profits and incidental damages caused by the breach.

FACTS: Neri (P) ordered a boat from Retail Marine (D) and tendered a deposit of $4,250. After delivery, Retail Marine (D) received a letter from Neri's (P) attorney indicating Neri (P) could not go through with the purchase and demanding return of the deposit. Retail Marine (D) refused and after several months resold the boat for the same price Neri (P) agreed to pay. Neri (P) sued to recover his deposit, and Retail Marine (D) filed a cross-complaint for lost profits, contending it would have sold two boats in the absence of Neri's (P) breach. It also sued for consequential damages in the form of storage costs incurred due to the delay in sale. Liability against Neri (P) was established by summary judgment, and the issue of damages was certified for appeal.

ISSUE: Under the Uniform Commercial Code, may the seller of goods rejected by a breaching buyer recover their lost profits and incidental damages caused by the breach?

HOLDING AND DECISION: (Gibson, J.) Yes. Under the Uniform Commercial Code, the seller of goods rejected by a breaching buyer may recover their lost profits and incidental damages caused by the breach. Had Neri (P) not breached, Retail Marine (D) clearly would have realized two boat sales instead of one, and, therefore, it is entitled to recover the lost profits as damages. Further, the storage costs were incidentally incurred due to the breach. Neri (P) is entitled to return of his deposit, subject to an offset for the recoverable damages.

ANALYSIS

This case illustrates a court protecting a nonbreaching party's expectancy interest in granting relief from breach. A party is granted not only out-of-pocket damages, but also what they expected to realize on the contract, placing them in the position they would have been in had the contract not been breached.

Quicknotes

BREACH OF CONTRACT Unlawful failure by a party to perform its obligations pursuant to contract.

LIABILITY Any obligation or responsibility.

Chatlos Systems, Inc. v. National Cash Register Corp.

Corporation (P) v. Corporation (D)

670 F.2d 1304 (3d Cir. 1982)

NATURE OF CASE: Appeal from an award of damages for breach of warranty.

FACT SUMMARY: Chatlos Systems, Inc. (P) contended the computer system it purchased from National Cash Register (D) did not function as warranted.

RULE OF LAW

For breach of warranty, the correct measure of damages is the difference between the fair market value of the goods accepted and the value they would have had if they had been as warranted.

FACTS: After negotiating for several months, Chatlos Systems, Inc. (Chatlos) (P) purchased an NCR model 399/656 computer from National Cash Register (NCR) (D) for $46,020. The computer system was warranted to have certain specified capabilities, which it failed to perform. Using a "benefit of the bargain" formula, the district court determined the damages to be $201,826.50. NCR (D) contended the contract price for the system was the only competent record evidence of the value of the system as warranted. However, the district court relied on the testimony of Chatlos's (P) expert witness, who estimated the value of a computer system that would perform all the functions that the purchased system had been warranted to perform to be in the $100,000 to $150,000 range. This appeal followed.

ISSUE: For breach of warranty, is the difference between the fair market value of the goods accepted and the value they would have had if they had been as warranted the correct measure of damages?

HOLDING AND DECISION: (Per curiam) Yes. For breach of warranty, the correct measure of damages is the difference between the fair market value of the goods accepted and the value they would have had if they had been as warranted. (N.J.S.A. § 12A:2714(2).) Contract price is not necessarily the same as market value. Chatlos (P) did not order merely a specific computer model, but an NCR (D) computer system with specified capabilities. The computer purchased, the NCR 399/656, would not perform the functions warranted. The trial court, confronted with conflicting value estimates submitted by the parties, made a credibility determination on the factual findings. That determination may be reversed only if the court's factual determinations were clearly erroneous. They were not so. Affirmed.

DISSENT: (Rosenn, J.) No probative evidence supports the award of damages for the breach of warranty in a sum amounting to almost five times the purchase price of the goods. The measure of damages has been misapplied. The focus of the statute is upon the goods accepted—not other hypothetical goods that may perform equivalent functions. The purpose of the statute is to put the buyer in the same position they would have been in if there had been no breach. The remedies for breach of warranty were intended to compensate the buyer for their loss, not to give them a windfall or treasure trove.

ANALYSIS

The dissent's point is that Chatlos (P) was not an unsophisticated purchaser. Further, they had bargained with NCR (D) for several months before deciding on the system eventually purchased. In other words, they bargained for a cheap system, and that is what they got. However, it appears NCR's (D) company officials knew in advance the system which they warranted and which was ordered by Chatlos (P) would not deliver the program bargained for and the program that was warranted.

Quicknotes

BREACH OF WARRANTY The breach of a promise made by one party to a contract on which the other party may rely, relieving that party from the obligation of determining whether the fact is true and indemnifying the other party from liability if that fact is shown to be false.

FAIR MARKET VALUE The price of particular property or goods that a buyer would offer and a seller would accept in the open market following full disclosure.

Smith v. Bolles

Individual (D) v. Individual (P)

132 U.S. 125 (1889)

NATURE OF CASE: Appeal from award of damages for fraud.

FACT SUMMARY: Bolles (P) was awarded damages based on the value of stock as it would have been had Smith's (D) fraudulent representations been true.

RULE OF LAW

The proper measure of damages for fraud in the sale of stock is the actual loss suffered that resulted from the deception, rather than the purported value of the stock as fraudulently misrepresented.

FACTS: Smith (D) fraudulently represented stock to have great value and sold it to Bolles (P) for $6,000. Bolles (P) sued for fraud and was awarded damages in an amount equal to what the stock would have been worth if the representations had been true. Smith (D) appealed, contending this was an improper measure of damages.

ISSUE: Is the proper measure of damages for fraud in the sale of stock the actual loss suffered that resulted from the deception, rather than the purported value of the stock as fraudulently misrepresented?

HOLDING AND DECISION: (Fuller, C.J.) Yes. The proper measure of damages for fraud in the sale of stock is the actual loss suffered that resulted from the deception, rather than the purported value of the stock as fraudulently misrepresented. The action here was not brought for breach of contract, thus no expectancy interest was lost. Bolles (P) was defrauded in the amount of the price paid for the stock, and this was the correct measure of damages. Reversed and remanded.

ANALYSIS

The key distinction in this case is the contrast between the remedial theories of tort and contract actions. Many commentators have criticized the unavailability of expectancy damages in tort, especially where the same set of facts could be used as the basis of a cause of action for tort or contract.

Quicknotes

MEASURE OF DAMAGES Monetary compensation that may be awarded by the court to a party who has sustained injury or loss to their person, property, or rights due to another party's unlawful act, omission, or negligence.

TORT A legal wrong resulting in a breach of duty by the wrongdoer, causing damages as a result of the breach.

Buck v. Morrow

Individual (P) v. Individual (D)

Tex. Civ. App. Ct., 21 S.W. 398 (1893)

NATURE OF CASE: Appeal from denial of damages for breach of lease.

FACT SUMMARY: The trial court held Buck (P) could not recover consequential damages for Morrow's (D) breach of lease.

RULE OF LAW

A party may recover any consequential damages reasonably anticipated by the parties for the breach of a lease of real property.

FACTS: Morrow (D) leased pastureland to Buck (P) for the latter's cattle. The lease included a clause requiring Morrow (D) to compensate Buck (P) for any damages that resulted from any sale of the land. Morrow (D) subsequently sold the land, and Buck (P) was dispossessed. He lost several head of cattle, was required to hire extra help to watch the cattle, and incurred other expenses in attempt to find alternative pastureland. Buck (P) sued, requesting damages not only for the lost value of the lease, but for the consequential damages incurred. The trial court held no consequential damages were recoverable, and Buck (P) appealed.

ISSUE: Are consequential damages recoverable for the breach of a lease?

HOLDING AND DECISION: (Stephens, J.) Yes. Consequential damages are recoverable for breach of lease. Such damages directly result from the breach and should be fully recoverable. Therefore, the trial court erred in refusing such an award. Reversed.

ANALYSIS

Traditionally the only damages recoverable for the breach of a lease were based upon the difference between the rent to be paid and the actual value of the unexpired lease term. Consequential damages are generally recognized; however, there are some areas, such as eminent domain, where they continue to be denied.

Quicknotes

BREACH The violation of an obligation imposed pursuant to contract or law, by acting or failing to act.

CONSEQUENTIAL DAMAGES Monetary compensation that may be recovered in order to compensate for injuries or losses sustained as a result of damages that are not the direct or foreseeable result of the act of a party, but that nevertheless are the consequence of such act and which must be specifically pled and demonstrated.

Meinrath v. Singer Co.

Individual (P) v. Corporation (D)

87 F.R.D. 422 (S.D.N.Y. 1980)

NATURE OF CASE: Action for damages for nonpayment of sums due under contract.

FACT SUMMARY: Meinrath (P) sought consequential damages for Singer's (D) failure to make timely bonus payments under a written agreement.

RULE OF LAW

A creditor may not recover consequential damages for a debtor's failure to timely pay sums owed.

FACTS: Meinrath (P) entered into a contract with Singer (D), which required the latter to pay him bonus compensation under certain circumstances. Meinrath (P) sued, contending Singer's (D) failure to make timely payments of such bonuses caused his other business ventures to fail. He contended such failures were consequential damages recoverable for Singer's (D) actions as Singer (D) knew of the dependency of such ventures on the timely payments. Singer (D) moved for summary judgment, contending consequential damages were not recoverable.

ISSUE: May a creditor recover consequential damages for a debtor's failure to timely pay sums owed?

HOLDING AND DECISION: (Weinfeld, J.) No. A creditor may not recover consequential damages for a debtor's failure to timely pay sums owed. The only type of damages available is interest payments at the legal limit. This case presents no agreement to pay consequential damages, and thus none are recoverable. Motion for summary judgment granted.

ANALYSIS

This case follows the holding in *Loudon v. Taxing District*, 104 U.S. 771 (1881). That case handed down the rule recognizing interest as the proper type of damages for failure to pay a money debt. This is true whether or not the consequential damages were well known by the debtor.

Quicknotes

CONSEQUENTIAL DAMAGES Monetary compensation that may be recovered in order to compensate for injuries or losses sustained as a result of damages that are not the direct or foreseeable result of the act of a party, but that nevertheless are the consequence of such act and which must be specifically pled and demonstrated.

Kearney & Trecker Corp. v. Master Engraving Co.

Corporation (D) v. Corporation (P)

N.J. Sup. Ct., 527 A.2d 429 (1987)

NATURE OF CASE: Appeal of an award of damages for breach of warranty.

FACT SUMMARY: Master Engraving Co. (Master) (P) bought a machine tool from Kearney & Trecker Corp. (D). The machine tool did not operate properly, and Master sought consequential damages for lost profits.

RULE OF LAW

A consequential damages disclaimer is not invalidated by the failure of a limited remedy provision unless it is unconscionable.

FACTS: Master Engraving Co. (Master) (P), a manufacturer of component parts for industrial application, bought a computer-controlled machine tool from Kearney & Trecker Corp. (K & T) (D) in 1978. The purchase price was $167,000, and the sales proposal from K & T (D) included a warranty provision that stated that consequential damages were disclaimed and that Master's (P) remedy was limited to repair or replacement. The machine tool malfunctioned frequently and was inoperable from 25 percent to 50 percent of the time in the first year. Master (P) brought suit for breach of warranty and introduced evidence regarding lost profits due to the breach. The trial court instructed the jury that it could award consequential damages if it found that K & T's (D) limited remedy provision had failed its essential purpose. The jury awarded $57,000 to Master (P), and K & T (D) appealed.

ISSUE: Is a consequential damages disclaimer invalidated by the failure of a limited remedy provision?

HOLDING AND DECISION: (Stein, J.) No. A consequential damages disclaimer is not invalidated by the failure of a limited remedy provision unless it is unconscionable. Under the Uniform Commercial Code, consequential damages are recoverable if the seller breaches. However, § 2719(3) provides that consequential damages may be limited or excluded unless it is unconscionable. Still, at least minimum adequate remedies must be available to the buyer. Section 2719(2) states that where a seller's limited remedy fails of its essential purpose, all remedies provided for in the Code are available. Limited remedies provisions are typically repair or replacement clauses included by the seller to allow for the opportunity to make the goods conform and limiting the risks of consequential damages. Where a limited warranty contains an express disclaimer of consequential damages, but the remedy fails of its essential purpose, courts are split on whether the disclaimer is still valid. Some courts have ruled that since there is an integral relationship between the exclusion and the limited remedy, the failure of the repair or replacement provision should invalidate the disclaimer. Other courts have concluded that the exclusion of consequential damages should be viewed independently. This is the better rule because sellers' immunity from liability for consequential damages is indispensable in routine transactions. The buyer is protected by other remedies in the Code and, also, when the disclaimer is unconscionable. Although K & T (D) was unable to repair or replace the machine tool sold to Master (P) so that is was operable during the first year, the exclusion of consequential damages contained in the sales agreement is not invalidated. Furthermore, Master (P) has an adequate remedy if it brings suit for breach of the limited warranty. Therefore, the award of damages must be reversed, and the case is remanded.

ANALYSIS

As the decision noted, there is significant split of authority on this issue. One court has staked out a middle position that holds the disclaimer does not survive if the breach is fundamental and total. See *RRX Industries v. LabCon*, 772 F.2d 543 (9th Cir. 1985). In a sales contract, the seller can either limit its warranty obligations or its liability for breach of the warranty. Only disclaimers of warranties must be conspicuous.

Quicknotes

BREACH OF WARRANTY The breach of a promise made by one party to a contract on which the other party may rely, relieving that party from the obligation of determining whether the fact is true and indemnifying the other party from liability if that fact is shown to be false.

CONSEQUENTIAL DAMAGES Monetary compensation that may be recovered in order to compensate for injuries or losses sustained as a result of damages that are not the direct or foreseeable result of the act of a party, but that nevertheless are the consequence of such act and which must be specifically pled and demonstrated.

Commercial Real Estate Investment, L.C. v. Comcast of Utah II, Inc.

Landlord (P) v. Commercial tenant (D)

Utah Sup. Ct., 285 P.3d 1193 (2012)

NATURE OF CASE: Appeal in action to, inter alia, enforce a liquidated damages clause in a commercial lease.

FACT SUMMARY: Comcast of Utah II, Inc. (D) contended that the liquidated damages clause in its lease for commercial space with Commercial Real Estate Investment, L.C. (P), which provided for double the rent amount for every day of a breach of the lease, was unenforceable because it was unconscionable.

RULE OF LAW

Liquidated damages clauses should be reviewed in the same manner as other contractual provisions, so that such clauses will be invalidated only when the facts clearly demonstrate that it would be unconscionable to decree enforcement of the terms of the contract.

FACTS: Commercial Real Estate Investment, L.C. (CRE) (P) bought a lot in an undeveloped industrial park and built a commercial building to the specifications of a company called TCI. TCI drafted the lease for the building, and, among other things, promised to pay as liquidated damages double the rent for each day of any breach. TCI performed for six years and then vacated the building. A year later, Comcast of Utah II, Inc. (Comcast) (D) acquired TCI and assumed its obligations under the lease. The building was vacant for five years. Although Comcast (D) paid the rent for those five years, it refused to pay any liquidated damages, which totaled $1.7 million, contending, inter alia, that they were unconscionable and grossly disproportionate to CRE's (P) actual damages. CRE (P) brought suit to enforce the liquidated damages provision of the lease. The state's highest court granted review. [The procedural posture of the case is not presented in the casebook extract.]

ISSUE: Should liquidated damages clauses be reviewed in the same manner as other contractual provisions, so that such clauses will be invalidated only when the facts clearly demonstrate that it would be unconscionable to decree enforcement of the terms of the contract?

HOLDING AND DECISION: (Durham, J.) Yes. Liquidated damages clauses should be reviewed in the same manner as other contractual provisions, so that such clauses will be invalidated only when the facts clearly demonstrate that it would be unconscionable to decree enforcement of the terms of the contract. Case law reflects several competing approaches to evaluating the enforceability of liquidated damages clauses. One approach is to invalidate a liquidated damages provision where it operates as a penalty—usually where the parties provide for the payment of money only, and where the agreement imposes several distinct duties or obligations of different degrees of importance, and the same sum is named as damages for the breach of either indifferently. Another approach is to compare the amount of liquidated damages versus actual damages. Under this approach, a liquidated damages provision will be invalidated where the liquidated damages bear no reasonable relationship to the actual damage or is so grossly excessive as to be entirely disproportionate to any possible loss that might have been contemplated such that it shocks the conscience. This is sometimes referred to as the "shock the conscience" standard. Although courts should focus on what the contracting parties knew at the time of contracting, in practice, they seem to have engaged frequently in post hoc weighing. A third approach is that taken by the Restatement of Contracts. Under this approach, a liquidated damages provision is invalid unless the amount it fixes is a reasonable forecast of just compensation for the harm that is caused by the breach, and the harm that is caused by the breach is one that is incapable or very difficult of accurate estimation. These factors are evaluated as of the time of contract formation, not breach. The final approach is to defer to the parties' freedom to contract where they have fairly bargained for the liquidated damages. Each of these approaches raises significant concerns. The determination of whether a liquidated damages clause appears to be a penalty imposes an unnecessary additional check on the enforceability of such clauses. First, it improperly reverses the general presumption that contractual provisions are enforceable, and, second, the penalty inquiry is motivated by the interest of justice and fairness, which can be adequately protected through general contractual remedies. The "shock the conscience" standard is problematic because cases employing this approach have tended to evaluate the enforceability of liquidated damages clauses with the benefit of hindsight, rather than as of the time of contract formation. The opinions thus tend to contain conclusory statements that the court's conscience was shocked and typically produce sharply divided opinions regarding the post hoc weighing. The Restatement test is problematic because it requires courts to evaluate the reasonableness of a forecast made when actual damages are almost impossible to estimate at the time of contract formation. For these reasons, liquidated damages clauses should be reviewed just like any other contract provisions and should be invalidated only when the facts clearly show that it would be unconscionable to enforce them. Comcast (D) unpersuasively argues that

Continued on next page.

reviewing liquidated damages clauses only for unconscionability would allow parties to effectively stipulate to permit punitive damages in the event of breach. However, reviewing liquidated damages clauses for unconscionability still preserves challenges to penalty clauses, as well as looking at the circumstances surrounding the parties at the time of the contract's execution. Under this approach, liquidated damages clauses are not subject to any form of heightened judicial scrutiny. Instead, courts should begin with the longstanding presumption that liquidated damages clauses are enforceable, and a party may challenge the enforceability of a liquidated damages clause only by pursuing one of the general contractual remedies, such as mistake, fraud, duress, or unconscionability. A two-pronged analysis is used in determining unconscionability. The first prong seeks to determine whether there was procedural unconscionability regarding the negotiations and the parties' circumstances. The second prong looks at substantive unconscionability, which focuses on the agreement's contents, the relative fairness of the obligations assumed, and whether the contract's terms are so one-sided as to oppress or unfairly surprise an innocent party or whether there exists an overall imbalance in the obligations and rights imposed by the bargain according to the mores and business practices of the time and place. Comcast (D) does not allege procedural unconscionability—nor could it—since Comcast (D) (through its predecessor TCI) drafted the contract in its entirety, including the liquidated damages clause, and presented the contract to CRE (P) for its approval. Thus, none of the hallmarks of procedural unconscionability are present in this case. Here, too, there are no signs of substantive unconscionability with respect to the liquidated damages clause. Although the clause may be more advantageous to CRE (P), it is not so one-sided as to oppress Comcast (D)—particularly where Comcast (D) stands in the shoes of the party that drafted the clause in the first instance. Moreover, the contractual amount of liquidated damages is not unreasonable as compensation for a breach of the contractual duty to continuously operate the building. Although Comcast (D) argues that over $1.7 million in liquidated damages is "grossly disproportionate" to CRE's (P) actual damages, this type of post hoc weighing does not bear on the question of substantive unconscionability, which focuses on the relative fairness of the obligations assumed at the time of contracting. Here, although TCI/Comcast (D) may have made an improvident bargain, the courts cannot supervise decisions made in the business world and provide relief for such bargains where no unconscionability is evident. [Judgment for CRE (P).]

CONCURRENCE AND DISSENT: (Lee, J.) The majority correctly repudiates the hindsight-based approach followed in some cases and correctly clarifies that the reasonableness evaluation must be made from the standpoint of the parties at the time they entered into the contract. However, there is no reason to abandon the Restatement test in its entirety. That test provides needed predictability for contracting parties seeking to anticipate the likely enforceability of the terms of their agreement. The test becomes problematic only when reasonableness is evaluated post hoc. Properly understood, there is no incompatibility between the two prongs of the Restatement inquiry: the reasonable forecast prong is the core standard under the Restatement; the difficulty of estimation prong is subsidiary and explanatory. When damages are difficult to estimate at the time of contract formation, a liquidated sum is more likely to be deemed reasonable (and vice versa). The Restatement's two-part inquiry is a sliding scale, with the degree of deference to the damages liquidated by contract depending on the degree of difficulty of estimating damages in advance. Moreover, the unconscionability standard that the majority adopts is not defined, and, because it is fuzzy, it does not necessarily serve the goal of foreclosing punitive damages for breach of contract and promoting efficient breach. Instead, the majority's standard is an invitation for arbitrariness and judicial decision-making. Under a properly applied Restatement standard, the judgment reached by the majority would still obtain. Under the Restatement test, Comcast (D) bore the burden of demonstrating that the damages liquidated by the parties in this case were a reasonable forecast of the damages they anticipated at the time of the execution of the contract. However, Comcast (D) failed to present any evidence of the nature of the damages anticipated by the parties or of the relationship the liquidated damages bore to those damages, so that its challenge to the liquidated damages clause in this case fails as a matter of law.

ANALYSIS

As a general principle, enforcement of liquidated damages clauses is intended to save the time of courts, juries, parties, and witnesses and reduce the expense of litigation. The majority criticizes the Restatement test, in part, on the grounds the test actually encourages litigation regarding the reasonableness of the forecast and the difficulty of estimating the harm. Justice Lee, however, views the Restatement test, when appropriately clarified, as serving those interests by providing needed predictability for contracting parties seeking to anticipate the likely enforceability of the terms of their agreement.

Continued on next page.

Quicknotes

LIQUIDATED DAMAGES An amount of money specified in a contract representing the damages owed in the event of breach.

POST HOC After this moment.

SHOCK THE CONSCIENCE This phrase is used to express judicial disapproval of some type of outrageous conduct or outcome.

SUBSTANTIVE UNCONSCIONABILITY Rule of law whereby a court may excuse performance of a contract, or of a particular contract term, if it determines that such terms are unduly oppressive or unfair to one party to the contract and violate the subordinate party's reasonable expectations.

S.J. Groves & Sons Co. v. Warner Co.

Corporation (P) v. Corporation (D)

576 F.2d 524 (3d Cir. 1978)

NATURE OF CASE: Appeal from award of damages for breach of contract.

FACT SUMMARY: The trial court held as a matter of law that S.J. Groves & Sons (Groves) (P) should have obtained concrete elsewhere, and its failure to do so precluded recovery of consequential damages.

RULE OF LAW

A buyer of goods may choose any one of several reasonable methods of mitigating damages in order to recover consequential damages caused by the seller's breach.

FACTS: Warner (D) contracted with S.J. Groves & Sons (Groves) (P) to supply concrete according to Groves's instructions. Warner Co. (D) consistently failed to make timely deliveries and the general contractor threatened to stop payment for services. Groves (P) continued to use Warner (D) even though another concrete company was available. Groves (P) subsequently sued and was awarded damages; however, consequential damages were denied on the basis Groves (P) failed to mitigate damages by employing the other concrete company. Groves (P) appealed.

ISSUE: May a buyer of goods choose any one of several reasonable methods of mitigating damages in order to recover consequential damages caused by the seller's breach?

HOLDING AND DECISION: (Weis, J.) Yes. A buyer of goods may choose any one of several reasonable methods of mitigating damages in order to recover consequential damages caused by the seller's breach. Groves (P) was not bound to drop Warner (D) in favor of another seller as the change may have incurred greater damages than those sustained with Warner (D). Therefore, Groves (P) cannot be penalized for choosing an available means of mitigation by staying with the breaching seller based upon assurances of satisfactory performance. Thus, consequential damages should have been awarded. Reversed in part and remanded.

ANALYSIS

The court in this case discussed and rejected the applicability of the avoidable-consequences doctrine. This doctrine holds a defendant harmless where the plaintiff could have avoided the consequences through affirmative action. The doctrine is analogous to contributory or comparative negligence theories.

Quicknotes

DAMAGES Monetary compensation that may be awarded by the court to a party who has sustained injury or loss to their person, property, or rights due to another party's unlawful act, omission, or negligence.

MITIGATION OF DAMAGES A plaintiff's implied obligation to take reasonable steps to attempt to minimize damages after injury has occurred.

Oden v. Chemung County Industrial Development Agency

Individual (P) v. Corporation (D)

N.Y. Ct. App., 661 N.E.2d 142 (1995)

NATURE OF CASE: Appeal from lower court decision regarding damages.

FACT SUMMARY: A falling steel column severely injured Oden (P). After a trial, the jury awarded the Oden (P) significant damages.

RULE OF LAW

Collateral-source payments to the plaintiff from a third party that actually replace a particular category of awarded damages may be used to reduce the damage award to the plaintiff.

FACTS: Oden (P), an ironworker, suffered severe and career-ending injuries when a falling steel column struck him. After a trial, the jury awarded him $5,752 for past medical expenses, $20,000 for pain and suffering, and $27,500 for lost past earnings. Significantly for the purposes of this decision, the jury also awarded $66,000 for lost ordinary pension benefits and $80,000 for future lost earnings and health and welfare benefits. Separately, it was offered into evidence that Oden (P) would receive $141,330 in disability retirement benefits. After the verdict, Chemung County Industrial Development Agency (Chemung County) (D) moved to reduce the amount of the jury's damage award by $141,330, based on New York's statutory provision that allows reduction of awards due to the presence of collateral-source payments. The trial court allowed the motion, but an intermediate appellate court reinstated the award of $80,000 for lost future earnings. Both parties appealed.

ISSUE: May collateral-source payments to the plaintiff from a third party that actually replace a particular category of awarded damages be used to reduce the damage award to the plaintiff?

HOLDING AND DECISION: (Titone, J.) Yes. Collateral-source payments to the plaintiff from a third party that actually replace a particular category of awarded damages may be used to reduce the damage award to the plaintiff. The traditional, common-law collateral-source rule held that personal injury awards could not be reduced or offset by the amount of any funds received by the plaintiff from a third party. Over the past 30 years, New York's legislature has whittled away at the common-law rule, which has been much criticized. The most recent statutory enactment, C.P.L.R. § 4545(c), allows a judge to reduce a damages award if the court finds that any portion of the damage award will, with reasonable certainty, be duplicated from a collateral source. The court should make a factual analysis of any possible duplication. The burden rests on the defendant to show that a particular portion of the award is duplicated by some outside source of funding. Here, two portions of the award are at issue—the $66,000 of lost ordinary pension benefits and the $80,000 in lost future earnings. Chemung County (D) contends Oden's (P) $141,330 in disability retirement benefits can be used to reduce both these categories of damage awards. The court agrees the disability retirement benefits should be used to reduce to zero the $66,000 award for lost ordinary pension benefits. The disability pension benefits Oden (P) will receive are duplicative of that portion of the award. However, the $80,000 in lost future earnings is not duplicative. Oden (P) would receive his disability retirement pension even if he did have the ability to continue working in other capacities following his retirement. Therefore, the $80,000 award for lost future earnings is not duplicative of his disability retirement pension benefits. Affirmed.

ANALYSIS

Not all states have modified the collateral-source rule as New York has done. The majority of states still follow the common-law rule that does not allow offsets for collateral-source payments. However, practitioners should be aware of their particular state's statutory efforts, if any, to modify the common-law rule.

Quicknotes

COLLATERAL-SOURCE RULE The doctrine that compensation given to an injured party from a third party should not be considered in assessing the damages to be paid by the party who inflicted the injury.

Pruitt v. Allied Chemical Corp.

Individuals (P) v. Corporation (D)

523 F. Supp. 975 (E.D. Va. 1981)

NATURE OF CASE: Action for damages for interference with business operations.

FACT SUMMARY: Pruitt (P) and others sued Allied Chemical (Allied) (D) for damage to their business from Allied's (D) pollution of various waterways.

RULE OF LAW

Recovery may be obtained for damages proximately caused by the defendant's negligence.

FACTS: Pruitt (P) and others who derive their income from the harvesting and sale of marine life in the James River and Chesapeake Bay sued Allied Chemical (Allied) (D), contending that Allied (D) polluted those waterways and materially affected the commercial worth of the wildlife. Allied (D) moved to dismiss the causes of action brought by merchants whose business allegedly suffered from the damage to the marine life in that the demand for such decreased due to the pollution. Allied (D) contended there was no direct injury to any property right held by those plaintiffs.

ISSUE: May recovery be obtained for damages proximately caused by the defendant's negligence?

HOLDING AND DECISION: (Merhige, J.) Yes. Recovery may be obtained for damages proximately caused by the defendant's negligence. In this case, while the injuries to the merchants may have been caused by and even foreseeable from the pollution, it is necessary to place a reasonable, if somewhat arbitrary limit on the recoverable damages. Granting recovery to the merchants as well as the fishermen would require Allied (D) to pay twice for the same injury. Thus, the more direct injury, i.e., that of the fishermen, must be recognized, while the injury to the merchants must be held not legally recognizable as too distant in the causal chain. Motion to dismiss granted.

ANALYSIS

This decision has been criticized on several grounds. First, the court recognized the direct causation, yet imposed a limit on liability from the water's edge. Second, it fails to meet the remedial goal of compensating for loss. However, many jurisdictions recognize that liability for foreseeable injury must, in some circumstances, be limited.

Quicknotes

PROXIMATE CAUSE The natural sequence of events without which an injury would not have been sustained.

PROXIMATE DAMAGES Damages that are the direct and foreseeable result of a particular act.

Sunnyland Farms, Inc. v. Central New Mexico Electric Cooperative, Inc.

Customer (P) v. Electrical utility (D)

N.M. Sup. Ct., 301 P.3d 387 (2013)

NATURE OF CASE: Appeal from reversal of award of consequential contract damages in action for breach of contract and tort.

FACT SUMMARY: Central New Mexico Electric Cooperative, Inc. (CNMEC) (D), an electrical utility, contended there were no special circumstances that would support consequential damages resulting from its negligent turning off of electricity to Sunnyland Farms, Inc. (Sunnyland) (P).

RULE OF LAW

In a contract action, a defendant is liable only for those consequential damages that were objectively foreseeable as a probable result of the defendant's breach when the contract was made.

FACTS: Sunnyland Farms, Inc. (Sunnyland) (P), a hydroponic grower of tomatoes, purchased its electricity from Central New Mexico Electric Cooperative, Inc. (CNMEC) (D), an electrical utility. CNMEC (D) turned off Sunnyland's (P) electricity for nonpayment, but negligently failed to give Sunnyland (P) advance notice prior to doing so. The next day, some Sunnyland (P) employees negligently started a fire that ultimately consumed Sunnyland's packhouse and operations building. When Sunnyland's (P) employees initially discovered the fire, they attempted to put it out using ordinary hoses, but without electricity, the Sunnyland (P) facility had no running water, and the fire grew. When firefighters arrived, they were unable to access well water for firefighting because there was no electricity to power the pumps. Sunnyland (P) had also failed to make alternative arrangements for emergency water in the event power failed. Firefighters attempted to use reservoir water and to preserve water by using foam and smaller hoses, but the buildings were nonetheless destroyed. Sunnyland (P) sued CNMEC (D) in contract and tort, among other causes of action, for damages resulting from the fire, alleging that if CNMEC (D) had taken adequate care prior to disconnecting Sunnyland's (P) electrical service, firefighters and Sunnyland (P) employees would have had access to water and the fire could have been contained. The trial court found CNMEC (D) liable both in contract and in tort. It calculated total consequential damages of over $21 million, of which $13.7 million was the net value of lost crops the facility would have been able to grow in the absence of the fire. The trial court reduced the damages in tort by 80 percent to account for Sunnyland's (P) comparative fault; however, in contract, the trial court awarded the entire almost $21.4 million. The trial court issued very limited conclusions of law regarding the issue of foreseeability and consequential damages, and it did not find special circumstances beyond the ordinary course of events. The trial court also did not distinguish between the proximate cause required for tort liability and the more stringent foreseeability required for consequential damages in contract. The state's intermediate appellate court reversed the award of contract damages, and the state's highest court granted review.

ISSUE: In a contract action, is a defendant liable only for those consequential damages that were objectively foreseeable as a probable result of the defendant's breach when the contract was made?

HOLDING AND DECISION: (Chávez, J.) Yes. In a contract action, a defendant is liable only for those consequential damages that were objectively foreseeable as a probable result of the defendant's breach when the contract was made. Under this standard, a defendant is liable for losses that were foreseeable at the time of contracting, regardless of whether the defendant actually contemplated or foresaw the loss. This foreseeability standard is more stringent than "proximate cause" in tort law, as the loss must have been foreseeable as the probable result of breach, not merely as a possibility. This is the approach taken by the Restatement (Second) of Contracts § 351. The Restatement asks whether there were "special circumstances, beyond the ordinary course of events, that the party in breach had reason to know." In the absence of such circumstances, the breaching party is liable only for general damages. Sunnyland (P) contended that it was sufficient to establish the presence of special circumstances that CNMEC (D) knew that Sunnyland (P) was a for-profit enterprise and that it depended on electricity. There are three problems with this contention. First, this is simply too speculative, since a reviewing court will not speculate about what the fact-finder (the trial court in this case) might have meant to say but did not. Second, Sunnyland's (P) injury was not directly caused by the lack of electricity. The actual harm was more attenuated: the lack of electricity interrupted Sunnyland's (P) water supply, which, in conjunction with Sunnyland's (P) lack of backup firefighting options, made it difficult for Sunnyland (P) to respond to the fire its employees negligently started. There were no findings that CNMEC (D) should have known that Sunnyland (P) was likely to start fires or was depending on electricity to fight any fires that occurred. Even if some damage to the tomato

Continued on next page.

crop was foreseeable from the disconnection of electricity, the particular damage that occurred was not. Third, even if CNMEC (D) had reason to know that Sunnyland (P) depended on its electricity to power water in the event of a fire, CNMEC (D) would still not be liable without the presence of additional special circumstances. CNMEC (D) would have needed to know not only that Sunnyland (P) depended on its electricity for access to water, but also that there was no backup power source, or that there was a particularized need for uninterrupted water or power. There was no evidence that CNMEC (D) had reason to know any of this. In particular, CNMEC (D) could not have been expected to know Sunnyland (P) did not have a separate power source, independent of the power for the main building, for the well that was to be used in the event of a fire. CNMEC (D) cannot have been expected to anticipate Sunnyland's (P) negligence in this regard. Accordingly, without findings or evidence of special circumstances, the award of consequential damages cannot stand, and the reversal of the trial court's award is, therefore, affirmed.

ANALYSIS

In its discussion of consequential damages, the court in this case cites the classic case in this area, the British case of *Hadley v. Baxendale,* 156 Eng. Rep. 145 (Ex. 1854). In that case, it was held that a common carrier could not have reasonably foreseen that a broken mill crankshaft had to be delivered with expedited service, so a new crankshaft could be built, and that the delay in the delivery would cause the mill to shut down. Although the defendant carrier knew that the crankshaft it was carrying was a broken part of a for-profit mill, the plaintiff never told the defendant exactly what was at stake, i.e., that there was no backup shaft or other alternative plan to keep the mill running. Although the state's (New Mexico's) Supreme Court had adopted the objective foreseeability test announced in *Hadley,* it had also incorporated the requirement that the nonperforming party had to explicitly or tacitly agree to respond in damages for the particular damages understood to be likely in the event of a breach. This made the New Mexico "tacit agreement" rule more limited and restrictive than the notion of foreseeability in the Restatement or the rule announced in *Hadley.* In *Sunnyland* the New Mexico Supreme Court abandoned the tacit agreement test, finding it to be confusing and antiquated.

Quicknotes

CONSEQUENTIAL DAMAGES Monetary compensation that may be recovered in order to compensate for injuries or losses sustained as a result of damages that are not the direct or foreseeable result of the act of a party, but that nevertheless are the consequence of such act and which must be specifically pled and demonstrated.

Brunswick Corp. v. Pueblo Bowl-O-Mat, Inc.

Corporation (D) v. Corporation (P)

429 U.S. 477 (1977)

NATURE OF CASE: Appeal from reversal of award of damages for violations of antitrust laws.

FACT SUMMARY: Pueblo Bowl-O-Mat (Pueblo) (P) sued Brunswick Corp. (D), contending the latter's acquisition of bowling centers violated the federal antitrust laws, requiring treble damages and an order of divestiture.

RULE OF LAW

Antitrust relief is not available in every case in which a large corporation takes over smaller businesses and causes readjustments in the market share of other participants.

FACTS: Pueblo Bowl-O-Mat (Pueblo) (P), the owner of several bowling centers, sued Brunswick Corp. (D), contending that by acquiring and operating bowling centers that otherwise would have gone bankrupt, Brunswick (D) had brought its deep pocket into the industry and decreased Pueblo's (P) profits. Pueblo (P) contended that it was damaged by the amount of profit it would have realized if the centers were allowed to close down. The trial court granted treble damages and enjoined further acquisitions by Brunswick (D). The court of appeals reversed and remanded, and the United States Supreme Court granted certiorari.

ISSUE: Is antitrust relief available in every case in which a large corporation takes over smaller businesses and causes readjustments in the market share of other participants?

HOLDING AND DECISION: (Marshall, J.) No. Antitrust relief is not available in every case in which a large corporation takes over smaller businesses and causes readjustments in the market share of other participants. An opposite rule would allow the imposition of antitrust relief in situations not within the general policy underlying the statutes. Every merger potentially causes market share readjustments. Because no anticompetitive effect was shown, no relief is available. Vacated and remanded.

ANALYSIS

In any type of case, remedial goals are intended to further substantive policy. The province of the judiciary is to shape remedies to further such goals. Thus each violation of substantive law should have a remedy shaped to discourage future violations and compensate for the present violation.

Quicknotes

ANTITRUST Body of federal law prohibiting business conduct that constitutes a restraint on trade.

Bigelow v. RKO Radio Pictures

Individual (P) v. Corporation (D)

327 U.S. 251 (1946)

NATURE OF CASE: Appeal from award of damages for violation of Sherman Act.

FACT SUMMARY: RKO Radio Pictures (RKO) (D) contended Bigelow (P) could not show damages with sufficient certainty to recover for violation of the Sherman Act.

RULE OF LAW

A jury may make a just and reasonable estimate of damages based on the evidence presented, and its award need not be based on precise mathematical computations.

FACTS: Bigelow (P) sued RKO Radio Pictures (RKO) (D) and others, contending they had engaged in a discriminatory system of film distribution that violated the Sherman Antitrust Act. The jury awarded damages, which were trebled, based upon evidence of the difference in profitability between Bigelow's (P) theater and a theater that was not a victim of the discrimination. RKO (D) appealed, contending the damage award was not sufficiently certain as the basis was not a precise measuring tool. The appellate court reversed, and the United States Supreme Court granted certiorari.

ISSUE: Must a damage award be based upon precise mathematical calculations?

HOLDING AND DECISION: (Stone, C.J.) No. A jury may make a just and reasonable estimate of damages based upon the evidence presented, and its award need not be based on precise mathematical calculations. In this case, it could not be established precisely what Bigelow's (P) profit would have been in the absence of the discriminatory practices. The comparison used offered a reasonable method of estimating damages and should be upheld. Reversed.

DISSENT: (Frankfurter, J.) In the absence of proof of actual injury, no violation of the Sherman Act can be found.

ANALYSIS

This case illustrates the requirement that damages be sufficiently certain to be recoverable. The Court noted that it has long been recognized that where the reason for the uncertainty is the act of one party, the issue is resolved in the other party's favor. This holds true in this case where the discriminatory enterprise caused the uncertainty.

Quicknotes

DAMAGES Monetary compensation that may be awarded by the court to a party who has sustained injury or loss to their person, property, or rights due to another party's unlawful act, omission, or negligence.

SHERMAN ACT Prohibits unreasonable restraint of trade.

Norfolk & Western Railway v. Liepelt

Corporation (D) v. Decedent's estate (P)

444 U.S. 490 (1980)

NATURE OF CASE: Appeal from exclusion of evidence and refusal to instruct jury.

FACT SUMMARY: Liepelt's (P) decedent was killed by the negligence of Norfolk & Western Railway (Norfolk) (D), his employer, and Norfolk (D) challenged the award of $775,000 in damages on the ground that the jury must have believed the award would be subject to federal income taxation, a matter about which the judge refused evidence and to instruct the jury.

RULE OF LAW

It is error for a trial judge to refuse to admit evidence of the nontaxability of jury awards or to instruct the jury thereof.

FACTS: Liepelt (P) represented a fireman killed through the negligence of his employer, Norfolk & Western Railway (Norfolk) (D). After trial on the matter, the jury awarded Liepelt (P) $775,000, though calculation by the decedent's life expectancy and expected salary would have placed the actual loss at approximately $302,000. Norfolk (D) appealed, challenging the award on the ground that the jury must have believed that the award would be subject to federal income taxation in order to have rendered so large a verdict, and that the trial judge refused to hear evidence on taxation and to instruct the jury regarding the freedom of jury awards from income taxation under the Internal Revenue Code. The appellate court found no error, and the Illinois Supreme Court denied hearing. The United States Supreme Court granted certiorari.

ISSUE: Is it error for a trial judge to refuse to admit evidence of the nontaxability of jury awards or to instruct the jury thereof?

HOLDING AND DECISION: (Stevens, J.) Yes. In the past, the tax liabilities that a person would incur in the future were regarded as too speculative for a jury to consider in calculating future earning power. The practical wisdom of the trial bar and the trial bench has developed effective methods of presenting essential elements of expert calculations in an understandable form. Despite today's increased general awareness of the realities of taxation, many are surely unaware that jury awards are nontaxable. Thus, it is error for a trial judge to refuse to admit evidence of the nontaxability of jury awards or to instruct the jury thereof. Reversed and remanded.

DISSENT: (Blackmun, J.) The proposed instruction to the jury is purely cautionary and does not implicate any federal interest. This issue is one of state procedure to be handled by state courts and legislatures. Moreover, Congress has bestowed a benefit on plaintiffs by prohibiting taxation of their wrong death awards. This decision effectively turns that benefit over to the tortfeasor at the expense of plaintiffs. In addition, such charges regarding collateral issues will confuse the jury.

ANALYSIS

Traditionally, no evidence was permitted as to the tax consequences of receipt of a jury award. The speculation and the complexity of the calculations required are attenuated by increased familiarity with tax law, and the practical effect of taxation is today far greater than in the past.

Quicknotes

DAMAGES Monetary compensation that may be awarded by the court to a party who has sustained injury or loss to their person, property, or rights due to another party's unlawful act, omission, or negligence.

WRONGFUL DEATH An action brought by the beneficiaries of a deceased person, claiming that the deceased's death was the result of wrongful conduct by the defendant.

City of Milwaukee v. Cement Division, National Gypsum Company

City government (D) v. Corporation (P)

515 U.S. 189 (1995)

NATURE OF CASE: Appeal from judgment denying prejudgment interest in an admiralty case.

FACT SUMMARY: National Gypsum Co. (P) sought prejudgment interest from the City of Milwaukee (D) after its ship sank in a City-owned slip.

RULE OF LAW

A genuine dispute over liability does not justify a court's departure from the general rule that prejudgment interest should be awarded in maritime cases.

FACTS: During a severe storm, the *E.M. Ford*, a ship owned by National Gypsum Co. (P), broke loose from her moorings and sank in a slip owned by the City of Milwaukee (City) (D). Invoking the federal district court's admiralty and maritime jurisdiction, National Gypsum (P) filed suit against the City (D) for negligence. National Gypsum alleged that the ship was assigned to an unsafe berthing slip without warning. The City (D) countered that National Gypsum (P) left the ship unmanned during the winter, with no means onboard for monitoring the weather or calling for help. The parties eventually settled the damages portion of the case and agreed to leave the prejudgment interest issue to the court's discretion. The district court declined to award prejudgment interest and National Gypsum (P) appealed. The Seventh Circuit Court of Appeals reversed and remanded, and the United States Supreme Court granted review.

ISSUE: Does a genuine dispute over liability justify a court's departure from the general rule that prejudgment interest should be awarded in maritime cases?

HOLDING AND DECISION: (Stevens, J.) No. A genuine dispute over liability does not justify a court's departure from the general rule that prejudgment interest should be awarded in maritime cases. A good faith dispute over liability and the existence of mutual fault do not qualify as "peculiar" or "exceptional" circumstance justifying the denial of prejudgment interest. Affirmed.

ANALYSIS

There has been much activity in courthouses and legislatures regarding the award and rate of prejudgment interest. The traditional common-law rule that prejudgment interest would be awarded only when damages were liquidated or "ascertainable" has been challenged, both successfully and unsuccessfully, in many states.

Quicknotes

ADMIRALTY That area of law pertaining to navigable waters.

LIABILITY Any obligation or responsibility.

NEGLIGENCE Conduct falling below the standard of care that a reasonable person would demonstrate under similar conditions.

Jones & Laughlin Steel Corp. v. Pfeifer

Corporation (D) v. Individual (P)

462 U.S. 523 (1983)

NATURE OF CASE: Appeal from award for future damages.

FACT SUMMARY: The district court held as a matter of law that in calculating an award of future damages that future inflation is presumed to equal future interest rates, and therefore these factors were offsetting.

RULE OF LAW

Federal courts may choose the manner in which to discount the present value of future earnings and are not bound by a rule of state law.

FACTS: Pfeifer (P) was injured in the course of his employment with Jones & Laughlin Steel (Jones) (D). The district court neither increased the award for future lost earnings to reflect inflation, nor discounted it to reflect its present value, holding it was bound by a Pennsylvania state court decision, which held that future inflation and future interest rates are presumed to be equal and the factors are offsetting. Pfeifer (P) appealed, contending the federal court was not bound by state law. The court of appeals affirmed, and the United States Supreme Court granted certiorari.

ISSUE: May federal courts choose the method to discount future earnings without being bound by state law?

HOLDING AND DECISION: (Stevens, J.) Yes. Federal courts may choose the manner in which to discount the value of future earnings. They are not bound by a rule of state law. There are several acceptable methods of calculating the present value of an award of future damages. Among these are to discount the award according to a market or real interest rate or to predict inflation and discount by a market interest rate. No matter which method is used, no exact figure can be arrived at with precision. Therefore, to adopt a single method as a federal rule of decision would be unworkable. Whatever method is used, the federal court is free to choose it and is not bound by a state rule of decision. Vacated and remanded.

ANALYSIS

This case illustrates the various methods available to courts to determine the present value of a lump sum award for future damages. The Court recognizes that the fluctuating nature of inflation renders any method used inexact. Because of this, some methods are more appropriate in some cases than in others, and it would not be beneficial to adopt a single method as a rule of decision applicable to all cases.

Quicknotes

DAMAGES Monetary compensation that may be awarded by the court to a party who has sustained injury or loss to their person, property, or rights due to another party's unlawful act, omission, or negligence.

Debus v. Grand Union Stores

Individual (P) v. Corporation (D)

Vt. Sup. Ct., 621 A.2d 1288 (1993)

NATURE OF CASE: Appeal from judgment awarding damages in a personal injury action.

FACT SUMMARY: Grand Union Stores (D) appealed from judgment awarding damages based upon a per diem argument.

RULE OF LAW

Per diem damage arguments are not overly prejudicial and should be allowed.

FACTS: Debus (P) was injured in a store owned by Grand Union Stores (D) when a palette of boxes fell on her. During closing argument, counsel for Debus (P) argued that the jury consider the injury in terms of daily pain and suffering. Counsel suggested a per diem figure and suggested the jury multiply the figure by the number of days in Debus's (P) life expectancy. The jury awarded Debus damages of $346,276.23. Grand Union Stores (D) appealed.

ISSUE: Should per diem damage arguments be disallowed as overly prejudicial?

HOLDING AND DECISION: (Johnson, J.) No. Per diem damage arguments are not overly prejudicial and should be allowed. A per diem argument is a useful tool of persuasion used by counsel to suggest how the jury can quantify damages related to evidence of pain and suffering. There is nothing inherently improper or prejudicial about per diem arguments if they are made under the ordinary supervision and control of the court. Plaintiffs, however, do not have "carte blanche" to depart from a reasonable view of the evidence. Affirmed.

DISSENT: (Allen, C.J.) The court should limit the arguments of counsel to the appropriateness of employing a time unit calculation method for fixing damages of pain and suffering but prohibit any suggestion of a specific monetary amount. The jury's determination is not aided by the suggestion of a lump sum amount for damages.

ANALYSIS

Jurisdictions are split over the propriety of per diem arguments on damages. Roughly equal numbers of states permit or forbid per diem arguments, while others require a corresponding cautionary instruction to accompany the arguments.

Quicknotes

DAMAGES Monetary compensation that may be awarded by the court to a party who has sustained injury or loss to their person, property, or rights due to another party's unlawful act, omission, or negligence.

Levka v. City of Chicago

Individual (P) v. City government (D)

748 F.2d 421 (7th Cir. 1984)

NATURE OF CASE: Motion for judgment n.o.v., new trial, or remittitur from civil rights verdict.

FACT SUMMARY: The City of Chicago (D) appealed from a decision denying its motion for judgment n.o.v., or alternatively for a new trial or remittitur, from a verdict rendered in Levka's (P) civil rights action, contending the circumstances attendant to the strip search that formed the basis of Levka's (P) suit did not justify the $50,000 verdict.

RULE OF LAW

A court may exercise its discretion in reducing a jury verdict when the evidence indicated the verdict is grossly excessive.

FACTS: Levka (P) brought a civil rights action to recover for a violation of her civil rights she claimed occurred when Chicago police subjected her to a strip search. Matrons conducted the search, and every arrestee was subjected to such a search by policy. There was only a visual inspection, conducted privately. When Levka (P) protested, she was told "just do it." She testified she felt debased and humiliated, and she called several witnesses to support her claims. Chicago (D) called several witnesses to refute Levka's (P) damages allegations. The jury awarded Levka (P) $50,000, solely for mental anguish, humiliation, embarrassment, etc., and nothing on her claims for lost earnings or loss of earning capacity. Chicago (D) challenged the award as excessive, moving for a judgment n.o.v., or in the alternative, for a new trial or a remittitur. From a denial of its motion, Chicago (D) appealed.

ISSUE: May a court exercise its discretion in reducing a jury verdict when the evidence indicates the verdict is grossly excessive?

HOLDING AND DECISION: (Pell, S.J.) Yes. The court may exercise its discretion in reducing a jury verdict when the evidence indicates the verdict is grossly excessive. Such indications are present in this case. The verdict is on the high end of verdicts rendered in similar cases. Further, aggravating circumstances in these other cases, such as vaginal or rectal probing, verbal abuse, etc., which justified a higher verdict, are not present here. This was a relatively straightforward visual strip search, done as privately as possible. Further, Chicago (D) was able to submit evidence sufficient to disallow Levka's (P) earnings claims. Deference to the jury is substantial, but, while not intending to minimize Levka's (P) humiliation, a verdict essentially punitive in nature cannot stand. The award is grossly excessive and subject to reduction. Reversed and remanded.

ANALYSIS

One of the cases referred to in the decision with a verdict higher than the present case was also reduced on appeal. The fact that Levka (P) was asserting constitutional claims was not essential and does not generally enhance one's ability to resist a motion for remittitur.

Quicknotes

DAMAGES Monetary compensation that may be awarded by the court to a party who has sustained injury or loss to their person, property, or rights due to another party's unlawful act, omission, or negligence.

JUDGMENT N.O.V. (JUDGMENT NOTHWITHSTANDING THE VERDICT) A judgment entered by the trial judge reversing a jury verdict if the jury's determination has no basis in law or fact.

REMITTITUR The authority of a court to reduce the amount of damages awarded by the jury.

Carey v. Piphus

Individual (P) v. Local school (D)

435 U.S. 247 (1978)

NATURE OF CASE: Appeal in action for denial of due process.

FACT SUMMARY: Carey (P), whose procedural due process was denied by his suspension from school without a proper hearing, sought damages.

RULE OF LAW

Absent proof of actual injury caused by a denial of procedural due process, only nominal damages may be awarded.

FACTS: Carey (P) was suspended from school without the proper procedural safeguards being taken. He sued under 42 U.S.C. § 1983, alleging that his Fourteenth Amendment right had been violated. The district court found that due process had been denied but declined to award damages since Carey (P) had not submitted evidence showing that he was so entitled. On appeal, the Seventh Circuit Court of Appeals held that the lower court should have heard evidence regarding the damages suffered by Carey (P), but that compensatory damages would not be recoverable for missed school time if the school (D) could show that the student would have been suspended even if a proper hearing had been held, i.e., there was just cause for the suspensions. However, even if just cause was found, Carey (P) would be entitled to recover substantial nonpunitive damages merely because of the denial of his due process, even if no proof is submitted as to the injuries thereby incurred. The United States Supreme Court granted certiorari.

ISSUE: May substantial damages be awarded for a denial of procedural due process, absent proof of actual injury?

HOLDING AND DECISION: (Powell, J.) No. Absent proof of actual injury caused by a denial of procedural due process, only nominal damages may be awarded. In many ways, a deprivation of a right under § 1983 creates a liability similar to traditional tort liability. As such, the court of appeals was correct in holding that damages for the deprivation of the substantive right, in this case the missed school time, can only be awarded where actual injury is evidenced in the record. Furthermore, the Court correctly asserted that in any case, if the school (D) shows that the suspension was for good cause, no injury can be found to have flowed from the denial of a hearing in this regard and therefore no damages are to be awarded. However, Carey (P) validly maintains that the denial of procedural due process is an injury, in and of itself. But the court of appeals incorrectly held that this deprivation may be compensated, without proof of actual damages suffered, by substantial damages. There is no basis for this holding. Reversed and remanded.

ANALYSIS

The issue of the kind of damages that may be awarded and the levels of proof required in suits for violations of constitutional rights was discussed thoroughly in *Basista v. Weir*, 340 F.2d 74 (3rd Cir. 1964). In *Basista*, the plaintiff was suing for injuries allegedly caused by unconstitutional beatings administered by police officers. The court acknowledged that 42 U.S.C. § 1983 was not specific as to the type of damages allowed for violations. However, after examining the section's history and analogizing to similar statutes, it was held that both compensatory and punitive damages could be recovered. Finally, the court stated that nominal damages automatically flow from the deprivation of a § 1983 right and specific injury need not be proven. Once nominal damages are awarded, punitive damages may also be granted. Apparently, the majority of the states are not in accord with the federal rule as enunciated in *Basista*. See *Hilbert v. Roth*, 395 Pa. 270 (1959).

Quicknotes

COMPENSATORY DAMAGES Measure of damages necessary to compensate victim for actual injuries suffered.

DAMAGES Monetary compensation that may be awarded by the court to a party who has sustained injury or loss to their person, property, or rights due to another party's unlawful act, omission, or negligence.

DUE PROCESS The constitutional mandate requiring the courts to protect and enforce individuals' rights and liberties consistent with prevailing principles of fairness and justice and prohibiting the federal and state governments from such activities that deprive its citizens of life, liberty, or property interest.

Arbino v. Johnson & Johnson

Individual (P) v. Corporation (D)

Ohio Sup. Ct., 880 N.E.2d 420 (2007)

NATURE OF CASE: Certified question of law from the federal court to the Ohio Supreme Court.

FACT SUMMARY: Arbino (P) suffered blood clots and side effects allegedly caused by Johnson & Johnson's (D) Ortho Evra Birth Control patch.

RULE OF LAW

Statutorily imposed caps on noneconomic damages are not unconstitutional.

FACTS: Arbino (P) suffered blood clots and other side effects allegedly caused by her use of Johnson & Johnson's (D) Ortho Evra Birth Control patch. Arbino (P) brought suit in federal district court. The district court certified a question of law as to whether Ohio's statutorily imposed cap on noneconomic damages is constitutional under the Ohio Constitution.

ISSUE: Are statutorily imposed caps on noneconomic damages unconstitutional?

HOLDING AND DECISION: (Moyer, C.J.) No. Statutorily imposed caps on noneconomic damages are not unconstitutional. Arbino (P) here has raised a facial challenge to Ohio Rev. Code Ann. § 2315.18. This statute limits noneconomic damages to the greater of (1) $250,000 or (2) three times the economic damages up to a maximum of $350,000 per person or $500,000 per single occurrence. Noneconomic damages consist of pain and suffering, loss of companionship, or mental anguish. The statute does not limit economic damages or punitive damages. In addition, there are exceptions for the limitation for noneconomic damages where the plaintiff suffers permanent physical deformities. Arbino (P) first argues the statute infringes upon her right to trial by jury. Any statute that prohibits a jury from determining all factual issues is unconstitutional. The statute does not alter a jury's factual findings. It simply limits the amount of a possible damage award as a matter of law. Accordingly, the statute does not restrict a plaintiff's right to trial by jury. Second, Arbino (P) argues the statute violates the Ohio Constitution's right to open court and to a remedy. The statute does not prohibit plaintiffs from obtaining a remedy, but only caps certain damage amounts. Third, Arbino (P) argues the statute violates the Ohio Constitution's due process clause. The statute does not restrict a fundamental right and is therefore reviewed under the rational basis test. The legislature made several economics-based findings, in particular that states with tort reform enjoy significant economic growth as a result of those reforms. Viewing these legislative findings, the court holds the statute bears a rational relationship to the public welfare. The statute is also not arbitrary. The statute still allows for full recovery of economic damages, punitive damages, and limitless noneconomic damages for catastrophic injuries. Fourth, Arbino (P) argues the statute violates equal protection. The statute is facially neutral and does not impinge on the rights of any suspect class. Thus, within the context of the equal protection analysis, we review the statute again on a rational basis test. The statute does not lack all rational relation to the legitimate state interest of protecting the state's economy and increasing judicial efficiency. Fifth, Arbino's (P) argument that the statute infringes upon the judicial role of deciding damages is without merit. The legislature has the power to limit damages in certain classes of cases. The statute is constitutional. Certified question answered in the affirmative.

CONCURRENCE: (Cupp, J.) The legislature has long held the power to alter or abolish common-law claims or remedies. Accordingly, while the legislature may not take away the right to a trial by jury, it may limit the amount of damages that one may legally recover.

DISSENT: (O'Donnell, J.) The cap on noneconomic damages is arbitrary. Under the state's Constitution, litigants have the right to a trial by jury. The right includes the right to have their damages decided by the jury, not the state legislature.

DISSENT: (Pfeifer, J.) Only juries have the power to determine facts and a damages award rests upon the factual findings of the jury. While the majority states that courts are not modifying a jury's ability to determine facts, the cap on damages essentially forces the judge to ignore those facts and limit any damage award arbitrarily. Because the cap infringes upon the right to a jury trial, it is unconstitutional. Moreover, the cap will ultimately only affect those plaintiffs who have meritorious claims and severe injuries. It does nothing to prevent frivolous lawsuits. In addition, the cap creates two classes of plaintiffs: those with catastrophic injuries or minor injuries, who can recover their full damages, and those with significant but not catastrophic injures, whose recoveries will be limited by this statute. There is no reasonable basis for this distinction. Hence, the statute fails the rational basis test and constitutes a violation of equal protection.

Continued on next page.

ANALYSIS

Many states limit damages in tort lawsuits in various forms. Some states apply hard caps on noneconomic and punitive damages. Others use varying ratios for a determination of noneconomic damages, capping the noneconomic damages at two or three times the amount of the economic damages.

Quicknotes

COMPENSATORY DAMAGES Measure of damages necessary to compensate victim for actual injuries suffered.

EQUAL PROTECTION CLAUSE A constitutional provision that each person be guaranteed the same protection of the laws enjoyed by other persons in like circumstances.

RATIONAL BASIS REVIEW A test employed by the court to determine the validity of a statute in equal protection actions, whereby the court determines whether the challenged statute is rationally related to the achievement of a legitimate state interest.

CHAPTER 3

Punitive Remedies

Quick Reference Rules of Law

Exxon Shipping Co. v. Baker

Corporation (D) v. Class (P)

554 U.S. 471 (2008)

NATURE OF CASE: Appeal from decision by the Ninth Circuit Court of Appeals to reduce damages award.

FACT SUMMARY: The *Exxon Valdez* ran aground in Prince William Sound, Alaska, spilling millions of gallons of oil.

RULE OF LAW

In federal maritime law cases, the ratio of punitive damages to compensatory damages shall be 1:1.

FACTS: The *Exxon Valdez's* captain, Joseph Hazelwood, was a relapsed alcoholic and there was evidence his superiors were aware of this. On the night of the grounding, he drank five double vodkas before boarding the ship. The ship left a channel to avoid ice. Hazelwood then left the bridge leaving instructions for the third mate to make a turn back to the channel. The mate missed the turn and the ship ran aground. Hazelwood then tried to rock the boat off of the reef, which actually would have allowed more oil to spill from the ship. Exxon (D) paid $2.1 billion in clean-up efforts, a $25 million criminal fine, and $100 million in criminal restitution. A class of Native Alaskans, local landowners, and commercial fisherman brought the instant suit. After a trial, a jury awarded $5 billion in punitive damages. The Ninth Circuit Court of Appeals reduced on constitutional grounds twice, but each time the district court judge reinstituted similar punitive awards. On a third appeal, the Ninth Circuit reduced the punitive damages to $2.5 billion. Exxon (D) appealed.

ISSUE: In federal maritime law cases, shall the ratio of punitive damages to compensatory damages be 1:1?

HOLDING AND DECISION: (Souter, J.) Yes. In federal maritime law cases, the ratio of punitive damages to compensatory damages shall be 1:1. This is not a constitutional law case. The class brought these claims under federal maritime law. Thus, this court will determine an issue of federal common law. The consensus today regarding punitive damages is that they are used for retribution and deterring harmful conduct. State policy varies. Some states bar punitive damages outright, while others impose caps or punitive to compensatory damages ratios. The main problem with punitive damages is their unpredictability. In addition, verbal jury instructions delineating varying tests for determining punitive damages have proven unreliable. Placing quantified limits on punitive damages is the better method to provide predictability. The median ratio for punitive to compensatory damages is typically 0.65:1. The court now establishes a 1:1 ratio for punitive to compensatory damages in cases brought under federal maritime law. In this case, the district court ordered $507.5 million dollars in compensatory damages. The amount of punitive damages shall be the same. Vacated and remanded.

CONCURRENCE: (Scalia, J.) While the court properly follows prior cases establishing constitutional limits on punitive damages, those prior cases were not properly decided.

CONCURRENCE AND DISSENT: (Stevens, J.) Caps on damages as well as ratios are better left to legislatures for determination. The court fails to cite to any state case where the state supreme court imposed the limitation. Congress is better suited to analyze and determine the proper limitations, if any. This award should be reviewed on an abuse of discretion standard. Under that standard, the $2.5 billion punitive damages award should be upheld.

CONCURRENCE AND DISSENT: (Ginsburg, J.) Congress is better suited to establish the limitation the court imposes here on punitive damages.

CONCURRENCE AND DISSENT: (Breyer, J.) The majority is correct that punitive damages should be awarded according to identifiable standards. However, existing legal standards can suffice rather than imposing a rigid formula that does not allow for exceptions. The Ninth Circuit's decision should be upheld.

ANALYSIS

This case underscores the wide range among state legislatures and the Supreme Court regarding options to limit tort and, more specifically, punitive damages. In addition, there appears to be a lack of consensus as to whether the legislative branch or the judicial branch of government should be the decision maker when it comes to tort reform.

Quicknotes

COMPENSATORY DAMAGES Measure of damages necessary to compensate victim for actual injuries suffered.

PUNITIVE DAMAGES Damages exceeding the actual injury suffered for the purposes of punishment of the defendant, deterrence of the wrongful behavior, or comfort to the plaintiff.

State Farm Mutual Automobile Insurance Co. v. Campbell

Insurance company (D) v. Insured (P)

538 U.S. 408 (2003)

NATURE OF CASE: Appeal from reinstatement of full punitive damages award in bad-faith insurance coverage claim.

FACT SUMMARY: State Farm Mutual Automobile Insurance Co. (State Farm) (D) claimed that a punitive damages award of $145 million was excessive and violated the Constitution's Due Process Clause. Campbell (P) claimed that this amount was appropriate in light of State Farm's (D) national scheme to fraudulently cap claim payments.

RULE OF LAW

A punitive damages award of $145 million, where full compensatory damages are $1 million, is excessive and violative of the Due Process Clause of the Constitution.

FACTS: Although investigators and witnesses concluded that Campbell (P) caused a car accident in which one person was killed and another permanently disabled, his insurer, State Farm Mutual Automobile Insurance Co. (State Farm) (D), contested liability, declined to settle the ensuing claims for the $50,000 policy limit, ignored its own investigators' advice, and took the case to trial, assuring Campbell (P) that he had no liability for the accident, that State Farm (D) would represent his interests, and that he did not need separate counsel. At trial, a jury, finding Campbell (P) 100 percent at fault, returned a judgment for over $185,000, which was three times the policy limit. State Farm (D) initially refused to pay the excess above the $50,000 coverage limit but ultimately paid the entire judgment. Campbell (P) then brought suit against State Farm (D) for bad-faith refusal to settle, fraud, and intentional infliction of emotional distress. At trial, Campbell (P) presented evidence that State Farm (D) had engaged in a national scheme to increase its profits by capping claim payouts at below fair value, which Campbell (P) referred to as the Performance, Planning and Review policy, or PP&R. While State Farm (D) objected to the introduction of evidence of this scheme based on 20 years' worth of its adjustment practices involving claims arising throughout the nation, the court admitted the evidence to determine whether State Farm's (D) conduct in the Campbell case was intentional and egregious to warrant punitive damages. The jury awarded Campbell (P) $2.6 million in compensatory damages and $145 million in punitive damages, which the trial court reduced to $1 million and $25 million respectively. The state's highest court reinstated the $145 million punitive damages award, which State Farm (D) challenged as an excessive award violative of the Constitution's Due Process Clause. The United States Supreme Court granted certiorari.

ISSUE: Is a punitive damages award of $145 million, where full compensatory damages are $1 million, excessive and violative of the Due Process Clause of the Constitution?

HOLDING AND DECISION: (Kennedy, J.) Yes. A punitive damages award of $145 million, where full compensatory damages are $1 million, is excessive and violative of the Due Process Clause of the Constitution. Compensatory damages are intended to redress a plaintiff's concrete loss, while punitive damages are aimed at the different purposes of deterrence and retribution. The Due Process Clause prohibits the imposition of grossly excessive or arbitrary punishments on a tortfeasor. To the extent that a punitive award is excessive, it serves no legitimate purpose and constitutes an arbitrary deprivation of property in violation of the Constitution. Punitive damages pose an acute danger of arbitrary deprivation of property, which is heightened when the jury is presented with evidence having little bearing on the amount that should be awarded. Thus, this Court has instructed courts reviewing punitive damages to consider three guideposts: (1) the degree of reprehensibility of the defendant's misconduct, (2) the disparity between the actual or potential harm suffered by the plaintiff and the punitive damages award, and (3) the difference between the punitive damages awarded by the jury and the civil penalties authorized or imposed in comparable cases. Punitive awards should be reviewed in light of these guideposts to ensure that they are the product of the application of law rather than passion, prejudice, or caprice. An application of these guideposts easily leads to the conclusion that the award at issue was excessive.

As to the first guidepost, which is to determine a defendant's reprehensibility—which is the most important indicator of a punitive damages award's reasonableness—a court must consider whether: the harm was physical rather than economic; the tortious conduct evinced an indifference to or a reckless disregard for the health or safety of others; the conduct involved repeated actions or was an isolated incident; and the harm resulted from intentional malice, trickery, or deceit, or mere accident. It should be presumed that a plaintiff has been made whole by compensatory damages, so punitive damages should be awarded only if the defendant's culpability is so reprehensible to warrant the imposition of further sanctions to achieve punishment or deterrence. Here, State Farm's

Continued on next page.

(D) handling of the claims against Campbell (P) was condemnable, but a more modest punishment could have satisfied the state's legitimate objectives. Instead, this case was avowedly used as a platform to expose, and punish, the perceived deficiencies of State Farm's operations throughout the country. However, a state cannot punish a defendant for conduct that may have been lawful where it occurred, nor does the state have a legitimate concern in imposing punitive damages to punish a defendant for unlawful acts committed outside of its jurisdiction. Campbell (P) argued that such evidence was used merely to demonstrate, generally, State Farm's motives against its insured. Lawful out-of-state conduct may be probative when it demonstrates the deliberateness and culpability of the defendant's action in the state where it is tortious, but that conduct must have a nexus to the specific harm suffered by the plaintiff. More fundamentally, in relying on such evidence, the state courts awarded punitive damages to punish and deter conduct that bore no relation to Campbell's (P) harm. Due process does not permit courts to adjudicate the merits of other parties' hypothetical claims under the guise of the reprehensibility analysis—but that is exactly what was done here. Punishment on these bases creates the possibility of multiple punitive damages awards for the same conduct, because nonparties are not normally bound by another plaintiff's judgment. Here, too, there was scant evidence of repeated misconduct of the sort that injured Campbell (P), and it seems that State Farm (D) was not being punished only for its actions toward Campbell (P). Because Campbell (P) did not show conduct similar to that which harmed him, the only relevant conduct to the reprehensibility analysis is that which actually harmed Campbell (P). As to the second guidepost, the Court has been reluctant to identify concrete constitutional limits on the ratio between harm, or potential harm, to the plaintiff and the punitive damages award, and declines to do so here. Nonetheless, in practice, few awards exceeding a single-digit ratio between punitive and compensatory damages will satisfy due process. Single-digit multipliers are more likely to comport with due process, while still achieving the state's deterrence and retribution goals, than are awards with 145:1 ratio, as in this case. Because there are no rigid benchmarks, ratios greater than those that this Court has previously upheld may comport with due process where a particularly egregious act has resulted in only a small amount of economic damages. However, when compensatory damages are substantial, then an even lesser ratio can reach the outermost limit of the due process guarantee. Here, there is a presumption against an award with a 145:1 ratio; the $1 million compensatory award for a year and a half of emotional distress was substantial; and the distress caused by outrage and humiliation Campbell (P) suffered is likely a component of both the compensatory and punitive damages awards. The state's highest court sought to justify the massive award based on premises bearing no relation to the award's reasonableness or proportionality to the harm actually sustained. In fact, its arguments sought to justify a departure from well-established constraints on punitive damages.

As to the third guidepost, the most relevant civil sanction under state law for the wrong done to Campbell (P) is a $10,000 fine for an act of grand fraud, which is dwarfed by the $145 million punitive damages award. The state's highest court's references to a broad fraudulent scheme drawn from out-of-state and dissimilar conduct evidence were insufficient to justify this amount. The proper amount of punitive damages should be determined by the state courts following the principles of this case. Reversed and remanded.

DISSENT: (Ginsburg, J.) The precedent the majority relies on is relatively new and cannot be said to be well established. It also departs from the Court's longstanding practice of not interfering with states' prerogatives to superintend punitive damages awards. While the state's highest court's very large award may warrant state damages-capping legislation, it does not warrant the Court's substitution of its judgment for that of the state's courts. Previously, the Court's intrusion on the purview of the state courts in this area was moderate, whereas here the majority shows no restraint. Not only does the majority not accord the state-court judgment a strong presumption of validity, it provides a formula pursuant to which punitive damages are presumptively unconstitutional. While rendering such a formula is appropriate for the legislature, it is inappropriate for the Court, which here oversteps its bounds of authority.

ANALYSIS

In *BMW of North America v. Gore,* 517 U.S. 559 (1996), the case on which the majority relies, and in which the Court enunciated the three guideposts it used in *Campbell,* in addition to finding that all three guideposts indicated that the punitive damages award was excessive, the Court found that *BMW*'s due process rights were also violated because it could not have possibly anticipated, nor did it receive fair notice, that it might face such a severe punishment. As in this case, Justice Scalia dissented, expressing the view that a state trial procedure that commits the decision whether to impose punitive damages, and the amount, to the discretion of the jury, subject to some judicial review for "reasonableness," furnishes a defendant with all the process that is "due," and that the Constitution does not contain any guarantees against unfairness, as where a punitive

Continued on next page.

damages award might be unfair but nonetheless the product of due process.

Quicknotes

DUE PROCESS CLAUSE Clauses found in the Fifth and Fourteenth Amendments to the United States Constitution providing that no person shall be deprived of "life, liberty, or property, without due process of law."

PUNITIVE DAMAGES Damages exceeding the actual injury suffered for the purposes of punishment of the defendant, deterrence of the wrongful behavior, or comfort to the plaintiff.

Philip Morris USA v. Williams

Tobacco company (D) v. Decedent's estate (P)

549 U.S. 346 (2007)

NATURE OF CASE: Appeal from the Oregon Supreme Court.

FACT SUMMARY: Williams (P) died of lung cancer after smoking Marlboro cigarettes for 40 years.

RULE OF LAW

A jury may not use punitive damages to punish a defendant directly for harm the defendant caused to nonparties to the litigation.

FACTS: Williams (P) died of lung cancer after smoking Marlboro cigarettes for 40 years. After a verdict for Williams's estate (P), the jury awarded $21,000 in economic damages, $800,000 in noneconomic damages, and $79.5 million in punitive damages. The Oregon Supreme Court upheld the punitive damages award on the grounds that Philip Morris USA's (D) conduct was unusually reprehensible. Philip Morris USA (D) appealed to the United States Supreme Court.

ISSUE: May a jury use punitive damages to punish a defendant directly for harm the defendant caused to nonparties to the litigation?

HOLDING AND DECISION: (Breyer, J.) No. A jury may not use punitive damages to punish a defendant directly for harm the defendant caused to nonparties to the litigation. Here, the Court is not concerned with the constitutional question of whether the award is grossly excessive. Rather, the Court's decision will focus on the procedures for determining the amount of punitive damages. Those procedures must pass constitutional muster. A defendant threatened during a trial with a charge of conduct that allegedly harmed nonparties has no opportunity to defend himself from those charges. A trial as to one plaintiff will not likely answer the question as to whether the defendant's conduct harmed others not a party to the litigation. This raises the due process concerns of risk of arbitrariness, uncertainty and lack of notice for defendants. However, a jury may take into account the defendant's conduct that risks harm to many other people. Evidence of this type goes to the reprehensibility of the conduct, which is a proper factor for juries to consider when awarding punitive damage. State courts must take steps to ensure that juries are not awarding punitive damages in order to punish defendants for harm caused to others. Vacated and remanded.

DISSENT: (Stevens, J.) The majority imposes a novel limit on the ability of state courts to determine punishment in civil litigation matters. A punitive damages award is by definition not compensatory. It serves the purpose of retribution and deterrence. There is even a greater justification in this case because the punitive damages award is paid in whole or part to the State of Oregon, pursuant to a state statute. Moreover, the majority's distinction between forbidding juries to punish defendants for harm caused to nonparties but then allowing them to consider that same conduct in terms of reprehensibility makes no sense. When a jury considers harm to others in the reprehensibility context, the jury is punishing the defendant for that same conduct.

DISSENT: (Ginsburg, J.) The Oregon Supreme Court's decision is not in conflict with the majority opinion here. That court agreed with the notion that punitive damages should not be used to punish defendants for harm caused to others. In addition, it does not appear Philip Morris (D) ever properly preserved any objections to the jury instructions given in the case.

ANALYSIS

The text notes that on remand, the Oregon Supreme Court entered the same punitive damages award, on the grounds that Philip Morris (D) had not properly preserved any claim of error. Regardless of the opinions here, it is always difficult to determine whether juries are meting out punitive damage awards for punishment or for the reprehensibility of the conduct.

Quicknotes

PUNITIVE DAMAGES Damages exceeding the actual injury suffered for the purposes of punishment of the defendant, deterrence of the wrongful behavior, or comfort to the plaintiff.

Formosa Plastics Corp. USA v. Presidio Engineers and Contractors, Inc.

Corporation (D) v. Corporation (P)

Tex. Sup. Ct., 960 S.W.2d 41 (1998)

NATURE OF CASE: Appeal from judgment awarding damages for fraud and breach of contract.

FACT SUMMARY: Presidio Engineers and Contractors, Inc. (P) sought damages stemming from its work as a contractor on a project owned by Formosa Plastics Corp. USA (D).

RULE OF LAW

A party may recover punitive damages for a fraud claim based upon economic losses related to the performance and subject matter of a breached contract.

FACTS: Presidio Engineers and Contractors, Inc. (Presidio) (P) submitted a construction bid on a project run by Formosa Plastics Corp. USA (Formosa) (D). In preparing its bid, Presidio (P) relied upon certain representations made by Formosa (D) regarding the scheduling and control of the project. When Presidio (P) discovered the representations were false after starting the project, it sued Formosa (D) for breach of contract and fraud. The district court found that Formosa (D) defrauded Presidio (P) and awarded damages, including exemplary damages based upon a finding of willfulness by Formosa (D). After Presidio accepted remittitur, Formosa (D) appealed. The court of appeals affirmed, and the Texas Supreme Court granted review.

ISSUE: May a party recover punitive damages for a fraud claim based upon economic losses related to the performance and subject matter of a breached contract?

HOLDING AND DECISION: (Abbott, J.) Yes. A party may recover punitive damages for a fraud claim based upon economic losses related to the performance and subject matter of a breached contract. With respect to the distinction between cases sounding in contract versus tort, cases of fraud fill a gray area. While a mere breach of contract cannot support recovery of punitive damages, such damages are not precluded simply because a fraudulent representation only results in an economic loss. If a plaintiff proves fraudulent inducement, the resulting damages sound in tort. Here, Presidio (P) demonstrated that Formosa (D) made untrue representations with no intention of performing on them in order to induce low bids. The district court's finding of fraud is legally sufficient. Affirmed.

ANALYSIS

While courts refuse to award punitive damages in breach of contract cases, such damages can be awarded if an independent tort is committed. In determining whether a claim sounds in tort versus contract, a court looks to the nature of the injury. If there is only economic loss, the case sounds in contract.

Quicknotes

BREACH OF CONTRACT Unlawful failure by a party to perform its obligations pursuant to contract.

FRAUD IN THE INDUCEMENT (contracts) A party's misleading another into entering a contract by providing false information or omitting important details, leading the deceived party to act to their detriment or disadvantage, and permitting the deceived party to recover damages or terminate the contract.

PUNITIVE DAMAGES Damages exceeding the actual injury suffered for the purposes of punishment of the defendant, deterrence of the wrongful behavior, or comfort to the plaintiff.

CHAPTER 4

Preventing Harm: The Measure of Injunctive Relief

Quick Reference Rules of Law

Almurbati v. Bush

Detainees (P) v. Federal government/Executive branch (D)

366 F. Supp. 2d 72 (D.D.C. 2005)

NATURE OF CASE: Detainees motion for a preliminary injunction.

FACT SUMMARY: Six Bahraini nationals (P) have been held at Guantanamo Bay and classified as enemy combatants. They seek a preliminary injunction against the Government (D) forbidding their transfer to another country without notice to a federal court.

RULE OF LAW

In order to obtain injunctive relief, a plaintiff must prove that the potential injury is not remote and speculative.

FACTS: The Government (D) held six Bahraini nationals (P) at Guantanamo Bay, Cuba, as enemy combatants. After hearing media reports that the government was going to transfer them to other countries, the six nationals (P) filed a motion for a preliminary injunction forbidding the Government (D) from carrying out such transfers without first providing 30-day notice to a federal court. The Bahraini nationals (P) cited media reports that other countries, such as Saudi Arabia and Yemen, employ inhumane interrogation techniques. There were also hearsay statements from guards that the Bahraini nationals (P) would be raped or "turned into women" after their transfers. The Government (D) provided affidavits in response that it was not the policy of the Government (D) to transfer individuals to countries that torture detainees. Also, the Government (D) averred that it seeks assurances that all detainees shall be treated humanely after a transfer.

ISSUE: In order to obtain injunctive relief, must a plaintiff prove that the potential injury is not remote and speculative?

HOLDING AND DECISION: (Walton, J.) Yes. In order to obtain injunctive relief, a plaintiff must prove that the potential injury is not remote and speculative. Here, the Bahraini nationals (P) have failed to show that their threatened harm is not remote and speculative. Their reliance on media reports and hearsay statements does not present a record on which this court may rely upon to enjoin the executive branch in its handling of detainees. There is no evidence the detainees will be transferred to any country other than their own, a prospect to which they have no objection. Motion denied.

ANALYSIS

Motions for preliminary injunction should be supported by admissible evidence in the form of affidavits based on personal knowledge, documents, or photographs that present a compelling case that the alleged injury is likely to occur without judicial intervention.

Quicknotes

PRELIMINARY INJUNCTION A judicial mandate issued to require or restrain a party from certain conduct; used to preserve a trial's subject matter or to prevent threatened injury.

Marshall v. Goodyear Tire & Rubber Co.

Federal government (P) v. Corporation (D)

554 F.2d 730 (5th Cir. 1977)

NATURE OF CASE: Appeal of permanent injunction prohibiting certain employment practices constituting age discrimination.

FACT SUMMARY: Following a successful suit on behalf of an employee illegally dismissed due to age, the U.S. Department of Labor (P) obtained a nationwide injunction against Goodyear Tire & Rubber Co. (D).

RULE OF LAW

The scope of injunctive relief should not be broader than the evidence warranting it.

FACTS: William G. Reed, Jr., was discharged due to his age by his employer, Goodyear Tire & Rubber Co. (Goodyear) (D). The U.S. Department of Labor (P) brought suit on his behalf. The district court ordered Reed be given back pay and issued a nationwide injunction barring such practices. No evidence of a nationwide age discrimination policy existed. Goodyear (D) appealed the injunction.

ISSUE: Should the scope of injunctive relief be broader than the evidence warranting it?

HOLDING AND DECISION: (Gewin, J.) No. The scope of injunctive relief should not be broader than the evidence warranting it. Injunctive relief is a drastic remedy and should not be applied lightly. It should only be granted as is appropriate to remedy the problem at issue in the suit before the court. Here, the discharge of a single employee was at issue, not a nationwide policy. The issuance of a nationwide injunction was far broader in scope than the situation before the court and was, therefore, not appropriate. Remanded.

ANALYSIS

Drafting an injunction can be quite difficult. Federal Rule of Civil Procedure 65(d) states that injunctions and the reasons therefore must be clearly spelled out. The purpose of such a rule is to force the issuing court to fully think through an injunction before issuing one. As the present case demonstrates, however, the plan does not always work.

Quicknotes

INJUNCTION An equitable remedy requiring a person, entity, or governmental unit to do, or prohibiting that person, entity, or governmental unit from doing, a specific act.

INJUNCTIVE RELIEF A court order issued as a remedy, requiring a person to do, or prohibiting that person from doing, a specific act.

United States v. W.T. Grant Co.

Federal government (P) v. Corporation (D)

345 U.S. 629 (1953)

NATURE OF CASE: Appeal of dismissal of suit for injunctive relief.

FACT SUMMARY: After Hancock (D) resigned from certain interlocking directorates, the Government (P) continued to petition for an injunction barring such activities.

RULE OF LAW

For a permanent injunction to issue, there must be some cognizable danger of recurrent violations.

FACTS: Hancock (D) was a director of several competing retail giants. Contending that this was in violation of the Clayton Act, the Government (P) brought an action seeking an injunction barring Hancock (D) and the retailing firms from such interlocking directorates. Hancock (D) resigned, although he refused to admit he had been violating the Act. The Government (P) continued to petition for an injunction, contending the danger of future violations existed. The Government (P) introduced no evidence of a plan by Hancock (D) or the retailers to renew the activity. The trial court rejected the petition, and the appellate court affirmed.

ISSUE: For a permanent injunction to issue, must there be some cognizable danger of recurrent violations?

HOLDING AND DECISION: (Clark, J.) Yes. For a permanent injunction to issue, there must be some cognizable danger of recurrent violations. While the voluntary cessation of an illegal activity does not render an action to enjoin it moot, proof that the relief is needed must be shown. More than a possibility must be shown. Here, no evidence that the conduct in question was apt to recur was shown, and therefore the trial court was well within the bounds of its discretion in denying the injunction. Affirmed.

DISSENT: (Douglas, J.) The proclivity of the defendants to engage in anticompetitive practices is fairly clear, and to enjoin such practices would be proper.

ANALYSIS

Mootness was not an issue here. Even though Hancock (D) resigned, the possibility that the conduct in question might repeat was sufficient to allow the court to retain jurisdiction. As the above demonstrates, the amount of proof necessary to avoid mootness and the amount necessary to justify relief are not at all coextensive.

Quicknotes

INJUNCTION An equitable remedy requiring a person, entity, or governmental unit to do, or prohibiting that person, entity, or governmental unit from doing, a specific act.

INJUNCTIVE RELIEF A court order issued as a remedy, requiring a person to do, or prohibiting that person from doing, a specific act.

MOOT Judgment on the particular issue that has previously been decided or settled.

Nicholson v. Connecticut Half-Way House, Inc.

Land owners (P) v. Corporation (D)

Conn. Sup. Ct., 218 A.2d 383 (1966)

NATURE OF CASE: Action to enjoin the use of property.

FACT SUMMARY: Halfway House, Inc. (D) wanted to use its residential property as a rehabilitation center for paroled convicts.

RULE OF LAW

Where a property owner's intended use of their property conforms to the law, such use will not be enjoined where the only injury claimed by a neighbor is the fear of future eventualities or a decline in the value of their property.

FACTS: Connecticut Half-Way House, Inc. (Half-Way House) (D) purchased a large home in a residential area. Half-Way House (D) planned to use the home to rehabilitate and counsel paroled felons. Adjoining landowners sought injunctive relief. They alleged that the intended use might increase the crime rate in the area and that it would detrimentally affect property values. The court granted the injunction.

ISSUE: Where a property owner's intended use of their property conforms to the law, will such use be enjoined where the only injury claimed by a neighbor is the fear of future eventualities or a decline in the value of their property?

HOLDING AND DECISION: (Thim, J.) No. Where a property owner's intended use of their property conforms to the law, such use will not be enjoined where the only injury claimed by a neighbor is the fear of future eventualities or a decline in the value of their property. The test of whether the intended use of private property constitutes a nuisance to other owners is one of reasonableness. A private property owner may not use their property in an unreasonable manner so as to injure their neighbors. Here, Half-Way House's (D) intended use is not prohibited by the zoning law. Nicholson (P) and its other neighbors are afraid of the effect it will have on the neighborhood and property values. They feel that crime may increase and their property will decline in value. The fear of future events or actions does not constitute irreparable injury for which equity will grant an injunction. The injury must be real and current. An injunction will not be granted for what may be groundless fears. Nor will it be granted because prospective buyers may have the same fears. Anticipatory claims such as this one are not grounds for injunctive relief. Injunction reversed.

ANALYSIS

Where the proposed use has known qualities so that a court may conclude that the use is unreasonable, an injunction may be issued. For example, in *Brainard v. Town of West Hartford*, 140 Conn. 631 (Conn. 1954), the defendant intended to use residential property as a garbage dump. The court held that the action to enjoin this use was not premature. The court felt that the presence of a dump in a residential neighborhood was an unreasonable use since the qualities of a dump were well known to the court and the fears of adjacent owners were not groundless.

Quicknotes

EQUITY Fairness; justice; the determination of a matter consistent with principles of fairness and not in strict compliance with rules of law.

INJUNCTION A court order requiring a person to do, or prohibiting that person from doing, a specific act.

PepsiCo, Inc. v. Redmond

Former employer (P) v. Departing employee (D)

54 F.3d 1262 (7th Cir. 1995)

NATURE OF CASE: Employer's motion for preliminary injunction against former employee.

FACT SUMMARY: Redmond (D) worked for PepsiCo, Inc. (P) for ten years and then accepted a job offer from a competitor.

RULE OF LAW

In litigation involving trade secrets, a court may enjoin the actual or threatened misappropriation of trade secrets.

FACTS: Redmond (D) worked for PepsiCo, Inc. (P) for ten years, eventually rising to the position of general manager of the business unit covering California. Redmond (P) signed a confidentiality agreement with PepsiCo (P) stating that he would not disclose confidential information. On November 8, 1994, Redmond (D) accepted an offer from Quaker Oats Co. (Quaker), a competitor of PepsiCo (P). On November 16, 1994, PepsiCo (P) filed a complaint and motion for preliminary injunction against Redmond (D). PepsiCo (P) sought an order enjoining Redmond (D) from taking the position at Quaker and to prevent him from disclosing trade secrets. PepsiCo (P) submitted evidence that Redmond had knowledge of PepsiCo's (P) strategic plans to manufacture, price, distribute, and market sport drinks that competed directly with Quaker's more successful Gatorade line of sport drinks. The district court allowed the motion, enjoining Redmond (D) from taking the position until May of 1995 and ordering him never to reveal PepsiCo's (P) trade secrets. Redmond (P) appealed to the Seventh Circuit Court of Appeals.

ISSUE: In litigation involving trade secrets, may a court enjoin the actual or threatened misappropriation of trade secrets?

HOLDING AND DECISION: (Flaum, J.) Yes. In litigation involving trade secrets, a court may enjoin the actual or threatened misappropriation of trade secrets. Trade secret law protects standards of commercial morality, but that same law should not be used to prevent employees from pursuing their livelihoods. Here, the alleged harm is not actual misappropriation of secrets but rather the threatened misappropriation thereof. A plaintiff may prove a claim of threatened misappropriation of trade secrets by successfully demonstrating that the employee will inevitably rely upon the trade secrets while in their new position. Here, PepsiCo (P) has successfully demonstrated that Redmond (D) had knowledge of PepsiCo's (P) plans to price, distribute and market its new age sport drinks. This will allow Quaker, armed unfairly with that knowledge, to anticipate PepsiCo's (P) strategic marketing moves. This is not unlike a star football player leaving one team for an opposing team with the playbook one day before the game. In addition, there was evidence that Redmond (D) was not entirely forthright with PepsiCo (P) as to his dealings with Quaker. Accordingly, the court properly allowed the motion for preliminary injunction on the grounds that PepsiCo (P) had demonstrated a likelihood of success of the merits of its statutory trade secrets claim. Affirmed.

ANALYSIS

A court faced with a typical motion for preliminary injunction will review the following four factors: (1) the plaintiff's likelihood of success on the merits of the underlying claim; (2) the likelihood of irreparable harm to the plaintiff; (3) the harm to the defendant caused by the injunction; and (4) the public's interest, if any, in the subject of the litigation.

Quicknotes

PRELIMINARY INJUNCTION A judicial mandate issued to require or restrain a party from certain conduct; used to preserve a trial's subject matter or to prevent threatened injury.

TRADE SECRET Consists of any formula, pattern, plan, process, or device known only to its owner and business, which gives an advantage over competitors; a secret formula used in the manufacture of a particular product that is not known to the general public.

Forster v. Boss

Individuals (P) v. Individuals (D)

97 F.3d 1127 (8th Cir. 1996)

NATURE OF CASE: Appeal from award of damages and a permanent injunction.

FACT SUMMARY: The district court awarded damages to the Forsters (P) because of the Bosses' (D) fraud in connection with the sale of their lakefront home, and it also granted their motion for a permanent injunction.

RULE OF LAW

In a case where either compensatory damages or an injunction would make the plaintiff whole, the plaintiff must choose which of the two remedies they want.

FACTS: The Forsters (P) were granted both a permanent injunction and compensatory damages due to the Bosses' (D) fraud in selling them lakefront property without a boat dock permit. The Bosses (D) appealed, claiming that the Forsters (P) were not entitled to a double recovery and that under the election of remedies doctrine, the Forsters (P) had to choose either the injunction or the compensatory damages.

ISSUE: In a case where either compensatory damages or an injunction would make the plaintiff whole, must the plaintiff choose which of the two remedies they want?

HOLDING AND DECISION: (Arnold, C.J.) No. In a case where either compensatory damages or an injunction would make the plaintiff whole, the plaintiff must choose which of the two remedies they want. Since the injunction made the Forsters (P) whole by granting them their boat dock permit and a swim dock, they could not also recover damages for the same loss. The award of punitive damages was not duplicative and was affirmed; the damages award was reduced to one dollar. Affirmed in part, reversed in part and remanded.

CONCURRENCE: (Kornmann, J.) The court should limit relief to the injunction sought by the Forsters (P) for the boat dock permit. It is unjust for the Forsters (P) to receive both the boat dock permit and monetary damages.

ANALYSIS

The court here reduced the compensatory damages award to one dollar to sustain the award of punitive damages. Since the Bosses' (D) fraud was found to be abusive, punitive damages were appropriate. A court of equity can award both injunctive relief and actual and punitive damages as an adjunct to its equitable jurisdiction.

Quicknotes

COMPENSATORY DAMAGES Measure of damages necessary to compensate victim for actual injuries suffered.

FRAUD A false representation of facts with the intent that another will rely on the misrepresentation to their detriment.

PERMANENT INJUNCTION A remedy imposed by the court ordering a party to cease the conduct of a specific activity until the final disposition of the cause of action.

PUNITIVE DAMAGES Damages exceeding the actual injury suffered for the purposes of punishment, deterrence, and comfort to plaintiff.

Winston Research Corp. v. Minnesota Mining & Manufacturing Co.

Corporation (D) v. Corporation (P)

350 F.2d 134 (9th Cir. 1965)

NATURE OF CASE: Appeal of injunction in unfair competition action.

FACT SUMMARY: Winston Research Corp. (D) developed a tape recorder with characteristics similar to one soon to be produced by Minnesota Mining & Manufacturing Co. (3M) (P). Winston (D) consisted of 3M (P) defectors.

RULE OF LAW

Unfair competition should be enjoined for the amount of time it would take to develop a similar product after public disclosure thereof.

FACTS: Minnesota Mining & Manufacturing Co. (3M) (P) developed a certain tape recorder. Prior to the recorder's marketing, Winston Research Corp. (D) had been formed by several defecting 3M (P) employees. When the intention of Winston Research (D) to market a similar recorder became known, 3M (P) brought an action to enjoin sales of the recorder. The trial court issued an injunction preventing Winston Research (D) from marketing the recorder for two years, which in the court's estimation was the time necessary for a competitor to develop a similar system after public disclosure thereof. Both sides appealed.

ISSUE: Should unfair competition be enjoined for the amount of time it would take to develop a similar product after public disclosure thereof?

HOLDING AND DECISION: (Browning, J.) Yes. Unfair competition should be enjoined for the amount of time it would take to develop a similar product after public disclosure thereof. An injunction of this nature should prevent unjust enrichment and protect trade secrets, but no more. Here, a permanent injunction would go beyond this goal in that Winston Research (D) would be denied the fruits of what normal research and development would produce. An injunction should not serve to chill the creation of new technologies. The approach of the district court was proper. Affirmed.

ANALYSIS

Permanent injunctions of the nature that 3M (P) wished to obtain in this action are punitive in nature. That is, they do more than compensate the plaintiff. Generally speaking, equity is compensatory, not punitive. Some courts, however, will indulge in punitive injunctions in egregious cases.

Quicknotes

EQUITY Fairness; justice; the determination of a matter consistent with principles of fairness and not in strict compliance with rules of law.

INJUNCTION An equitable remedy requiring a person, entity, or governmental unit to do, or prohibiting that person, entity, or governmental unit from doing, a specific act.

PERMANENT INJUNCTION A remedy imposed by the court ordering a party to cease the conduct of a specific activity until the final disposition of the cause of action.

Bailey v. Proctor

Individuals (P) v. Receiver (D)

160 F.2d 78 (1st Cir. 1947)

NATURE OF CASE: Appeal of court-ordered liquidation of investment trust.

FACT SUMMARY: A court ordered the liquidation of a barely solvent trust organized before the Investment Company Act of 1940.

RULE OF LAW

A court may order the liquidation of an investment enterprise when necessary to protect investors.

FACTS: The Aldred Investment Trust (Trust) had been set up prior to the Investment Company Act of 1940. Its structure was characterized by concentrated decision-making power with the prospect of high profits for the controlling shareholders to the detriment of the other investors. The Trust became insolvent, and a receiver was appointed. The management of the Trust was changed. The Trust became solvent again. Nonetheless, the court issued an injunction liquidating the Trust. Bailey (P) and others in the control group appealed this order.

ISSUE: May a court order the liquidation of an investment enterprise when necessary to protect investors?

HOLDING AND DECISION: (Mahoney, J.) Yes. A court may order the liquidation of an investment enterprise when necessary to protect investors. Insolvency is not a necessary prerequisite to liquidating an investment enterprise. When it appears that the continuation of the enterprise presents a threat to investors, liquidation may be ordered. Here, although new management had been installed, the structural defects in the trust that permitted the problems to arise in the first place still existed, and the court could legitimately conclude that the Trust's termination was necessary to protect noncontrolling investors. Affirmed and remanded.

ANALYSIS

Like injunction, receivership is an equitable remedy. It, like the injunction, finds its origins in the chancery courts of England. Receivership is thus characterized by the flexibility and wide applicability of injunctions and other equitable remedies.

Quicknotes

INSOLVENT One's liabilities exceed one's assets; inability to pay one's debts.

LIQUIDATION The reduction to cash of all assets for distribution to creditors.

RECEIVERSHIP Proceeding or condition whereby a receiver is appointed in order to maintain the holdings of a corporation, individual, or other entity that is insolvent.

Brown v. Plata

State governor (D) v. Mentally or physically ill state prisoner (P)

563 U.S. 493 (2011)

NATURE OF CASE: Appeal from decision of three-judge district court convened under the Prison Litigation Reform Act of 1995 (PLRA) ordering the release of prisoners to remedy the unconstitutional consequences of overcrowding in the California (D) prison system.

FACT SUMMARY: California (D) contended that a remedial order issued by a three-judge district court pursuant to the Prison Litigation Reform Act of 1995 (PLRA), which required California (D) to significantly reduce its prison population within two years, was erroneous because it did not comply with the PLRA's requirements and procedures.

RULE OF LAW

A remedial order issued by a three-judge district court convened pursuant to the Prison Litigation Reform Act of 1995 (PLRA), which requires a state to significantly reduce its prison population to remedy Eighth Amendment violations resulting from overcrowding, meets the PLRA's requirements and procedures where: the PLRA's requirement of allowing a state reasonable amount of time to comply with previous court orders is satisfied; evidence supports the court's finding that overcrowding is the primary cause of Eighth Amendment violations; evidence supports the court's finding that no other relief would remedy the Eighth Amendment violations; the court has given substantial weight to public safety; and the evidence supports the court's determination of the appropriate number at which the prison population should be capped.

FACTS: California's (D) prisons were designed to house a population just under 80,000, but its prison population had grown to almost double that. In other words, the prison population was at about 200 percent of design capacity. This resulted, on average, in an inmate in one of California's (D) prisons needlessly dying every six to seven days due to constitutional deficiencies in the California (D) prisons' medical delivery system. The consequences of overcrowding also included needless suffering and pain, the increased, substantial risk for transmission of infectious illness, and a suicide rate approaching an average of one per week. The resulting conditions were the subject of two federal class actions. In *Coleman v. Brown,* filed in 1990, the district court found that prisoners (P) with serious mental illness did not receive minimal, adequate care. A Special Master appointed to oversee remedial efforts reported 12 years later that the state of mental health care in California's (D) prisons was deteriorating due to increased overcrowding. In *Plata v. Brown,* filed in 2001, California (D) conceded that deficiencies in prison medical care violated prisoners' (P) Eighth Amendment rights and stipulated to a remedial injunction. However, when California (D) had not complied with the injunction by 2005, the court appointed a Receiver to oversee remedial efforts. Three years later, the Receiver described continuing deficiencies caused by overcrowding. Believing that a remedy for unconstitutional medical and mental health care could not be achieved without reducing overcrowding, the *Coleman* and *Plata* plaintiffs (P) moved their respective district courts to convene a three-judge district court empowered by the Prison Litigation Reform Act of 1995 (PLRA), 18 U.S.C. § 3626, to order reductions in the prison population. The judges in both actions granted the request, and the cases were consolidated before a single three-judge court. Under the PLRA, only a three-judge court may limit a prison population. Before convening such a court, a district court must have entered an order for less-intrusive relief that failed to remedy the constitutional violation and must have given the defendant state a reasonable time to comply with its prior orders. Once convened, the three-judge court must find by clear and convincing evidence that crowding is the primary cause of the violation, and that no other relief will remedy the violation. The court must also ensure that the relief is narrowly drawn, extends no further than necessary, and is the least intrusive means necessary to correct the violation. Additionally, the court must give substantial weight to any adverse impact on public safety or the operation of a criminal justice system caused by the ordered relief. After hearing testimony and making extensive findings of fact, the court ordered California (D) to reduce its prison population to 137.5 percent of design capacity within two years. Assuming California (D) would not be able to increase capacity through new construction, the order required a prison population reduction of 38,000 to 46,000 persons. Because it appeared all but certain that California (D) could not complete sufficient construction to comply fully with the order, the prison population would have to be reduced to at least some extent. The court did not order California (D) to achieve this reduction in any particular manner. Instead, the court ordered California (D) to formulate a plan for compliance and submit its plan for approval by the court. California (D), contending that the remedial order did not satisfy the

Continued on next page.

PLRA's requirements and procedures, appealed directly to the United States Supreme Court, as authorized by federal law, and the Court granted review.

ISSUE: Does a remedial order issued by a three-judge district court convened pursuant to the Prison Litigation Reform Act of 1995 (PLRA), which requires a state to significantly reduce its prison population to remedy Eighth Amendment violations resulting from overcrowding, meet the PLRA's requirements and procedures where: the PLRA's requirement of allowing a state reasonable amount of time to comply with previous court orders is satisfied; evidence supports the court's finding that overcrowding is the primary cause of Eighth Amendment violations; evidence supports the court's finding that no other relief would remedy the Eighth Amendment violations; the court has given substantial weight to public safety; and the evidence supports the court's determination of the appropriate number at which the prison population should be capped?

HOLDING AND DECISION: (Kennedy, J.) Yes. A remedial order issued by a three-judge district court convened pursuant to the Prison Litigation Reform Act of 1995 (PLRA), which requires a state to significantly reduce its prison population to remedy Eighth Amendment violations resulting from overcrowding, meets the PLRA's requirements and procedures where: the PLRA's requirement of allowing a state reasonable amount of time to comply with previous court orders is satisfied; evidence supports the court's finding that overcrowding is the primary cause of Eighth Amendment violations; evidence supports the court's finding that no other relief would remedy the Eighth Amendment violations; the court has given substantial weight to public safety; and the evidence supports the court's determination of the appropriate number at which the prison population should be capped.

California (D) contended that it was error to convene the three-judge court without affording it more time to comply with the prior orders in *Coleman* and *Plata*. This contention is without merit. The district court orders in those cases were intended to remedy constitutional violations and were given ample time to succeed—12 years in *Coleman*, and 5 years in *Plata*. Contrary to California's (D) claim, the district courts were not required to wait to see whether their more recent efforts would yield equal disappointment and thus were not required to give more time for subsequent remedial efforts to succeed. The district courts had a solid basis to doubt that additional efforts to build new facilities and hire new staff would achieve a remedy, given the ongoing deficiencies recently reported by both the Special Master and the Receiver. Therefore, the district courts acted reasonably in convening the three-judge district court.

Also contrary to California's (D) assertion, the three-judge court did not err in finding that crowding was the primary cause of Eighth Amendment violations in the California (D) prison system. The trial record documented the severe impact of burgeoning demand on the provision of care. The evidence showed that there were high vacancy rates for medical and mental health staff, e.g., 20 percent for surgeons and 54.1 percent for psychiatrists; that these numbers understated the severity of the crisis because California (D) had not budgeted sufficient staff to meet demand; and that even if vacant positions could be filled, there would be insufficient space for the additional staff. Such a shortfall contributed to significant delays in treating mentally ill prisoners, who were housed in administrative segregation for extended periods while awaiting transfer to scarce mental health treatment beds. There were also backlogs of up to 700 prisoners waiting to see a doctor for physical care. Crowding created unsafe and unsanitary conditions that hampered the effective delivery of medical and mental health care. It also promoted unrest and violence. Increased violence requires increased reliance on lockdowns to keep order, and lockdowns further impede the effective delivery of care. Overcrowding's effects were particularly acute in prison reception centers, which processed 140,000 new or returning prisoners annually, and which housed some prisoners for their entire incarceration period. Numerous experts testified that crowding was the primary cause of the constitutional violations. Further, California's (D) complaint that the three-judge court excluded evidence of current conditions in the prisons lacked a factual basis, as California (D) failed to point to any significant evidence that it was unable to present and that would have changed the outcome of the proceedings.

The three-judge court acknowledged that the violations were caused by factors in addition to overcrowding and that reducing crowding in the prisons would not entirely cure the violations. The three-judge court nevertheless did not err in finding that overcrowding was the primary cause in the sense of being the foremost cause of the violation. This understanding of the primary cause requirement is consistent with the text of the PLRA. Overcrowding need only be the foremost, chief, or principal cause of the violation. If Congress had intended to require that crowding be the only cause, it would have said so. A reading of the PLRA that would render population limits unavailable in practice would raise serious constitutional concerns. A finding that overcrowding is the "primary cause" of a violation is therefore permissible, despite the need for additional steps to remedy the violation.

The evidence supported the three-judge court's finding that "no other relief [would] remedy the violation." California (D) argues that the violation could have been remedied through a combination of new construction,

Continued on next page.

transfers of prisoners out of state, hiring of medical personnel, and continued efforts by the *Plata* Receiver and *Coleman* Special Master. The order in fact permits California (D) to comply with the population limit by transferring prisoners to county facilities or facilities in other states, or by constructing new facilities to raise the prisons' design capacity. If California (D) does find an adequate remedy other than a population limit, it may seek modification or termination of the three-judge court's order on that basis. The evidence at trial, however, supports the three-judge court's conclusion that an order limited to other remedies would not provide effective relief—especially given that the California (D) legislature has not been willing or able to allocate the resources necessary to meet the prison crisis absent a reduction in overcrowding, and there is no reason to believe it will begin to do so in the face of unprecedented budgetary shortfalls.

Furthermore, the prospective relief ordered here was narrowly drawn, extended no further than necessary to correct the violation, and was the least intrusive means necessary to correct the violation. The population limit does not fail narrow tailoring simply because prisoners beyond the plaintiff class will have to be released through parole or sentencing reform to meet the required reduction, or because reducing overcrowding will have positive effects beyond facilitating timely and adequate access to medical care, such as reducing violence and ameliorating unsafe living conditions. A narrow and otherwise proper remedy for a constitutional violation is not invalid simply because it will have collateral effects. Nor does the PLRA require that result. The PLRA states that a remedy shall extend no further than necessary to remedy the violation of the rights of a "particular plaintiff or plaintiffs." This means only that the scope of the order must be determined with reference to the constitutional violations established by the specific plaintiffs (P) before the court. Even prisoners with no present physical or mental illness might become afflicted, and all prisoners in California (D) are at risk so long as they are provided inadequate care. Prisoners in the general population will become sick, and will become members of the plaintiff classes, with routine frequency. Relief targeted only at present members of the plaintiff classes might therefore fail to adequately protect future class members who will develop serious physical or mental illness.

The three-judge court also gave "substantial weight" to any potential adverse impact on public safety from its order. The PLRA's "substantial weight" requirement does not require the court to certify that its order has no possible adverse impact on the public. Here, statistical evidence showed that prison populations had been lowered without adversely affecting public safety in some California counties, several states, and Canada. The court found that various available methods of reducing overcrowding—good time credits and diverting low-risk offenders to community programs—would have little or no impact on public safety, and its order took account of such concerns.

To comply with the PLRA, a court must set a population limit at the highest level consistent with an efficacious remedy, and it must order the population reduction to be achieved in the shortest period of time reasonably consistent with public safety. Here, the three-judge court's conclusion that the prison population should be capped at 137.5 percent of design capacity was not clearly erroneous. The court concluded that the evidence supported a limit between a 130 percent limit and a 145 percent limit. The court made the most precise determination it could in light of the record before it. The PLRA's narrow tailoring requirement is satisfied so long as such equitable, remedial judgments are made with the objective of releasing the fewest possible prisoners consistent with an efficacious remedy. In light of substantial evidence supporting an even more drastic remedy, the three-judge court complied with the requirement of the PLRA in this case.

Finally, the three-judge court did not err in providing a two-year deadline for relief. The court has the authority, and responsibility, to amend its order as warranted by the exercise of sound discretion, and the court must remain open to a showing by either California (D) or the plaintiffs (P) that its injunction should be altered to ensure that the rights and interests of the parties are given all due and necessary protection. For example, the court may grant a motion to extend the deadline if California (D) meets appropriate preconditions designed to ensure that the plan will be implemented without undue delay. Such observations reflect the fact that the existing order, like all ongoing equitable relief, must remain open to appropriate modification, and are not intended to cast doubt on the validity of the order's basic premise. Affirmed.

DISSENT: (Scalia, J.) The institutional reform the three-judge court has undertaken violates the PLRA's terms, ignores bedrock limitations on the power of Article III judges, and takes federal courts beyond their institutional capacity. This case alleges a prison system with inadequate medical facilities, but it is inconceivable that anything more than a small proportion of prisoners (P) in the plaintiff classes have personally received sufficiently atrocious treatment that their Eighth Amendment right was violated. No tenable procedural principles justify certifying a class of plaintiffs so they may assert a claim of systemic unconstitutionality. One possible justification is that although some or most plaintiffs in the class do not individually have viable Eighth Amendment claims, the class as a whole has collectively suffered an Eighth Amendment violation. That theory, however, is contrary to the bedrock rule that the sole purpose of class-wide

Continued on next page.

adjudication is to aggregate claims that are individually viable. A second possibility is that every member of the plaintiff class has suffered an Eighth Amendment violation merely by virtue of being a patient in a poorly run prison system, and the purpose of the class is merely to aggregate all those individually viable claims. Under this theory, each and every prisoner who happens to be a patient in a system that has systemic weaknesses has suffered cruel or unusual punishment, even if that person cannot make an individualized showing of mistreatment. Such a theory, however, is contrary to established Eighth Amendment jurisprudence. Nevertheless, even assuming, arguendo, that the plaintiffs (P) have established a systemic Eighth Amendment violation, the three-judge court's de-crowding order, which is in the form of a structural injunction, is unsupportable. Structural injunctions depart from the historical practice of courts issuing injunctions that require a single act, turning judges into long-term administrators of complex social institutions such as schools, prisons, and police departments. Indeed, they require judges to play a role essentially indistinguishable from the role ordinarily played by executive officials. The majority's decision not only affirms the structural injunction but vastly expands its use, by holding that an entire system is unconstitutional because it *may produce* constitutional violations. One of the most pernicious aspects of structural injunctions is that they force judges to engage in a form of fact-finding-as-policymaking that is outside the traditional judicial role. The fact-finding in which judges traditionally engage primarily involves the determination of past or present facts based exclusively upon a closed trial record. In a very limited category of cases, judges have also traditionally been called upon to make some predictive judgments. However, a judge that manages a structural injunction will inevitably be required to make very broad empirical predictions necessarily based in large part upon policy views—the sort of predictions regularly made by legislators and executive officials, but inappropriate for the judiciary. Here, for example, the three-judge court cast its predictions of the effect on public safety of its de-crowding order as findings, based on expert testimony. The notion that the judges relied solely on this testimony is fanciful: it is impossible for judges to make "factual finding" without inserting their own policy judgments, when the factual findings are, in fact, policy judgments. When, as in this case, a court issues an injunction, it must make a factual assessment of the anticipated consequences of the injunction. When the injunction undertakes to restructure a social institution, assessing the factual consequences of the injunction is necessarily the sort of predictive judgment that our system of government allocates to other government officials. The court's reliance on the un-cross-examined findings in the reports of the Receiver and Special Master likewise bears no resemblance to ordinary judicial decision-making. Further, a court may not order a prisoner's release unless it determines that the prisoner's constitutional rights are being violated, and that such release, and no other relief, will remedy the violation. A court may not, however, order the release of prisoners who have suffered no violations of their constitutional rights, merely to make it less likely that that will happen to them in the future. The PLRA states that it shall not be construed to repeal or detract from otherwise applicable limitations on the remedial powers of the courts; the PLRA is therefore best understood as an attempt to constrain the discretion of courts issuing structural injunctions—not as a mandate for their use.

DISSENT: (Alito, J.) Undesirable prison conditions that do not violate the Constitution are beyond the federal courts' reach. Both the PLRA and general principles concerning injunctive relief dictate that a prisoner release order cannot properly be issued unless the relief is necessary to remedy an ongoing violation. Thus, the propriety of the relief ordered here cannot be assessed without ascertaining the nature and scope of any ongoing constitutional violations. The three-judge court, however, erroneously relied heavily on outdated information and findings and refused to permit California (D) to introduce new evidence. Additionally, the power of the federal courts to restructure the operation of state and local entities is not plenary, and once a constitutional violation is found, a federal court is required to tailor the scope of the remedy to fit the nature and extent of the violation. Here, however, the majority's conclusion that no remedy short of a massive release of prisoners can remedy California's (D) failure to provide constitutionally adequate health care is implausible on its face and is not supported by the requisite clear and convincing evidence. Although general overcrowding contributes to many of California's (D) prison system's healthcare problems, it by no means follows that reducing overcrowding is the only or the best or even a particularly good way to alleviate those problems. Although some class members will presumably be among those who are discharged, the decrease in the number of prisoners needing mental health treatment or other forms of extensive medical care will be much smaller than the total number of prisoners released, and thus the release will produce at best only a modest improvement in the burden on the medical care system. The three-judge court, seemingly intent on attacking the broader problem of general overcrowding, rejected all of California's (D) proposals that did not involve prisoner release. In doing so, the court made three critical errors. First, the court did not assess those proposals and other remedies in light of conditions proved to exist at the time the release order was framed. Second, the court failed to distinguish between conditions that fall below the level

Continued on next page.

that may be desirable as a matter of public policy and conditions that do not meet the minimum level mandated by the Constitution. Third, the court rejected alternatives that would not have provided immediate relief, notwithstanding that nothing in the PLRA suggests that public safety may be sacrificed to implement an immediate remedy rather than a less dangerous one that requires a more extended but reasonable period of time. Absent these errors, it is possible that a less drastic, yet adequate, remedial plan could have been crafted. For example, sanitary procedures could be improved, or sufficient medical supplies and equipment could be purchased. Perhaps the number of medical and other staff positions could be increased by increasing salaries, improving working conditions, and providing better training and performance monitoring. Measures such as these—all of which will require expenditures—could be combined with targeted reductions in critical components of the prison population. Finally, the three-judge court erred in concluding that loosing 46,000 criminals would not have an adverse impact on public safety. When a trial court selects between the competing views of experts on broad empirical questions such as the efficacy of preventing crime through the incapacitation of convicted criminals, the trial court's choice is very different from a classic finding of fact and is not entitled to the same degree of deference on appeal.

ANALYSIS

In contradistinction to structural injunctions, such as the one issued by the three-judge court in this case, mandatory injunctions that are issued upon termination of litigation usually require a single simple act. In fact, courts of equity historically avoided rendering decrees that called for more than a single affirmative act. For example, where specific performance of contracts was sought, it was the categorical rule that no decree would issue that required ongoing supervision. Thus, by avoiding ongoing involvement with litigants, courts can simplify their workloads by avoiding prolonged entanglement with litigants. Once the ordered act is achieved, the litigant's obligation to the court, and the court's coercive power over the litigant, ceases, and the court does not need to engage in any ongoing supervision of the litigant's conduct, which, presumably results in greater efficiency of the court system.

Quicknotes

EIGHTH AMENDMENT The Eighth Amendment to the federal constitution prohibits the imposition of excessive bail, fines, and cruel and unusual punishment.

INJUNCTION An equitable remedy requiring a person, entity, or governmental unit to do, or prohibiting that person, entity, or governmental unit from doing, a specific act.

INJUNCTIVE RELIEF A court order issued as a remedy, requiring a person to do, or prohibiting that person from doing, a specific act.

PLENARY Unlimited and open; as broad as a given situation may require.

REMEDIAL ACTION An action for compensation or indemnity.

Horne v. Flores

Parents (P) v. State (D)

557 U.S. 443 (2009)

NATURE OF CASE: Appeal from the circuit court of appeals' decision in favor of the plaintiffs.

FACT SUMMARY: Students and their parents sued various Arizona state officials for allegedly failing to properly support Congress's English Learners Language program.

RULE OF LAW

A court may modify an injunction pursuant to Federal Rule of Civil Procedure 60(b)(5) if a significant change in the factual conditions or in the law renders the continued enforcement of the injunction detrimental to the public interest.

FACTS: The Equal Educational Opportunities Act of 1974 requires states to take "appropriate action" to overcome language barriers faced by some students. In 1992, students in the English Language Learners (ELL) program and their parents of Nogales, Arizona, sued various state officials on the grounds the state was not properly funding the program. The district court entered a declaratory judgment that the state was in violation of the act due to the lack of funding. The court issued an injunction that the state must set up a funding scheme to comply with the federal mandate. The court extended this injunction from Nogales to the entire state. The state defendants did not appeal this decision. The state legislature increased funding; but did so by diverting federal funds from other programs. The district court held this funding was not sufficient. The defendants then filed a motion to modify the injunction. At this stage of the litigation, the State's Board of Education (P) sided with the plaintiffs. The remaining state defendants were the legislature's Speaker of the House and Senate President (D). The Board of Education (P) consisted of all Democrats while the Speaker and Senate President (D) were Republicans. The district court denied the defendants' motion to modify the judgment and the circuit court of appeals affirmed. The Speaker and Senate President (D) appealed.

ISSUE: May a court modify an injunction pursuant to Federal Rule of Civil Procedure 60(b)(5) if a significant change in the factual conditions or in the law renders the continued enforcement of the injunction detrimental to the public interest?

HOLDING AND DECISION: (Alito, J.) Yes. A court may modify an injunction pursuant to Federal Rule of Civil Procedure 60(b)(5) if a significant change in the factual conditions or in the law renders the continued enforcement of the injunction detrimental to the public interest. A party seeking to modify the injunction bears the burden of proof. Motions to modify are particularly important in these "institutional reform litigation cases." These cases raise serious federalism concerns because the litigation involves core areas of state responsibility. Also, the dynamics in these cases often have parties switching sides in order to support a federal injunction as a method to circumvent the normal legislative process. This Court's prior cases have mandated a flexible approach to ensure federal court injunctions are discontinued, and control is returned to the state when the circumstances warrant it. Rule 60(b)(5) permits relief from judgment when: (1) the judgment has been satisfied or discharged; (2) it is based on an earlier judgment that has been vacated; or (3) its continued application is no longer equitable. A continued injunction must be supported by an ongoing violation of federal law. If the violation no longer exists, the injunction, not should, but must be vacated. This case must be remanded to the district court for a review of the following four factors: the state's adoption of a new instruction method for the ELL program, the increased funding through the No Child Left Behind Act, management reforms in the Nogales school district, and increased state funding for education overall. These changes may establish that Nogales and the state are no longer in violation of the federal statute. The district court must consider these in the context of the motion to modify the injunction. Reversed and remanded.

DISSENT: (Breyer, J.) The majority's decision is incorrect for several reasons. First, the court considers issues that neither party raised in their briefs. Second, the majority fails to apply its own principle that the party seeking to modify an injunction has the burden of proof. Third, the court fails to state a longstanding principle that to set aside an injunction, the moving party must show the injunction's purposes have been attained and that that it is unlikely the violations will occur again. Fourth, Rule 60(b)(5) motions to modify cannot be used to attach the legal conclusions of the original injunction. Fifth, the standard of review is abuse of discretion for these cases. The district court did not abuse its discretion by denying the motion to modify.

ANALYSIS

The evidentiary requirements for motions to modify are very flexible and they are normally reviewed under an abuse of discretion standard. Separately, underscoring

Continued on next page.

the division between the five-member conservative block of the court and the four-member liberal wing is a disagreement regarding federalism. The conservative block believes core state interests should not be co-opted by a federal judge, while the liberal wing believes Congress may properly regulate state action through its power of the purse.

Quicknotes

PRELIMINARY INJUNCTION A judicial mandate issued to require or restrain a party from certain conduct; used to preserve a trial's subject matter or to prevent threatened injury.

Hills v. Gautreaux

Federal agency (D) v. Individuals (P)

425 U.S. 284 (1976)

NATURE OF CASE: Appeal of court order compelling desegregation of public housing.

FACT SUMMARY: Having found the Department of Housing and Urban Development (HUD) to be subsidizing segregated housing in Chicago, a district court ordered a remedial plan encompassing the metropolitan area.

RULE OF LAW

A court may order a housing authority to correct segregation it has facilitated over an area outside the locality in question.

FACTS: The Department of Housing and Urban Development (HUD) had been subsidizing segregated public housing in the city of Chicago. A district court ordered HUD to remedy this situation by subsidizing desegregated housing. The court of appeals entered an order in this regard encompassing areas outside of Chicago. This was challenged on appeal to the United States Supreme Court.

ISSUE: May a court order a housing authority to correct segregation it has facilitated over an area outside the locality in question?

HOLDING AND DECISION: (Stewart, J.) Yes. A court may order a housing authority to correct segregation it has facilitated over an area outside the locality in question. It is true that a remedy cannot go beyond the scope of a constitutional violation. For that reason, a court cannot include nonviolating local authorities in a remedial plan, as was the case in *Milliken I* [*Milliken v. Bradley*, 418 U.S. 717 (1974)]. However, a violation by HUD was shown here, and the court properly formulated a remedial plan involving HUD. The fact that the violations occurred in Chicago and some of the remedial action will take place in the suburbs does not challenge the authority of local political subdivisions, as it is HUD that is being coerced, not the local authorities. Affirmed.

ANALYSIS

The Court did not discuss the extent to which coercion of HUD constituted coercion of local housing authorities. It seems that this case says that a wrongdoer can be forced to take remedial action affecting third parties to whom a court cannot dictate. It would appear the court has left open a method for courts to sidestep *Milliken I*.

Quicknotes

REMEDIAL ACTION An action for compensation or indemnity.

REMEDY Compensation for violation of a right or for injuries sustained.

SEGREGATION The use of separate institutions and facilities for persons of different races, nationalities, religions, etc.

General Building Contractors Association v. Pennsylvania

Union (D) v. State (P)

458 U.S. 375 (1982)

NATURE OF CASE: Appeal of injunction against discriminatory union practices.

FACT SUMMARY: A district court enjoined certain discriminatory union practices and included several nondiscriminating parties within the scope of the injunction.

RULE OF LAW

A party not violating antidiscrimination laws may not be assessed a share of the costs of implementing a decree remedying the discrimination of others.

FACTS: The International Union of Operating Engineers had a contract with local employers wherein all hiring was to be done through the local union hall. Certain minorities and the Commonwealth (P) challenged the practices. The district court held the practices discriminatory. The court issued an injunction requiring changes in the hiring system and assessed the costs of this against the union, which had been found to be discriminating, and against certain employers, which had not been found to be discriminating. The injunction was affirmed on appeal.

ISSUE: May a party not violating antidiscrimination laws be assessed a share of the costs of implementing a decree remedying the discrimination of others?

HOLDING AND DECISION: (Rehnquist, J.) No. A party not violating antidiscrimination laws may not be assessed a share of the costs of implementing a decree remedying the discrimination of others. An injunctive remedy of this nature can go no further than the scope of the violation. Since the employers were not found to be discriminating, a remedy including them exceeds the scope of the violation. Reversed and remanded.

CONCURRENCE: (O'Connor, J.) Minor ancillary remedies may include parties not found to be liable for a violation of antidiscrimination laws.

ANALYSIS

Despite the holding here, it seems clear that in this area third parties can be affected by injunctions issued to prevent or remedy discrimination. The Court in this case would allow minor "ancillary remedies" against an innocent third party. Future decisions will have to answer exactly how minor an issue is.

Quicknotes

DISCRIMINATION Unequal treatment of a class of persons.

INJUNCTION An equitable remedy requiring a person, entity, or governmental unit to do, or prohibiting that person, entity, or governmental unit from doing, a specific act.

REMEDY Compensation for violation of a right or for injuries sustained.

CHAPTER 5

Choosing Remedies

Quick Reference Rules of Law

Pardee v. Camden Lumber Co.

Individual (P) v. Corporation (D)

W. Va. Sup Ct. App., 73 S.E. 82 (1911)

NATURE OF CASE: Appeal of denial of injunction preventing cutting of timber.

FACT SUMMARY: Pardee (P) brought an action to enjoin Camden Lumber Co. (D) from felling trees on his land.

RULE OF LAW

An injunction against the felling of trees on another's property is appropriate.

FACTS: Camden Lumber Co. (D) began felling trees on Pardee's (P) property without his consent. Pardee (P) brought an action to enjoin the practice. The court, not believing equitable relief appropriate, denied the injunction. Pardee (P) appealed.

ISSUE: Is an injunction against the felling of trees on another's property appropriate?

HOLDING AND DECISION: (Poffenbarger, J.) Yes. An injunction against the felling of trees on another's property is appropriate. Where the legal remedy is inadequate, equity will intervene. Timber cut is plainly not the same thing as a standing tree. Money damages will not restore the appearance of the land. When the destruction of something not amenable to replacement is threatened, equity will intervene. The legal remedy here will not replace the character of Pardee's (P) land, and an injunction is therefore appropriate. Reversed, injunction reinstated, and remanded.

ANALYSIS

The decision of the court focused on the unique nature of land. As the court stated, where land is involved, equity will usually be appropriate. This certainly was correct in this instance, as denuded land is not the same as forest. The court really did not discuss irreparable injury, another prerequisite of equity, but the irreparable (within a lifetime) character of the wrong was obvious here.

Quicknotes

EQUITY Fairness; justice; the determination of a matter consistent with principles of fairness and not in strict compliance with rules of law.

INJUNCTION A court order requiring a person to do, or prohibiting that person from doing, a specific act.

IRREPARABLE HARM Such harm that because it is either too great, too small, or of a continuing character that it cannot be properly compensated in damages, and the remedy for which is typically injunctive relief.

Brook v. James A. Cullimore & Co.

Individual (D) v. Corporation (P)

Okla. Sup. Ct., 436 P.2d 32 (1967)

NATURE OF CASE: Appeal of court-ordered delivery of personal property.

FACT SUMMARY: Brook (D), liable to James A. Cullimore & Co. (P) for certain collateral, offered instead to deliver cash of equivalent value.

RULE OF LAW

A successful litigant in a replevin action has a right to the subject property, rather than cash.

FACTS: Brook (D) borrowed approximately $8,000 from Cullimore (P). Brook (D) gave Cullimore (P) a security interest in certain property valued at around $2,500. Brook (D) defaulted on the note, and Cullimore (P) brought an action to obtain possession of the property. Brook (D) offered cash equivalent to the value of the property. Cullimore (P) refused, desiring the property. The court ordered Brook (D) to deliver the property, and Brook (D) appealed.

ISSUE: Does a successful litigant in a replevin action have a right to the subject property, rather than cash?

HOLDING AND DECISION: (McInerney, J.) Yes. A successful litigant in a replevin action has a right to the subject property, rather than cash. A replevin action is at common law an action to recover property, not money. Statutes have modified replevin to allow for damages if the property is unavailable, but this is at the option of the plaintiff, not the defendant. Here, since Cullimore (P) was successful, it had a right to demand the property itself, not a cash equivalent. Affirmed.

ANALYSIS

Replevin is a very old remedy, predating equity. As the case indicates, it is employed in cases where delivery of personal property is required. The remedy has some flaws; for instance, hearings are often delayed, and the property can be secreted. Some equitable remedies, such as temporary restraining orders, can ameliorate this.

Quicknotes

EQUITY Fairness; justice; the determination of a matter consistent with principles of fairness and not in strict compliance with rules of law.

REPLEVIN An action to recover personal property wrongfully taken.

TEMPORARY RESTRAINING ORDER A court order preserving the status quo pending a hearing regarding injunctive relief.

Continental Airlines, Inc. v. Intra Brokers, Inc.

Corporation (P) v. Corporation (D)

24 F.3d 1099 (9th Cir. 1994)

NATURE OF CASE: Appeal from order granting injunction.

FACT SUMMARY: Continental Airlines, Inc. (P) sought an injunction against Intra Brokers, Inc.'s (D) sale of travel discount coupons.

RULE OF LAW

A party is entitled to equitable relief of injunction when economic damages would be difficult and expensive to prove.

FACTS: Intra Brokers, Inc. (Intra) (D) acquired travel discount coupons published by Continental Airlines, Inc. (Continental) (P) and sold them to travel agents for resale to their customers. The coupons contained a clause-prohibiting sale of the coupon, though Continental (P) stated it would not enforce the clause. When Continental (P) later decided to enforce the clause, Intra (D) did not comply with the new policy. Neither side presented evidence of harm or benefit to Continental (P) on Intra's (D) refusal to comply.

ISSUE: Is a party entitled to equitable relief of injunction where economic damages would be difficult and expensive to prove?

HOLDING AND DECISION: (Kleinfeld, J.) Yes. A party is entitled to equitable relief of injunction when economic damages would be difficult and expensive to prove. For equitable relief to be appropriate, there must generally be no adequate legal remedy. While Continental (P) did not demonstrate any economic harm, the hardship it would have to undertake to prove damages is considered in deciding whether to grant an injunction. The possible immeasurability of harm does not mean Continental (P) was not harmed. The difficulty of establishing the amount of economic harm supports the proposition that damages would be an inadequate remedy. The harm here was to Continental's (P) right to control its own discounting policies. Affirmed.

ANALYSIS

It is often difficult to decide what makes a legal remedy inadequate with regard to injuries parties deem to be irreparable. Parties often argue that economic damages are inadequate in cases of personal and commercial property. While this case does not directly address the irreparability issue, it clearly shows Continental's (P) right to control its own policies is very difficult to value.

Quicknotes

EQUITABLE REMEDY A remedy that is based upon principles of fairness as opposed to rules of law; a remedy involving specific performance rather than money damages.

INJUNCTIVE RELIEF A court order issued as a remedy, requiring a person to do, or prohibiting that person from doing, a specific act.

Campbell Soup Co. v. Wentz

Corporation (P) v. Individual (D)

172 F.2d 80 (3d Cir. 1948)

NATURE OF CASE: Appeal from dismissal of breach of contract action for specific relief.

FACT SUMMARY: Wentz (D) contracted to sell carrots to Campbell Soup Co. (P) but instead sold them to Lojeski (D).

RULE OF LAW

Even though a contract may be perfectly legal, entitling both parties to legal relief, equity will not provide specific relief to any party who has driven too hard a bargain or obtained too one-sided an agreement.

FACTS: On June 21, 1947, Wentz (D) contracted to sell all the Chantenay red cored carrots to be grown on a certain 15-acre parcel of his farm to Campbell Soup Co. (Campbell) (P) for a price between $23 and $30 per ton. The contract, drawn up by and in the primary interest of Campbell (P), provided several conditions. Paragraph 2 set out a very particular manner of delivery and further stated that Campbell (P) was to be judge of conformance with all specifications. Paragraphs 3 and 4 provided Campbell (P) could refuse all carrots in excess of 12 tons per acre but that Wentz (D) could only sell such excess carrots after Campbell (P) rejected them. Paragraph 9 provided certain circumstances under which Campbell (P) would be excused from accepting delivery of any carrots but provided that, even if it was, Wentz (D) could not sell the carrots elsewhere without Campbell's (P) approval. By January 1948, the price of Chantenay carrots had risen to $90 per ton. Wentz (D) thereupon notified Campbell (P) that it would no longer deliver carrots to them, selling instead to Lojeski (D), a neighbor, who in turn sold to Campbell (P). Campbell instituted this action, as a result, for specific performance of its contract with Wentz (D). The trial court dismissed, and this appeal followed.

ISSUE: Even though a contract may be perfectly legal, entitling both parties to legal relief, will equity provide specific relief to any party who has driven too hard a bargain or obtained too one-sided an agreement?

HOLDING AND DECISION: (Goodrich, J.) Yes. Even though a contract may be perfectly legal, entitling both parties to legal relief, equity will not provide specific relief to any party who has driven too hard a bargain or obtained too one-sided an agreement. The general policy of liberality in the granting of specific relief favors the granting of it as long as the court is not forced to undertake too burdensome or time-consuming a supervisory role in the process. As such, the trial court below erred in dismissing the suit because of the purported adequacy of the legal remedy here. (The relative "uniqueness" of these carrots is really immaterial.) But the dismissal was nevertheless proper considering the excessively burdensome provisional that Campbell (P) obtained in its contract with Wentz (D). Affirmed.

ANALYSIS

This case points up what has been termed "equity's middle course" in the question of whether courts should enforce contracts that, though unfair, fall short of being unconscionable. Essentially equitable (though not legal) relief will be denied wherever the evidence supports a finding of misrepresentation, unclean hands (from overreaching), inadequate consideration, equitable estoppel, etc. Note also, here, the fact that the court skirts the question of adequacy of the legal remedy which the trial court had held dispositive below. As a general rule, inadequacy of the legal remedy (i.e., damages) must be established before a party may obtain equitable relief. "Uniqueness" of the subject matter of a contract (carrots, above) will often make damages inadequate. In *Campbell* the court in essence said that mere need for product uniformity by Campbell (P) in its soups made Wentz's (D) Chantenay red carrots unique.

Quicknotes

EQUITABLE REMEDY A remedy that is based upon principles of fairness as opposed to rules of law; a remedy involving specific performance rather than money damages.

EQUITY Fairness; justice; the determination of a matter consistent with principles of fairness and not in strict compliance with rules of law.

Van Wagner Advertising Corp. v. S & M Enterprises

Corporation (P) v. Corporation (D)

N.Y. Ct. App., 492 N.E.2d 756 (1986)

NATURE OF CASE: Appeal from denial of specific performance in breach of contract action.

FACT SUMMARY: Van Wagner Advertising Corp. (Van Wagner) (P) contended that S & M Enterprises' (S & M's) (D) cancellation of a lease of billboard space on the side of a building was ineffective because only an owner making a bona fide sale could terminate the lease, and Van Wagner's (P) lease had not been terminated by the former owner of the building, Michaels, before she sold it to S & M (D).

RULE OF LAW

The point at which breach of contract will be redressable by specific performance lies not in any inherent physical uniqueness of the property but, instead, in the uncertainty of valuing it.

FACTS: Michaels leased billboard space on the side of a building she owned to Van Wagner Advertising Corp. (Van Wagner) (P). Van Wagner (P) erected a sign on the building and leased it to Asch Advertising, Inc. for three years. Michaels sold the building to S & M Enterprises (S & M) (D), and S & M (D) canceled the lease with Van Wagner (P). Van Wagner (P) sued for specific performance and damages for breach of contract, contending that only an owner making a bona fide sale could terminate the lease and that Michaels had not terminated the lease before she sold the building to S & M (D). The trial court ruled for Van Wagner (P), stating that the parties did not intend that once a sale had been made that any future purchaser could terminate the lease at will. The court would not, however, order specific performance, and Van Wagner (P) appealed.

ISSUE: Does the point at which breach of a contract will be redressable by specific performance lie not in any inherent physical uniqueness of the property but, instead, in the uncertainty of valuing it?

HOLDING AND DECISION: (Kaye, J.) Yes. The point at which breach of a contract will be redressable by specific performance lies not in any inherent physical uniqueness of the property but, instead, in the uncertainty of valuing it. In stating that the subject matter of a contract is unique and has not established market value, a court is really saying that it cannot obtain, at reasonable cost, enough information about substitutes to permit it to calculate an award of money damages without imposing an unacceptably high risk of undercompensation on the injured promisee. Here, the trial court correctly concluded that the value of the "unique qualities" of the demised space could be fixed with reasonable certainty and without imposing an unacceptably high risk of undercompensating the injured tenant. Thus, the court correctly concluded that specific performance should be denied Van Wagner (P) because such relief would be inequitable in that its effect would be disproportionate in its harm to S & M (D) and in its assistance to Van Wagner (P). Affirmed as modified.

ANALYSIS

Specific performance is an equitable remedy. Its availability is severely restricted by the necessity of meeting the traditional prerequisite of equitable relief—a showing that the available legal remedies would be inadequate. This most often means that if the contracted-for performance is available from any other source, specific performance will be denied, and plaintiff will have to settle for money damages.

Quicknotes

BREACH OF CONTRACT Unlawful failure by a party to perform its obligations pursuant to contract.

EQUITABLE REMEDY A remedy that is based upon principles of fairness as opposed to rules of law; a remedy involving specific performance rather than money damages.

SPECIFIC PERFORMANCE An equitable remedy whereby the court requires the parties to perform their obligations pursuant to a contract.

Whitlock v. Hilander Foods, Inc.

Homeowner (P) v. Corporation (D)

Ill. App. Ct., 720 N.E.2d 302 (1999)

NATURE OF CASE: Appeal from the granting of summary judgment to the defendant.

FACT SUMMARY: Hilander Foods, Inc. (Hilander) (D) began construction of an addition to its grocery store. Whitlock (P) alleged that Hilander (D) was building a retaining wall's footing on his property.

RULE OF LAW

In encroachment cases, a court may issue an injunction to a builder to remove an encroachment if the plaintiff can prove the encroachment was deliberate.

FACTS: Whitlock (P) discovered that Hilander Foods, Inc. (Hilander) (D) had placed the footings of a retaining wall on his adjoining property. Whitlock (P) first met with workers from Hilander (D) and requested that if the footings were to remain, he would like a lease. Over the next six months, the parties and their lawyers exchanged offers to resolve the issue. There was an allegation by Hilander (D), based on a survey, that in fact the new wall's footings may actually have been placed in the same spot, where on older retaining wall had existed. Whitlock (P) brought suit and a motion for an injunction ordering Hilander (D) to remove the wall. There was evidence this would cost Hilander (D) $1.5 million. Hilander (D) moved for summary judgment, which the trial court granted on the grounds the encroachment was not intentional and that Whitlock had unreasonably delayed in bringing the suit. Whitlock (P) appealed.

ISSUE: In encroachment cases, may a court issue an injunction to a builder to remove an encroachment if the plaintiff can prove the encroachment was deliberate?

HOLDING AND DECISION: (Bowman, J.) Yes. In encroachment cases, a court may issue an injunction to a builder to remove an encroachment if the plaintiff can prove the encroachment was deliberate. The lower court erred as a matter of law that the encroachment was not intentional. There is at least evidence supporting the existence of a genuine issue of fact on the intent issue. Normally, a court will weigh and balance the hardships to defendants for having to remove the encroaching structure with the benefit to the property owner. However, if the encroachment is intentional, a court may order removal of the offending structure. A fact finder could infer that Hilander (D) knew or should have known that the retaining wall was on Whitlock's (P) property. In addition, Hilander (D) continued building the wall even though Whitlock (P) had put it on notice the wall was on his property. Separately, the court improperly found that laches barred Whitlock's (P) complaint. Laches applies when a plaintiff's unreasonable delay in filing a claim causes a defendant to be misled or prejudiced. There are no fixed rules with the defense of laches. Courts should examine both plaintiff's and defendant's conduct. This issue turns on issues of fact to be determined by a jury, and not a judge, at the summary judgment stage. There is evidence Hilander (D) assured Whitlock (P) the issue would be resolved, in addition to the negotiation between the parties to reach an agreement prior to the filing of the suit. Reversed and remanded.

ANALYSIS

Trial courts are oftentimes reluctant to grant summary judgment because the much safer course of action is to simply deny the motion on the grounds there are genuine issues of material fact to be decided by a jury. Here, the multiple issues of fact should have precluded the original granting of summary judgment.

Quicknotes

ENCROACHMENT The unlawful intrusion onto another's property.

LACHES An equitable defense against the enforcement of rights that have been neglected for a long period of time.

Lord & Taylor, LLC v. White Flint, L.P.

Retailer (P) v. Real estate developer (D)

780 F.3d 211 (4th Cir. 2015)

NATURE OF CASE: Appeal from denial of permanent injunction in action for breach of a restrictive covenant.

FACT SUMMARY: Lord & Taylor, LLC (P), a department store retailer that was the anchor tenant of a mall developed and operated by White Flint, L.P. (D), pursuant to a long-term reciprocal easement agreement (REA), asserted that White Flint's (D) plan to redevelop the mall site, which had experienced a significant decline in business, violated the REA. Lord & Taylor (P) accordingly sought a permanent injunction to enjoin the redevelopment in any way inconsistent with the REA, contending that the requested injunction would be feasible.

RULE OF LAW

(1) Given that trial courts retain discretion to deny specific performance or injunctive relief where enforcement would be unreasonably difficult or require long-continued supervision by the court, a trial court may deny an injunction to enforce a restrictive covenant as infeasible if it would compel the parties to continue a commercial relationship, or require the court to closely monitor the caliber of their performance.

(2) A trial court does not err in denying a permanent injunction to enforce a restrictive covenant on feasibility grounds where its determination that injunctive relief is infeasible is neither a clear error of judgment nor an abuse of discretion.

FACTS: Around 1975, Lord & Taylor, LLC (P), a department store retailer, entered into a long-term reciprocal easement agreement (REA) with Bloomingdale's, another retailer, and White Flint, L.P. (D), a real estate developer, for the development and operation of a shopping mall (Mall). Lord & Taylor (P) and Bloomingdale's agreed to lease land immediately adjacent to the Mall and serve as anchor tenants. White Flint (D) agreed to construct and maintain a "first class high fashion" regional shopping center on the Mall property. Under the REA, Lord & Taylor (P) had the right of approval of any structural changes or design alterations, and all the agreement's conditions were treated by the REA as restrictive covenants running with the land. The REA would terminate in 2042, but it could be extended through 2057. The Mall opened in 1977 and operated smoothly for many years. By 2012, however, the Mall began to experience a significant decline in business, and Bloomingdale's did not renew its lease. By 2013, 75 percent of Mall tenants had left. Thereafter, the Bloomingdale's building was demolished, and the remaining businesses had closed. The Mall was shuttered permanently in 2015; Lord & Taylor (P) alone remained open. To address this situation, in 2011 White Flint (D) released a preliminary plan to redevelop the site ("Sketch Plan"). This was part of the county government's larger initiative to redevelop the area as a public-private undertaking that would involve $1 billion in new public works ("Sector Plan"). The Sketch Plan would transform the Mall site into a mixed-use development, with a 45-acre town center including 2,400 apartment units, parks and schools, a hotel, and at least three high-rise office buildings. The Lord & Taylor (P) store would remain, but the enclosed Mall would be demolished, along with portions of the parking lots and internal roadways surrounding Lord & Taylor (P). Lord & Taylor (P) objected to the Sketch Plan, asserting that it would violate the REA and negatively impact its business. Accordingly, Lord & Taylor (P) brought suit seeking, inter alia, a permanent injunction compelling White Flint (D) to honor the terms of the REA. Specifically, Lord & Taylor (P) asked the district court to enjoin White Flint (D) from taking any steps to carry out or construct the redevelopment in a manner inconsistent with the REA and to require White Flint (D) to abide by its obligations under the REA to operate a first-class high-fashion regional retail shopping center. The district court assumed for purposes of its decision that the proposed redevelopment would breach the REA, and that Lord & Taylor (P) would be entitled to damages for any harm that resulted. It concluded, however, that injunctive relief would be infeasible under the circumstances, since an injunction requiring White Flint (D) to operate a "first class" shopping center contemplated by the REA would require the court to supervise rebuilding and bringing tenants back to the Mall—a task the court deemed outside its competence. Therefore, the district court denied the injunction, Lord & Taylor (P) appealed, and the court of appeals granted review.

ISSUE:

(1) Given that trial courts retain discretion to deny specific performance or injunctive relief where enforcement would be unreasonably difficult or require long-continued supervision by the court, may a trial court

Continued on next page.

deny an injunction to enforce a restrictive covenant as infeasible if it would compel the parties to continue a commercial relationship, or require the court to closely monitor the caliber of their performance?

(2) Does a trial court err in denying a permanent injunction to enforce a restrictive covenant on feasibility grounds where its determination that injunctive relief is infeasible is neither a clear error of judgment nor an abuse of discretion?

HOLDING AND DECISION: (Harris, J.)

(1) Yes. Given that trial courts retain discretion to deny specific performance or injunctive relief where enforcement would be unreasonably difficult or require long-continued supervision by the court, a trial court may deny an injunction to enforce a restrictive covenant as infeasible if it would compel the parties to continue a commercial relationship or require the court to closely monitor the caliber of their performance. Lord & Taylor (P) argues that under controlling law (Maryland state law), injunctive relief for breaches of restrictive covenants is so strongly favored that injunctions are granted almost as a matter of course and regardless of factors like the public interest or the availability of monetary damages to compensate for a breach, so that the district court had little equitable discretion and erroneously denied the requested injunction. This argument is rejected. Although an injunction typically is an appropriate remedy for breach of a restrictive covenant, such relief is not automatic, and the presumption in its favor does not displace a trial court's traditional equitable discretion. Moreover, it is clear under established law that trial courts may take account of feasibility concerns in considering injunctive relief for breach of a restrictive covenant. Trial courts retain discretion to deny specific performance or injunctive relief where enforcement would be "unreasonably difficult" or require "long-continued supervision" by the court, so that, for example, an injunction may be denied as infeasible if it would compel the parties to continue a commercial relationship, or require the court to closely monitor the caliber of their performance. Because such affirmative injunctions are difficult to draft clearly and even harder to enforce, courts typically will issue them only where no other relief is possible. Also, when considering feasibility, courts should consider broadly the "advantages to be gained" from injunctive relief as well as "the harm to be suffered" if an injunction is denied as infeasible. For these reasons, the district court did not err in going beyond the presumption in favor of injunctive relief and considering the feasibility of the requested injunction. Affirmed as to this issue.

(2) No. A trial court does not err in denying a permanent injunction to enforce a restrictive covenant on feasibility grounds where its determination that injunctive relief is infeasible is neither a clear error of judgment nor an abuse of discretion. The review of a trial court's feasibility determination is highly deferential when it rests on equitable considerations or other discretionary factors and will be overturned only for abuse of discretion and a clear error of judgment. Given the practical realities of the situation, Lord & Taylor's (P) argument that injunctive relief would be entirely feasible is unconvincing. Restoring the Mall to its former glory would have required more than a negative prohibition on the site's redevelopment; it would have necessitated an affirmative injunction ordering White Flint (D) to transform the now-fading, almost defunct Mall back into a "first class high fashion regional retail [s]hopping [c]enter"—the kind of order that is so hard to draft with specificity and then to enforce that courts generally will grant it only as a last resort. Affirmative injunctive relief would have been even more impractical than usual, given the highly detailed provisions of the REA. An order that White Flint (D) abide by its obligations under the REA would require judicial oversight of compliance with the myriad of REA conditions that controlled every facet of the Mall's operations, from the distribution of parking and interior access roads to the placement of entrances to the design of the various retail stores and restaurants that populate the Mall. Also, once it had ascertained that the Mall's operations were again compliant with every provision of the REA, the district court would still have to ensure that the Mall remained in compliance for the duration of the REA, at least until 2042 and potentially until 2057—or for over 40 years. Even a revised injunction that would simply prohibit White Flint (D) from proceeding with destruction of the Mall and its adjacent parking area—as proposed by Lord & Taylor (P) at oral argument—was appropriately rejected by the district court, which deemed it unrealistic to require White Flint (D) to maintain the status quo of a mostly empty Mall with a demolished "anchor" store on one side. The district court determined that such a negative injunction would freeze in place a vacant and partially demolished Mall and would be tantamount to a judicially mandated blight on the area. That outcome would serve neither party to the dispute, let alone the interests of the general public. Indeed, it is so patently unworkable that Lord & Taylor (P) defends it not on its own terms, but as a form of leverage that might encourage White Flint (D) to resume Mall operations, consistent with the REA. However, the district

Continued on next page.

court cannot simply assume that best-case scenario, and must instead contend with the very real possibility that a negative injunction would produce nothing but an empty and unusable 45-acre Mall site within the county's redevelopment project. Even if such an injunction would force White Flint (D) to attempt to repopulate and restore the Mall, feasibility concerns would remain. For instance, if the parties disputed whether White Flint (D) had lived up to its highly detailed obligations under the REA, the district court would find itself inserted once again into the thick of ongoing and complex commercial relationships, and any effort to resolve that dispute by way of injunctive relief would raise precisely the feasibility issues already described. For these reasons, the district court did not commit a clear error of judgment, and it did not abuse its discretion to manage its own affairs. Affirmed as to this issue. Affirmed.

ANALYSIS

Instances where courts in Maryland had issued injunctions involving the use of real estate for retail purposes involved situations that were significantly less complex and of shorter duration than Lord & Taylor's (P) proposed injunction. For example, Maryland courts had prohibited the operation of a single nearby competitor by enjoining the operation of a rival grocery store in the same strip mall [*Redner's Mkts., Inc.,* 2013 WL 2903285 (Md. D.C.)], or had resolved a single dispute over misused office space by enjoining the operation of a dance studio [*City of Bowie v. MIE, Props., Inc.*, 398 Md. 657, 922 A.2d 509 (2007)]. By comparison, Maryland courts had found injunctive relief infeasible under circumstances far more streamlined and straightforward than those presented by the case at bar, where purely bilateral commercial relations were involved. For example, Maryland courts had refused to order a tenant to reoccupy leased retail space on feasibility grounds [*M. Leo Storch L.P. v. Erol's, Inc.,* 95 Md. App. 253, 620 A.2d 408 (Md. Ct. Spec. App. 1993)]. In fact, the scale and complexity of the Mall's operations—spread over 45 acres, and potentially involving dozens of new counter-parties as the Mall repopulated—and the over 40-year duration of the proposed injunction, had no parallel in the Maryland case law.

Quicknotes

ABUSE OF DISCRETION A determination by an appellate court that a lower court's decision was based on an error of law.

FEASIBILITY Capable of being completed, executed, or accomplished with reasonable assurance of success.

SPECIFIC PERFORMANCE An equitable remedy whereby the court requires the parties to perform their obligations pursuant to a contract.

Willing v. Mazzocone

Individual (D) v. Law firm (P)

Pa. Sup. Ct., 393 A.2d 1155 (1978)

NATURE OF CASE: Appeal of injunction prohibiting exhibiting of defamatory sign.

FACT SUMMARY: Willing (D), believing herself to have been defrauded by Mazzocone (D) and his law firm, walked around city hall with a defamatory sign.

RULE OF LAW

A court may not enjoin defamatory speech.

FACTS: Willing (D) had been represented by the law firm of Quinn & Mazzocone in a worker's compensation action. Willing (D) formed the belief that Quinn & Mazzocone (P) cheated her. She began walking around the outside of city hall with a placard that stated the firm had stolen money from her and had sold her out to the insurance company. Quinn & Mazzocone (P) brought an action to enjoin this behavior. The evidence at the hearing indicated that Quinn & Mazzocone (P) had done nothing unethical, and that Willing (D) was either eccentric or mentally ill. The court issued an injunction, and Willing (D) appealed. Willing (D) was indigent.

ISSUE: May a court enjoin defamatory speech?

HOLDING AND DECISION: (Manderino, J.) No. A court may not enjoin defamatory speech. Prior restraints of free speech are repugnant to the American political heritage, and an injunction such as that issued would undoubtedly be highly suspect from a constitutional standpoint. However, the constitutional issue need not be addressed, because the legal remedy in a defamation is adequate. A suit for libel or slander, if successful, serves to exonerate a party and compensates for actual damages, if any exist. The fact that Willing (D) is indigent is irrelevant. A legal remedy does not become inadequate because it appears uncollectible. Reversed.

CONCURRENCE: (Roberts, J.) Conditioning the propriety of equitable relief on a party's indigence is clearly wrong.

DISSENT: (Eagen, C.J.) Prior restraints consist only of administrative or licensing schemes that operate before first publication of a statement. Even this narrow class of prior restraints is not absolute.

ANALYSIS

One must question some aspects of the court's opinion. It would seem a successful verdict in a libel suit would not, absent some unusual publicity, restore a reputation. Also, to say that an uncollectible legal remedy is adequate is a suspect conclusion. It may be that the court was stretching to avoid discussing the constitutional issues.

Quicknotes

DEFAMATORY Subjecting one to statements meant to injure one's reputation or to adversely affect one's business.

INDIGENT A person who is poor and thus is unable to obtain counsel to defend themself in a criminal proceeding and for whom counsel must be appointed.

LIBEL A false or malicious publication subjecting a person to scorn, hatred, or ridicule, or injuring them in relation to their occupation or business.

SLANDER Defamatory statement communicated orally.

eBay, Inc. v. MercExchange, LLC

Internet company (D) v. Patent-holder (P)

547 U.S. 388 (2006)

NATURE OF CASE: Appeal from reversal of denial of permanent injunctive relief in patent infringement action.

FACT SUMMARY: eBay, Inc. and its subsidiary, Half.com (collectively, eBay) (D) contended that the four-factor test historically used by courts sitting in equity to determine whether to grant an injunction applied to disputes arising under the Patent Act, rather than a "general rule" that courts will issue permanent injunctions against patent infringement absent exceptional circumstances.

RULE OF LAW

The four-factor test historically used by courts sitting in equity to determine whether to grant an injunction applies to disputes arising under the Patent Act.

FACTS: eBay, Inc. and its subsidiary, Half.com (collectively, eBay) (D) operated popular auction websites that enabled private sellers to list goods they wished to sell. MercExchange, LLC (P), which held several patents, sought to license a business method patent to eBay (D), but no agreement was reached. MercExchange (P) subsequently brought a patent infringement suit, and a jury found that its patent was valid, that eBay (D) had infringed the patent, and that damages were appropriate. MercExchange (P) also moved for permanent injunctive relief, which the district court denied. In reversing, the court of appeals applied a "general rule" that courts will issue permanent injunctions against patent infringement absent exceptional circumstances. The United States Supreme Court granted review.

ISSUE: Does the four-factor test historically used by courts sitting in equity to determine whether to grant an injunction apply to disputes arising under the Patent Act?

HOLDING AND DECISION: (Thomas, J.) Yes. The four-factor test historically used by courts sitting in equity to determine whether to grant an injunction applies to disputes arising under the Patent Act. That test requires a plaintiff to demonstrate: (1) that it has suffered an irreparable injury; (2) that remedies available at law are inadequate to compensate for that injury; (3) that considering the balance of hardships between the plaintiff and defendant, a remedy in equity is warranted; and (4) that the public interest would not be disserved by a permanent injunction. The decision to grant or deny such relief is an act of equitable discretion by the district court, reviewable on appeal for abuse of discretion. These principles apply with equal force to Patent Act disputes. "[A] major departure from the long tradition of equity practice should not be lightly implied." Nothing in the Act indicates such a departure, and, to the contrary, it indicates that injunctions may issue in accordance with equity principles. Although the Act creates in the patent-holder a right to exclude others from benefiting from the patented invention, a right should not be confused with a remedy such as an injunction. Such an approach is consistent with the approach the Court has taken under the Copyright Act. Because neither court below correctly applied the traditional four-factor test, the case must go back to the district court for a correct application of that test. Vacated.

CONCURRENCE: (Roberts, C.J.) The majority is correct that a major departure from historical equity practice should not be undertaken lightly. Part of that history is that injunctions have issued for patent infringement in the vast majority of infringement cases. This makes sense, given that money damages may not be sufficient to prevent an infringing use of a patented invention. While such historic practice does not entitle a patent-holder to an injunction or justify a general rule in support of granting patent-holders injunctions, when there has been infringement, it should be considered by courts when they exercise their equitable discretion in evaluation of the test's four factors.

CONCURRENCE: (Kennedy J.) The historic trend of granting injunctions in cases of patent infringement may just be reflection of the application of the four-factor test to patented inventions at a time when patents were used as a basis for producing and selling goods. In contrast, in many modern patent cases, the nature of the patent being enforced and the economic function of the patent-holder present considerations that were unlike those in earlier cases since in many instances nowadays the patent is used primarily for extracting licensing fees. Therefore, it is possible that in the context of the current use of patents, legal remedies may be adequate to compensate for infringement. The equitable discretion over injunctions, granted by the Patent Act, is thus well suited to allow courts to adapt to the rapid technological and legal developments in the patent system. In light of changed use of patents, district courts should look to historic practice, but should also consider whether the results from prior cases fit the circumstances of today's cases.

Continued on next page.

ANALYSIS

The Supreme Court noted that although the district court recited the traditional four-factor test, the lower court appeared to adopt certain expansive principles suggesting that injunctive relief could not issue in a broad swath of cases. Most notably, the district court concluded that a "plaintiff's willingness to license its patents" and "its lack of commercial activity in practicing the patents" would be sufficient to establish that the patent-holder would not suffer irreparable harm if an injunction did not issue. The Supreme Court found that traditional equitable principles do not permit such broad classifications and that there would be certain types of patent-holders that would be able to satisfy the test. The example the court gave was of university researchers or self-made inventors who might reasonably prefer to license their patents, rather than undertake efforts to secure the financing necessary to bring their works to market themselves. In doing so, the Supreme Court seemed to be indicating that equity requires discretion based on particular circumstances rather than categorical rules that may not fit all circumstances.

Quicknotes

EQUITY Fairness; justice; the determination of a matter consistent with principles of fairness and not in strict compliance with rules of law.

INJUNCTIVE RELIEF A court order issued as a remedy, requiring a person to do, or prohibiting that person from doing, a specific act.

PERMANENT INJUNCTION A remedy imposed by the court ordering a party to cease the conduct of a specific activity until the final disposition of the cause of action.

Winter v. Natural Resources Defense Council, Inc.

United States Navy official (D) v. Advocacy group (P)

555 U.S. 7 (2008)

NATURE OF CASE: Appeal from the granting of a preliminary injunction against the United States Navy.

FACT SUMMARY: The Natural Resources Defense Council, Inc. (NRDC) (P) brought a motion for a preliminary injunction to force the United States Navy (D) to complete an environmental impact statement before continuing with its use of active sonar, which allegedly harmed marine life.

RULE OF LAW

As one factor in the preliminary injunction analysis, an injunction may only be issued where the plaintiff demonstrates a likelihood of irreparable harm and not just the possibility of harm.

FACTS: The United States Navy's (Navy's) (D) use of active sonar is critical to its ability to detect other submarines. Training in the use of this sonar is also essential to the Navy (D). The Natural Resources Defense Council, Inc. (NRDC) (P) alleges that active sonar injures marine life, the extent to which the parties vehemently disagree. The National Environmental Policy Act (NEPA) requires the Navy (D) to prepare an environmental impact statement (EIS) before continuing with the active sonar training. The EIS would not be completed until the training was finished. The NRDC (P) brought a motion for a preliminary injunction seeking an order that the Navy (D) cease training until the EIS is complete. The district court issued the injunction and the Ninth Circuit Court of Appeals affirmed. The Navy (D) appealed.

ISSUE: As one factor in the preliminary injunction analysis, may an injunction only be issued where the plaintiff demonstrates a likelihood of irreparable harm and not just the possibility of harm?

HOLDING AND DECISION: (Roberts, C.J.) Yes. As one factor in the preliminary injunction analysis, an injunction may only be issued where the plaintiff demonstrates a likelihood of irreparable harm and not just the possibility of harm. A plaintiff seeking a preliminary injunction must establish the following four elements: a likelihood of success on the merits, that irreparable harm is likely without an injunction, that the balance of the equities favors the plaintiff, and that the injunction is in the public's interest. On the issue of harm specifically, this Court's prior decisions have held that the irreparable injury must be likely, and not just a possibility. The NRDC (P) has only put forth evidence of a "possible" harm to marine life. However, even if the injury here was likely, it is outweighed by two other factors in the analysis. First, the balance of the equities tips clearly in the Navy's (D) favor. The NRDC (P) alleges only harm to an unknown amount of marine animals. In contrast, forcing the Navy (D) to deploy a submarine fleet not fully trained places the entire Naval fleet in jeopardy. The injunction also does not serve the public interest as it jeopardizes national security. While the Navy (D) should complete the EIS, an injunction ordering the cessation of training is improper. Reversed.

DISSENT: (Ginsburg, J.) The Navy (D) should have completed the EIS before it began the training exercises. The majority is incorrect when it states that plaintiffs must show a likelihood of irreparable harm in all cases. Rather, prior decisions have allowed a lesser showing of harm where the likelihood of success on the merits was high. Here, the Navy (D) was in violation of NEPA for failing to conduct the EIS. Accordingly, the NRDC's (P) burden to show harm was less than the normal case. Moreover, environmental harm cases are ripe for equitable remedies such as injunctions because remedies at law often come much later after harm to the environment has already occurred.

ANALYSIS

It is interesting that the majority did not even consider the NRDC's (P) likelihood of success of the merits. In addition, Justice Ginsburg is correct that there have been prior decisions allowing for a lower level of injury where the likelihood of success on the merits is high.

Quicknotes

INJUNCTION An equitable remedy requiring a person, entity, or governmental unit to do, or prohibiting that person, entity, or governmental unit from doing, a specific act.

IRREPARABLE HARM Such harm that because it is either too great, too small, or of a continuing character that it cannot be properly compensated in damages, and the remedy for which is typically injunctive relief.

National Collegiate Athletic Association v. Governor of New Jersey

Sports association (P) v. State official (D)

939 F.3d 597 (3d Cir. 2019)

NATURE OF CASE: Appeal from denial of motion for recovery on judgment bond.

FACT SUMMARY: Collegiate and professional sports associations (P) sought to enjoin a New Jersey (D) law authorizing certain types of sports gambling as violating a federal statute, the Professional and Amateur Sports Protection Act (PASPA). The New Jersey Thoroughbred Horsemen's Association (NJTHA) (D) intervened as a defendant, asserting, inter alia, that PASPA was unconstitutional. The sports associations (P) sought a temporary restraining order (TRO) preventing any sports gambling while the case proceeded, and had to post a judgment bond, which totaled $3.4 million. The district court held for the sports associations (P), and the Third Circuit affirmed. However, on further appeal, the United States Supreme Court held that PAPSA was unconstitutional. On remand, NJTHA (D) moved to collect on the judgment bond, contending that its members had been wrongfully enjoined throughout the proceedings. The district court denied the motion, ruling that NJTHA (D) members had not been wrongfully enjoined, and further ruling that even if they had, there was good cause to deny recovery on the bond because NJTHA (D) and the other defendants had prevailed through a change in the law.

RULE OF LAW

(1) A party is wrongfully enjoined when it turns out that that party had a right all along to do what it was enjoined from doing.

(2) In an action where a judgment bond has been posted as a condition of the issuance of a temporary restraining order (TRO), there is a rebuttable presumption that a wrongfully enjoined party is entitled to recover provable damages up to the bond amount.

FACTS: In 2014, the National Collegiate Athletic Association (NCAA) (P) and several professional sports associations (P) brought suit in federal district court to enjoin New Jersey (D) from implementing a law that authorized sports gambling in the state, on the grounds that the New Jersey (D) law violated a federal statute, the Professional and Amateur Sports Protection Act (PASPA). The New Jersey Thoroughbred Horsemen's Association (NJTHA) (D) intervened as a defendant, asserting, inter alia, that PASPA was unconstitutional. The sports associations (P) sought a temporary restraining order (TRO) preventing any sports gambling while the case proceeded and had to post a judgment bond per Federal Rule of Civil Procedure 65(c), which totaled $3.4 million and was based on NJTHA's (D) assertion that its members would lose $1.7 million per week during which sports gambling was enjoined. The district court held for the sports associations (P), and the Third Circuit Court of Appeals affirmed. However, on further appeal, the United States Supreme Court in 2018 held that PAPSA was unconstitutional, thus reversing the Third Circuit. On remand, NJTHA (D) moved to collect on the judgment bond, contending that its members had been wrongfully enjoined throughout the proceedings. The district court denied the motion, ruling that NJTHA (D) members had not been wrongfully enjoined, and further ruling that even if they had, there was good cause to deny recovery on the bond because NJTHA (D) and the other defendants had prevailed through a change in the law. The district court had reasoned that the law in the case had changed, characterizing PASPA as "constitutionally valid" in 2014, when the TRO was entered, and invalid in 2018. NJTHA (D) appealed the denial of its motion, contending that the district court had erred in both rulings it had made. The Third Circuit granted review, noting that both issues were matters of first impression in the circuit.

ISSUE:

(1) Is a party wrongfully enjoined when it turns out that that party had a right all along to do what it was enjoined from doing?

(2) In an action where a judgment bond has been posted as a condition of the issuance of a temporary restraining order (TRO), is there a rebuttable presumption that a wrongfully enjoined party is entitled to recover provable damages up to the bond amount?

HOLDING AND DECISION: (Rendell, J.)

(1) Yes. A party is wrongfully enjoined when it turns out that that party had a right all along to do what it was enjoined from doing. Federal Rule of Civil Procedure 65(c) requires a judgment bond to cover "the costs and damages sustained by any party found to have been wrongfully enjoined or restrained." Other circuits that have considered this issue have held that a party is wrongfully enjoined when it turns out that that party had a right all along to do what it was enjoined from doing. Although the parties agree that this is the correct standard to apply, they disagree as to how the standard should be applied in the case at bar. NJTHA (D) urges that, because the Supreme

Continued on next page.

Court ultimately held that PASPA is unconstitutional, it "turned out" that it had a right all along to conduct sports gambling and was, therefore, "wrongfully enjoined." The sports associations (P) argue that because the constitutionality of PASPA was settled law in this circuit at the time the temporary restraining order (TRO) was entered and because the district court's holding on the only issue before it at that time was confirmed on appeal, NJTHA (D) was not "wrongfully enjoined," and they also argue that a determination that NJTHA (D) was wrongfully restrained would require a retroactive application of the Supreme Court's holding. However, the district court wrongly conflates the standard for "wrongfully enjoined" with whether it had abused its discretion in entering the TRO in 2014. The entire concept of "wrongfully enjoined" envisions a look back from the ultimate conclusion of the case and asks whether the enjoined party should have been permitted to do what it was prevented from doing. Thus, whether a party was wrongfully enjoined depends upon the final judgment on the merits. The use of the past tense in Rule 65(c), which allows defendants to collect on the bond if they are "found to have been wrongfully enjoined or restrained," confirms this conclusion. In other words, the Rule's focus is on the right of an enjoined party to engage in certain conduct, not on whether the court entering the TRO acted erroneously. As to the retroactive application of the law, retroactivity is not implicated when a court is asked to determine whether a party was "wrongfully enjoined." The only pertinent question is whether it turned out that NJTHA (D) had the right all along to do what they were enjoined from doing, and there is no way that the answer to that question could be "no." The lookback that is envisioned in the Rule is not an issue of retroactivity, or of applying a ruling to undo or affect previous rulings; instead, it requires a simpler inquiry as to whether, if we knew then what we know now, should the enjoined party have been restrained? This does not require the court at the bond hearing to ask whether the TRO was wrongfully issued, or to nullify any intervening action as invalid. Because it turns out that PASPA was unconstitutional all along, it turns out that NJTHA (D) had the right all along to engage in sports gambling, and, therefore, was "wrongfully enjoined" and is entitled to call on the bond.

(2) Yes. In an action where a judgment bond has been posted as a condition of the issuance of a temporary restraining order (TRO), there is a rebuttable presumption that a wrongfully enjoined party is entitled to recover provable damages up to the bond amount. A majority of circuits have held that there is such a rebuttable presumption, in part because they have concluded that such a presumption is strongly implied by Rule 65(c), and because the presumption increases predictability of the law, discourages parties from requesting injunctions based on tenuous legal grounds, and conserves judicial resources, since a defendant who can recover damages against a preliminary injunction bond will be less likely to file a separate malicious prosecution action. Moreover, the rebuttability of the presumption in favor of recovery affords courts some, albeit limited, discretion to decline to impose damages on the rare party who has lost a case on the merits but, nevertheless, for good cause, should not suffer the execution of the judgment bond. For these reasons, this presumption is adopted in this circuit. Applying the rebuttable presumption here, the district court focused only on one factor that courts consider in determining whether the presumption has been rebutted, namely whether NJTHA (D) prevailed on the merits as a consequence of a change in law. However, circuit courts that have considered this issue have ruled that a court must consider all relevant factors, including, but not limited to, a defendant's failure to mitigate damages, the reasonableness of the damages sought, the outcome of the underlying suit, and the parties' resources, as well as a change in the law. Here, none of these factors rebut the presumption that NJTHA (D) is entitled to the bond damages. The sports associations (P) did not claim that NJTHA (D) failed to mitigate its damages or that the bond amount was unreasonable, and the underlying suit resulted in a judgment in NJTHA's (D) favor. As to a change in the law, this case did not involve the type of "change in law" that is required to rebut the presumption. Instead, there was no change in the state of the law while the case was in the federal court. NJTHA (D) and the other defendants successfully challenged the constitutionality of PASPA on appeal, such that they ultimately prevailed. "That is not a change in the law; that is success on the merits." Accordingly, NJTHA (D) is entitled to recover provable damages up to the bond amount. Reversed.

DISSENT: (Porter, J.) The majority incorrectly holds that NJTHA (D) was wrongfully enjoined, because the district court's TRO was not based on PASPA's constitutionality, but was based on whether New Jersey (D) law complied with PASPA itself, and because relying on the Supreme Court's holding as to PASPA's constitutionality requires indulging the fiction—not available to the district court—that PASPA never existed at all. Although the majority adopts the correct standard for determining when a party is wrongfully enjoined, the majority's application of that standard was erroneous. In the sister circuit

Continued on next page.

cases cited by the majority, the injunction and full merits proceedings addressed essentially the same issues, but none of these cases involved an appellate court expressly upholding the basis of the injunction while nonetheless deciding for the enjoined party on other grounds.

ANALYSIS

As the Third Circuit Court of Appeals in this case notes, Rule 65(c), which states in relevant part, "[t]he court may issue a preliminary injunction or a temporary restraining order only if the movant gives security in an amount that the court considers proper to pay the costs and damages sustained by any party found to have been wrongfully enjoined or restrained," itself only implies that when a party has been "wrongfully enjoined," the restrained party may collect some or all of the security, but the Rule does not explicitly address when an enjoined party may recover on a bond, nor does it indicate whether and to what extent a district court has discretion to deny damages. Thus, in the absence of statutorily articulated standards and requirements for these terms and concepts, the circuit courts have supplied them as a matter of statutory construction and interpretation. As the Third Circuit observes in this case, although it is possible to read Rule 65(c) as asking whether a district court abused its discretion in granting a TRO or temporary injunction, such a reading would distort the plain meaning and purpose of the rule, and, in any event, the Third Circuit's precedents had already made clear that "wrongfully enjoined" does not necessarily mean that the district court abused its discretion in granting the relief in the first place and that whether a party is wrongfully enjoined depends upon whether it turns out that that party had a right all along to conduct the activity it was enjoined from doing.

Quicknotes

INJUNCTION An equitable remedy requiring a person, entity, or governmental unit to do, or prohibiting that person, entity, or governmental unit from doing, a specific act.

INJUNCTION BOND A type of surety bond required by a court when a party to an action seeks to enjoin another party, which surety bond serves as a financial guarantee that the enjoined party will be compensated for any damages if it is later determined that the injunction was wrongful, and the enjoined party was wrongfully enjoined.

INJUNCTIVE RELIEF A court order issued as a remedy, requiring a person to do, or prohibiting that person from doing, a specific act.

PERMANENT INJUNCTION An equitable remedy imposed by a court ordering a party to do or refrain from doing a specific activity, which remedy is issued as part of the court's final judgment, and which remains in effect until it is modified or terminated by the court.

PREEMPTION (FEDERAL/STATE) Doctrine holding that matters of national interest take precedence over matters of local interest; federal law takes precedence over state law where federal law exists, as in federal common law, or where the clear and manifest purpose of Congress in a statute is to displace state law, but only as to statutes that pertain to Congress's constitutionally enumerated legislative powers, as all other legislative powers are reserved to the states by the Tenth Amendment.

PRESUMPTION A rule of law requiring the court to presume certain facts to be true based on the existence of other facts, thereby shifting the burden of proof to the party against whom the presumption is asserted to rebut.

REBUTTABLE PRESUMPTION A rule of law inferred from the existence of a particular set of facts that is conclusive in the absence of contrary evidence.

SURETY A party who guarantees payment of the debt of another party to a creditor.

SURETY BOND A three-party agreement where one party (the surety) guarantees the performance or obligations of a second party (the principal) to a third party (the obligee), whereby the surety compensates the obligee for any losses suffered by the obligee in the event that the principal fails to compensate the obligee when the principal is required to.

TEMPORARY RESTRAINING ORDER (TRO) A court order preserving the status quo pending a hearing regarding injunctive relief.

Carroll v. President and Commissioners of Princess Anne

Individuals (P) v. Municipality (D)

393 U.S. 175 (1968)

NATURE OF CASE: Appeal of temporary restraining order.

FACT SUMMARY: Authorities of the town of Princess Anne (P) obtained an ex parte TRO preventing a political rally.

RULE OF LAW

In the absence of a showing of impossibility, ex parte abridgements of First Amendment rights without notice are improper.

FACTS: In the town of Princess Anne (P), a white supremacist organization held a political rally filled with potentially inflammatory speech. Upon hearing that another rally was planned for the next day, the authorities obtained an ex parte temporary restraining order (TRO) prohibiting the rally. No notice of the application was given or even attempted. The TRO was obtained. The court later issued an injunction prohibiting rallies for 10 months. The state appellate court reversed the injunction but allowed the TRO to stand. Carroll (D) and other organization members appealed.

ISSUE: In the absence of a showing of impossibility, are ex parte abridgements without notice of First Amendment rights proper?

HOLDING AND DECISION: (Fortas, J.) No. In the absence of a showing of impossibility, ex parte abridgements of First Amendment rights without notice are improper. It is impossible for a court to intelligently weigh the issues in as delicate a situation as is a First Amendment issue without an adversary hearing. An order must be framed in the narrowest terms possible, and such precise tailoring is impossible without a full hearing. Reversed.

CONCURRENCE: (Douglas, J.) A TRO can never constitutionally restrain speech.

ANALYSIS

Federal Rule of Civil Procedure 65 provides the parameters of TROs. The Rule provides that notice must be given or an affidavit explaining the reasons for lack of notice must be presented. This is consistent with the rule of the Court given here.

Quicknotes

TEMPORARY RESTRAINING ORDER A court order preserving the status quo pending a hearing regarding injunctive relief.

Sampson v. Murray

Federal government (D) v. Individual (P)

415 U.S. 61 (1974)

NATURE OF CASE: Appeal of an issuance of a preliminary injunction barring termination of employment.

FACT SUMMARY: Murray (P), terminated by the Government (D), filed a wrongful discharge claim and obtained a preliminary injunction compelling the Government (D) to rehire her.

RULE OF LAW

A preliminary injunction is not proper in a wrongful discharge suit.

FACTS: Murray (P) was employed by the Government (D). The Government (D) terminated her. Murray (P) filed an action with the Civil Service Commission claiming wrongful discharge and, also, sought an injunction forcing the Government (D) to rehire her. The injunction was issued. The court of appeals affirmed, and the Government (D) appealed.

ISSUE: Is a preliminary injunction proper in a wrongful discharge suit?

HOLDING AND DECISION: (Rehnquist, J.) No. A preliminary injunction is improper in a wrongful discharge suit. It is basic in equitable relief that legal remedies must be inadequate. Wrongful termination can lead to lost income, which is compensable at law. While the argument can be made that a loss of reputation may result from a wrongful discharge, if the claimant prevails, the claimant will be vindicated. The damage therefore will not be irreparable. For this reason, the injunction was improper. Reversed.

DISSENT: (Marshall, J.) No appealable order has been entered, and this court lacks jurisdiction. Turning to the merits, the indignities of wrongful discharge constitute irreparable injury.

ANALYSIS

The district court called its order a temporary restraining order but extended it beyond the 10-day limit of Federal Rule of Civil Procedure 65. For this reason, the Court considered it a preliminary injunction. Justice Marshall did not agree with this, and for that reason argued that no jurisdiction existed.

Quicknotes

INJUNCTION An equitable remedy requiring a person, entity, or governmental unit to do, or prohibiting that person, entity, or governmental unit from doing, a specific act.

IRREPARABLE HARM Such harm that because it is either too great, too small, or of a continuing character that it cannot be properly compensated in damages, and the remedy for which is typically injunctive relief.

WRONGFUL DISCHARGE Unlawful termination of an individual's employment.

Edelman v. Jordan

State (D) v. Individual (P)

415 U.S. 651 (1974)

NATURE OF CASE: Appeal of injunction ordering welfare payments.

FACT SUMMARY: A district court issued an injunction compelling Illinois to make certain welfare payments to Jordan (P).

RULE OF LAW

A federal court cannot fashion an equitable remedy compelling a state to make payments out of its treasury.

FACTS: Illinois participated in a federal program wherein the United States matched certain welfare payments if the participating state agreed to follow federal Social Security regulations. Illinois failed to commence welfare payments to Jordan (P), an eligible beneficiary, in the required time. Jordan (P) sued Edelman (D), the responsible official, to recover for the time he should have been receiving benefits. The district court issued an injunction compelling Edelman (D) to comply with the time guidelines and awarding "equitable restitution" in the amount Jordan (P) would have obtained had payments started in a timely fashion. The court of appeals affirmed. The United States Supreme Court granted review.

ISSUE: Can a federal court fashion an equitable remedy compelling a state to make payments out of its treasury?

HOLDING AND DECISION: (Rehnquist, J.) No. A federal court cannot fashion an equitable remedy compelling a state to make payments out of its treasury. The sole exception to the Eleventh Amendment prohibition on federal actions where states are real parties in interest or defendants is when an action is brought under the Fourteenth Amendment or a statute thereunder. Even then, only prospective relief may be given; a state cannot be forced to make payments out of its treasury. Whether the relief is called "damages" or, as here, "equitable restitution" is irrelevant. A state cannot be compelled to make payments out of its treasury in a federal action, either in a legal or equitable action. Reversed and remanded.

DISSENT: (Douglas, J.) Where a state consents to participate in a federal program involving grants, it has waived its Eleventh Amendment immunities.

DISSENT: (Brennan, J.) The Eleventh Amendment does not bar federal suits against states by its own citizens.

DISSENT: (Marshall, J.) When a state voluntarily participates in a federal grant program, it waives its Eleventh Amendment protections, particularly where, as here, evidence of congressional intent that beneficiaries should have an avenue of redress exists.

ANALYSIS

In terms of strict construction, the dissent of Justice Brennan is quite correct. The Eleventh Amendment, in its wording, does not bar federal suits against states by its own citizens. However, it is by now a well-established rule that the Eleventh Amendment does apply to suits brought against states by its own citizens. Some have argued that such immunities are inherent in the American federal system, and the Eleventh Amendment merely reflects preexisting principles.

Quicknotes

ELEVENTH AMENDMENT The Eleventh Amendment to the United States Constitution prohibits the extension of the judicial powers of the federal courts to suits brought against a state by citizens of another state, or of a foreign state, without the state's consent.

EQUITABLE Just; fair.

Harlow v. Fitzgerald

Federal government (D) v. Individual (P)

457 U.S. 800 (1982)

NATURE OF CASE: Appeal of denial of summary judgment in action for conspiracy.

FACT SUMMARY: Fitzgerald (P) brought an action against former Nixon White House aides for conspiring to oust him from his job.

RULE OF LAW

Presidential aides have only a qualified immunity from suit for acts done in their official capacities.

FACTS: Fitzgerald (P), a management analyst in the Air Force, "blew the whistle" regarding certain questionable weapons procurement practices. His job was subsequently taken out from under him, and he eventually brought suit against Harlow (D), a White House aide, and others for conspiring to retaliate against him. Fitzgerald (P) alleged that Harlow (D) conspired with the other defendants to achieve a reduction in force in his department merely to get him out of the civil service. Harlow (D) moved for summary judgment based on a contention of absolute immunity. This was denied, and the court of appeals affirmed.

ISSUE: Do presidential aides have only a qualified immunity for acts done in their official capacities?

HOLDING AND DECISION: (Powell, J.) Yes. Presidential aides have only a qualified immunity for acts done in their official capacities. Immunity is based on the notion that an official must be able to perform their tasks without worrying about potential legal liability. However, immunity extracts a social price, and therefore absolute immunity will be granted only when necessary. By and large, presidential aides can be given such immunity only when they are acting as direct alter egos of the President, something not often occurring. Other than at those times, the privilege White House aides should enjoy is one of "good faith." If the official was reasonably unaware that their conduct constituted a violation of the Constitution or statutes, they will be granted immunity. This action must be remanded to allow Harlow (P) to plead facts that will defeat this sort of privilege. Vacated and remanded.

ANALYSIS

Both the Court's opinion and Chief Justice Burger's dissent discuss "derivative immunity." As the name indicates, it is immunity deriving from another source, here the President. This sort of immunity is recognized in legislative aides. However, the circumstances under which this immunity applies are narrow.

Quicknotes

IMMUNITY Exemption from a legal obligation.

SUMMARY JUDGMENT Judgment rendered by a court in response to a motion made by one of the parties, claiming that the lack of a question of material fact in respect to an issue warrants disposition of the issue as a matter of law without consideration at trial by a fact-finder.

CHAPTER 6

Remedies and Separation of Powers

Quick Reference Rules of Law

Stone v. North Carolina Department of Labor

Individual (P) v. State (D)

N.C. Sup. Ct., 495 S.E.2d 711 (1998)

NATURE OF CASE: Appeal from denial of motion to dismiss a negligence action.

FACT SUMMARY: After sustaining injury in a fire at a food products plant, Stone (P) filed a negligence suit against the North Carolina Department of Labor (D) for failure to inspect the plant.

RULE OF LAW

The public duty doctrine immunizes state agencies from suits alleging negligent failure to perform an obligation to the public.

FACTS: Stone (P) was injured when he could not escape a fire at a food products plant due to inaccessible or blocked exits. After the fire, the North Carolina Department of Labor (Department) (D) conducted its first inspection of the plant and found many violations of the state health and safety act. Stone (P) filed suit alleging that the Department's (D) failure to properly inspect the plant before the fire caused the injuries. The Department moved to dismiss the action on the grounds that it was immune from prosecution under the public duty doctrine. The state's Industrial Commission denied the motion, and the court of appeals affirmed. The Department (D) appealed.

ISSUE: Does the public duty doctrine immunize state agencies from individual suits alleging negligent failure to perform an obligation to the public?

HOLDING AND DECISION: (Whichard, J.) Yes. The public duty doctrine immunizes state agencies from suits alleging negligent failure to perform an obligation to the public. While the Department of Labor (D) bears an obligation to inspect facilities for safety violations, it is not liable to a private person injured in such a facility. The Department (D), in the performance of its public obligations, owes no legal duty to individual plaintiffs, only to the public at large. The Department (D) cannot be treated as a private person under the state Tort Claims Act because such persons do not possess public duties. This rule applies to municipalities as well as state agencies. The rule is necessary to prevent the placement of a great burden of liability upon financially limited government agencies. Reversed and remanded.

DISSENT: (Orr, J.) The common-law public duty doctrine only applies to municipalities, not state agencies. The granting of immunity under the public duty doctrine effectively undermines the legislature's intent in giving private citizens the right to sue the state government in tort.

ANALYSIS

Tort claims acts have been widely adopted by state legislatures. The acts allow private citizens to bring a range of lawsuits against state and local governments. Some state courts have abolished the public duty doctrine, only to have state legislatures codify the doctrine's principal protections.

Quicknotes

CLAIM The demand for a right to payment or equitable relief; the fact or facts giving rise to such demand.

TORT A legal wrong resulting in a breach of duty by the wrongdoer, causing damages as a result of the breach.

Van de Kamp v. Goldstein

Individual (P) v. District Attorney's office (D)

555 U.S. 335 (2009)

NATURE OF CASE: Appeal from the affirmation of the denial of defendant's motion to dismiss.

FACT SUMMARY: In 1980, a jury convicted Van de Kamp (P) of murder. In 1998, a federal court granted Van de Kamp habeas corpus on the grounds a witness lied during Van de Kamp's (P) trial.

RULE OF LAW

Prosecutors involved in administrative duties such as supervision, training, or information system management that are related to a specific criminal case enjoy absolute immunity.

FACTS: In 1980, a jury convicted Van de Kamp (P) of murder. In 1998, Van de Kamp (P) filed a petition for habeas corpus on the grounds the prosecution knowingly used a prosecution witness, Edward Fink, who lied on the stand by stating that Van de Kamp (P) admitted the murder to Fink. In addition, there was evidence that the Los Angeles County District Attorney's Office (D) had used Fink before in prior trials and given him reduced criminal sentences in return. Van de Kamp (P) alleged in his habeas petition that the Office had failed to divulge that information to his attorney at the criminal trial. The district court allowed the petition and ordered the District Attorney's Office (D) to offer Van de Kamp (P) a new trial or release him. The District Attorney's Office (D) decided to release Van de Kamp (P) after 24 years of incarceration. Van de Kamp (P) then filed this § 1983 action against the District Attorney's Office (D) alleging the Office: (1) failed to properly train prosecutors; (2) failed to supervise the prosecutors; and (3) failed to establish an information sharing system containing impeachment material on informants. The District Attorney's Office (D) moved to dismiss, which the district court denied. The Ninth Circuit affirmed. The District Attorney's Office (D) appealed.

ISSUE: Do prosecutors involved in administrative duties such as supervision, training, or information system management that are related to a specific criminal case enjoy absolute immunity?

HOLDING AND DECISION: (Breyer, J.) Yes. Prosecutors involved in administrative duties such as supervision, training, or information system management that are related to a specific criminal case enjoy absolute immunity. In *Imbler v. Pachtman*, 424 U.S. 409 (1976), this Court held that prosecutors enjoyed absolute immunity from liability in § 1983 actions where the alleged unlawful conduct was "intimately associated with the judicial phase of the criminal process." Prosecutors enjoy absolute immunity because concern over unfounded litigation may cause prosecutors to make decisions based upon liability concerns. Usually, the immunity does not apply to administrative tasks, such as hiring and payroll administration. However, the administrative issues here—training and supervision of prosecutors—require legal knowledge and the exercise of discretion and as a result have an impact on specific cases. Whether the claim is failure to train or supervise a specific attorney on a specific case or a more general claim of failure to train is immaterial. Such a claim necessarily arises from some specific alleged mistake in the plaintiff's underlying criminal trial. Consequently, members of large prosecutors' offices could have liability in mind when they are considering general decisions regarding training and when they are making decisions specific to a particular case. Both types of decisions will impact specific cases. Moreover, allowing such general supervision and training claims to go forward would create an anomaly. A prosecutor handling a specific case would be immune even if they intentionally committed a constitutional violation. However, their supervisor could be liable for their negligent failure to supervise or train that particular prosecutor. Separately, the decision to create an information system involves decisions about whether to have such a system at all and what information would be included. These types of decisions are legal in nature and are associated with the judicial phase of a criminal process. Accordingly, absolute immunity applies there as well. Reversed and remanded.

ANALYSIS

This decision makes the piercing of a prosecutor's immunity extremely difficult. Essentially, the decision extends liability protection from decisions involving specific cases to those regarding the general supervision of cases within a district attorney's office. The decision is practical because of the difficulty in separating decisions over general policy within the office from those relating to a specific case.

Quicknotes

IMMUNITY Exemption from a legal obligation.

Bivens v. Six Unknown Named Agents

Suspect (P) v. Federal agents (D)

403 U.S. 388 (1971)

NATURE OF CASE: Appeal from dismissal of private action for violation of the Fourth Amendment.

FACT SUMMARY: The district court dismissed Bivens's (P) private damages action against six federal agents holding no such cause of action existed under the Fourth Amendment.

RULE OF LAW
A private cause of action exists for the violation of constitutional rights under color of federal law.

FACTS: Bivens (P) sued six agents of the Federal Bureau of Narcotics, contending they physically abused and arrested him without a warrant. He contended this action, under color of law, violated his Fourth Amendment rights and entitled him to damages. The district court dismissed the action for failure to state a claim upon which relief could be granted. Bivens (P) appealed, and the Second Circuit Court of Appeals affirmed. The Unites States Supreme Court granted certiorari.

ISSUE: Does a private cause of action exist for the violation of constitutional rights under color of federal law?

HOLDING AND DECISION: (Brennan, J.) Yes. A private cause of action exists for the violation of constitutional rights under color of federal law. Where legal rights have been invaded, courts must fashion remedies to provide relief. The Fourth Amendment grants freedom from unreasonable searches and seizures. If the facts in this case allow a finding of unreasonableness, a damages award would be appropriate. Thus, the lower courts erred in dismissing the action. Reversed and remanded.

CONCURRENCE: (Harlan, J.) State remedies for trespass to the person do not preclude a federal cause of action where the tortfeasor acts under color of federal law.

DISSENT: (Burger, C.J.) This decision violates the separation of powers doctrine by creating a cause of action judicially.

DISSENT: (Black, J.) Congress is the appropriate branch of government to create a private cause of action.

ANALYSIS

This case is the key case creating a private action for violation of constitutional rights. The defense had argued that Bivens (P) should have been required to sue under state tort law. However, this opened the door for the argument that federal agents acting under color of state law have authority exceeding state law.

Quicknotes

CAUSE OF ACTION A fact or set of facts, the occurrence of which entitles a party to seek judicial relief.

FOURTH AMENDMENT Provides that persons be secure as to their person and private belongings against unreasonable searches and seizures.

Armstrong v. Exceptional Child Center, Inc.

State official (D) v. In-home health services provider (P)

575 U.S. 320 (2015)

NATURE OF CASE: Appeal from affirmance of summary judgment granted to providers of in-home care health services in action seeking an injunction to compel a state to increase its rates of reimbursement to the providers under Medicaid.

FACT SUMMARY: Providers of in-home health services (P) brought suit against Idaho (D), claiming that Idaho (D) violated Section 30A of the Medicaid Act (Act) by reimbursing the providers (P) at rates lower than permitted in § 30A. Idaho (D) contended that such an action was permitted neither implicitly under the Supremacy Clause nor at equity.

RULE OF LAW

(1) The Supremacy Clause does not implicitly create a right of action in Medicaid providers to challenge a state's alleged violations of the state's Medicaid plan.

(2) Medicaid providers may not challenge a state's alleged violations of the state's Medicaid plan in an action brought in equity.

FACTS: Providers (P) of in-home health care for individuals who, but for the provision of such services, would require the level of care provided in a hospital or a nursing facility or intermediate care facility for the cognitively disabled—under Idaho's (D) Medicaid plan were reimbursed by the State's Department of Health and Welfare. Section 30(A) of the Medicaid Act (Act) required Idaho's (D) plan to "assure that payments are consistent with efficiency, economy, and quality of care" while "safeguard[ing] against unnecessary utilization of . . . care and services." The providers (P) sued Idaho Health and Welfare Department officials (D), claiming that Idaho (D) reimbursed them at rates lower than permitted by § 30(A), and sought to enjoin Idaho (D) to increase these rates. The district court entered summary judgment for the providers (P). The court of appeals affirmed, concluding that the Supremacy Clause gave the providers (P) an implied right of action, and that they could sue under this implied right of action to seek an injunction requiring Idaho (D) to comply with § 30(A). The United States Supreme Court granted certiorari.

ISSUE:

(1) Does the Supremacy Clause implicitly create a right of action in Medicaid providers to challenge a state's alleged violations of the state's Medicaid plan?

(2) May Medicaid providers challenge a state's alleged violations of the state's Medicaid plan in an action brought in equity?

HOLDING AND DECISION: (Scalia, J.)

(1) No. The Supremacy Clause does not implicitly create a right of action in Medicaid providers to challenge a state's alleged violations of the state's Medicaid plan. The Supremacy Clause instructs courts to give federal law priority when state and federal law clash. However, it is not a source of any federal rights, and it certainly does not create a cause of action. Nothing in the Clause's text suggests otherwise, and nothing suggests it was ever understood as conferring a private right of action. Article I vests Congress with broad discretion over the manner of implementing its enumerated powers. It is unlikely that the Constitution gave Congress broad discretion with regard to the enactment of laws, while simultaneously limiting Congress's power over the manner of their implementation, making it impossible to leave the enforcement of federal law to federal actors. In other words, if the Supremacy Clause includes a private right of action, then the Constitution requires Congress to permit the enforcement of its laws by private actors, significantly curtailing its ability to guide the implementation of federal law. It would be strange indeed to give a clause that makes federal law supreme a reading that limits Congress's power to enforce that law, by imposing mandatory private enforcement. Moreover, interpreting the Supremacy Clause not to confer a private right of action is consistent with the Court's preemption jurisprudence. The ability to sue to enjoin unconstitutional actions by state and federal officers is the creation of courts of equity and reflects a long history of judicial review of illegal executive action, tracing back to England. The Court has never held nor suggested that this judge-made remedy, in its application to state officers, rests upon an implied right of action contained in the Supremacy Clause. Reversed as to this issue.

(2) No. Medicaid providers may not challenge a state's alleged violations of the state's Medicaid plan in an action brought in equity. The power of federal courts of equity to enjoin unlawful executive action is subject

Continued on next page.

to express and implied statutory limitations. Here, the express provision of a single remedy for a state's failure to comply with Medicaid's requirements—the withholding of Medicaid funds by the Secretary of Health and Human Services (Secretary)—and the sheer complexity associated with enforcing § 30(A) combine to establish Congress's intent to foreclose equitable relief. The provision for the Secretary's enforcement by withholding funds might not, by itself, preclude the availability of equitable relief, but it does so when combined with the judicially unadministrable nature of § 30(A)'s text, since it is difficult to imagine a requirement broader and less specific than § 30(A)'s mandate that state plans provide for payments that are "consistent with efficiency, economy, and quality of care," all the while "safeguard[ing] against unnecessary utilization of . . . care and services." Explicitly conferring enforcement of this standard upon the Secretary alone establishes that Congress wanted to make the agency remedy that it provided exclusive. The sheer complexity associated with enforcing § 30(A), coupled with the express provision of an administrative remedy, shows that the Medicaid Act precludes private enforcement of § 30(A) in the courts. This is the fairest reading of the Act, and the Court—contrary to the dissenters' assertion—is not authorized to revise Congress's scheme simply because it did not affirmatively and explicitly preclude the availability of a judge-made action at equity. Finally, the Medicaid Act itself is not a source of action for the providers (P), given that Section 30(A) lacks the sort of rights-creating language needed to imply a private right of action. It is phrased as a directive to the federal agency charged with approving state Medicaid plans, not as a conferral of the right to sue upon the beneficiaries of the state's decision to participate in Medicaid. Reversed as to this issue. Reversed.

CONCURRENCE: (Breyer, J.) The correct characterization of the question presented is whether federal courts may, under the circumstances presented by this case, grant injunctive relief against state official who are violating, or planning to violate, federal law. The answer is no; but it does not follow from the application of a simple, fixed legal formula, but rather follows from characteristics of the Medicaid Act that make clear that Congress intended to foreclose a private action for equitable relief under § 30(A). The statute's broad standards apply to rate setting, a task that is much better left for administrative agencies, rather than judges. Additionally, it is not clear that other forms of relief are inadequate, since the Secretary can withhold federal funds, or sue a State to compel compliance. Moreover, providers (P) could ask the Secretary to interpret the agency's rules to the providers' (P) satisfaction, to modify those rules, to promulgate new rules or to enforce old rules. Normally, when such requests are denied, an injured party can seek judicial review of the agency's refusal. Although it may be difficult for providers (P) to prevail on their claim unless it results from the agency's particularly egregious failure to act, that would be the case because Congress vested broad discretion in the agency to interpret and enforce § 30(A).

DISSENT: (Sotomayor, J.) The majority fails to point to the sort of detailed remedial scheme the Court previously has deemed necessary to establish congressional intent to preclude resort to equity. Instead, the majority relies on Congress's provision for agency enforcement of § 30(A)—an enforcement mechanism of the sort the Court already definitively has determined does not foreclose private actions—and on the mere fact that § 30(A) contains relatively broad language. In fact, this equitable authority is exceedingly well established. Because Congress is undoubtedly aware of the federal courts' long-established practice of enjoining preempted state action, it should generally be presumed to contemplate such enforcement unless it affirmatively manifests a contrary intent. The use of equity in such situations—to halt or prevent constitutional violations—is warranted because a plaintiff otherwise would have little or no recourse in the face of constitutional violations. By contrast, a plaintiff invoking a statute that provides damages, or an implied statutory cause of action, may seek a variety of remedies—including damages—from a potentially broad range of parties. Rather than simply pointing to background equitable principles authorizing the action that Congress presumably has not overridden, such a plaintiff must demonstrate specific congressional intent to create a statutory right to these remedies. Here, the providers (P) do not have an adequate remedy at law for a Section 30(A) violation. As one possible remedy, the majority points to the Act's section that authorizes the Secretary to withhold federal Medicaid payments to a state in whole or in part if the Secretary determines that the state has failed to comply with the obligations set out in the Act, including § 30(A). However, such a remedy is inadequate, since the Act provides no specific procedure that parties actually affected by a state's violation of its statutory obligations may invoke in lieu of an equitable action, thus leaving them without any other avenue for seeking relief from the state. Moreover, this mechanism may be self-defeating if federal funding to the state is reduced or eliminated. Second, perhaps attempting to reconcile its treatment of the Act with the Court's longstanding precedent, the majority focuses on the particular language of § 30(A), contending that this provision, at least, is so "judicially unadministrable" that Congress must have intended to preclude its enforcement in private suits. Although the standard set out in § 30(A) admittedly is fairly broad, mere breadth of statutory language

Continued on next page.

does not require the Court to give up all hope of judicial enforcement or, more importantly, to infer that Congress must have done so. In fact, the contention that § 30(A)'s language was intended to foreclose private enforcement actions entirely is difficult to square with the provision's history. To the contrary, the breadth of § 30(A) counsels in favor of interpreting it to provide substantial leeway to states, so that only in rare and extreme circumstances could a state actually be held to violate its mandate. When the agency has made a determination with respect to what legal standard should apply, or the validity of a state's procedures for implementing its Medicaid plan, that determination should be accorded the appropriate deference. Finally, because the authority invoked for enforcing § 30(A) is equitable in nature, a plaintiff is not entitled to relief as of right, but only in the sound discretion of the court. Given the courts' ability to both respect states' legitimate choices and defer to the federal agency when necessary, there is no reasoned basis for presuming that Congress believed the courts to be completely incapable of enforcing § 30(A). Under the majority's decision, it must suffice that a federal agency, with many programs to administer, has the authority to address § 30(A) violations through the drastic and often counterproductive measure of withholding funds, instead of permitting those affected by the violation to compel the State to respect its obligations under the statute. This will have very real consequences.

ANALYSIS

Justice Scalia responded to the dissenters' objection that this decision would leave those seeking to enforce the Act without recourse by pointing out that relief sought for Act violations would have to be sought initially through the Secretary rather than through the courts, and that the dissenters' view that the sanction available to the Secretary (the cut-off of funding) would be too massive to be a realistic source of relief was mistaken. In this respect, Justice Scalia expressed doubt that the Secretary's notice to a state that its compensation scheme was inadequate would be ignored. Justice Breyer, who concurred in the decision, emphasized that the rate-setting nature of § 30(A) was key in precluding judicial relief for its violation. Justice Breyer observed that the history of rate making demonstrates that administrative agencies are far better suited to this task than judges and emphasized that the language of § 30(A) underscores the complexity and nonjudicial nature of the rate-setting task involved. Although he recognized that federal courts have long become accustomed to reviewing for reasonableness or constitutionality the rate-setting determinations made by agencies, Justice Breyer expressed the opinion that § 30(A)'s rate-setting scheme was not susceptible to such review, since finding in the law a basis for courts to engage in direct rate-setting could set a precedent for allowing other similar actions, potentially resulting in rates set by federal judges outside the ordinary channel of federal judicial review of agency decision-making.

Quicknotes

ENUMERATED POWERS Those powers expressly delegated by the U.S. Constitution to a particular branch of government.

SUPREMACY CLAUSE Article VI, § 2 of the U.S. Constitution, which provides that federal action must prevail over inconsistent state action.

Securities & Exchange Commission v. Jarkesy

Federal agency (P) v. Investment adviser (D)

603 U.S. 109 (2024)

NATURE OF CASE: Appeal from judgment vacating order of federal agency imposing civil penalties, on the grounds that the adjudication of the matter by the agency deprived the defendants of their Seventh Amendment right to a jury trial.

FACT SUMMARY: The Securities & Exchange Commission ("SEC" or "Commission") (P) brought an enforcement action against Jarkesy (D) and his firm for securities fraud, and, after the action was adjudicated in-house, the SEC levied a civil penalty of $300,000 against the defendants and barred Jarkesy (D) from the securities industry. Jarkesy (D) appealed, contending that by adjudicating the action in-house, the SEC (P) deprived him of his Seventh Amendment right to a jury.

RULE OF LAW

When the Securities & Exchange Commission (SEC) seeks civil penalties against a defendant for securities fraud, the Seventh Amendment entitles the defendant to a jury trial.

FACTS: The Securities & Exchange Commission ("SEC" or "Commission") (P) brought an enforcement action against Jarkesy (D) and his firm for securities fraud. The SEC (P) may bring an enforcement action in one of two forums. It can file suit in federal court, where a jury decides the fact issues, or it can adjudicate the matter itself in-house, in the absence of a jury. The SEC (P) decided to bring the matter in-house, without a jury. The matter was heard by an administrative law judge (ALJ), and the Commission (P) imposed a civil penalty of $300,000 against the defendants and barred Jarkesy (D) from the securities industry. Jarkesy (D) petitioned for judicial review, which the Fifth Circuit Court of Appeals granted. The Fifth Circuit vacated the SEC's (P) order on the ground that adjudicating the matter in-house violated the defendants' (D) Seventh Amendment right to a jury trial. The United States Supreme Court granted certiorari.

ISSUE: When the Securities & Exchange Commission (SEC) seeks civil penalties against a defendant for securities fraud, does the Seventh Amendment entitle the defendant to a jury trial?

HOLDING AND DECISION: (Roberts, C.J.) Yes. When the Securities & Exchange Commission (SEC) seeks civil penalties against a defendant for securities fraud, the Seventh Amendment entitles the defendant to a jury trial. The threshold issue here is whether the action implicates the Seventh Amendment. It does, because the SEC's (P) antifraud provisions replicate common-law fraud, and it is well established that common law claims must be heard by a jury. The right to trial by jury is of such importance and occupies so firm a place in the country's history and jurisprudence that any seeming curtailment of the right has always been and should be scrutinized with the utmost care. When the British attempted to evade American juries by siphoning adjudications to juryless admiralty, vice admiralty, and chancery courts, the Americans protested and eventually cited the British practice as a justification for declaring Independence. In the Revolution's aftermath, concerns that the proposed Constitution lacked a provision guaranteeing a jury trial right in civil cases was perhaps the "most success[ful]" critique leveled against the document during the ratification debates. The Federalist No. 83, p. 495. To fix that flaw, the Framers promptly adopted the Seventh Amendment, and ever since, every encroachment upon the jury trial right has been scrutinized very closely. The Seventh Amendment guarantees that in "[s]uits at common law . . . the right of trial by jury shall be preserved." The Court has construed this text to mean that the right itself is not limited to the common-law forms of action recognized when the Seventh Amendment was ratified. Instead, it embraces all suits that are legal in nature and that are not of equity or admiralty jurisdiction, including statutory claims that are legal in nature. To determine whether a suit is legal in nature, courts must consider whether the cause of action resembles common-law causes of action, and whether the remedy is the sort that was traditionally obtained in a court of law. Of these factors, the remedy is the more important. In the case at bar, the remedy is all but dispositive. Here, the SEC (P) sought civil penalties for Jarkesy's (D) fraud. Such relief is a form of monetary relief and is legal in nature when it is designed to punish or deter the wrongdoer rather than solely to "restore the status quo." Here, the civil penalty was meant to punish Jarkesy (D), rather than compensate any victims, so that the action was one at law. Additionally, the availability and size of the civil penalties available to the SEC (P) are based on considerations such as culpability, deterrence, and recidivism, which are factors that go beyond restoring the status quo, and, so, are legal in nature. Moreover, the SEC (P) is not obligated to use civil penalties to compensate victims. Finally, the close relationship between federal securities fraud and common-law fraud, with both targeting the same basic conduct—misrepresenting or concealing material facts—confirms that SEC (P) civil

Continued on next page.

penalties are a type of remedy at common law that could only be enforced in courts of law. Accordingly, the enforcement action at issue here implicates the Seventh Amendment right to a jury trial, and a defendant would be entitled to a jury on these claims, unless the "public rights" exception applies. Under this exception, Congress may assign the matter for decision to an agency without a jury, consistent with the Seventh Amendment. The Court has also held that the Constitution prevents Congress from withdrawing from judicial cognizance any matter that, from its nature, is the subject of a suit at the common law. Once such a suit is brought within the bounds of federal jurisdiction, an Article III court must decide it, with a jury if the Seventh Amendment applies. On that basis, this Court has repeatedly explained that matters concerning private rights may not be removed from Article III courts, and that, if a suit is in the nature of an action at common law, the matter presumptively concerns private rights, and adjudication by an Article III court is mandatory. Nonetheless, the Court has also recognized a class of cases concerning "public rights." Such matters historically could have been determined exclusively by the executive and legislative branches, and no involvement by an Article III court in the initial adjudication of such public rights claims is necessary. The key to determining whether an action qualifies for the public rights exception is the substance of the suit, regardless whether the claims originate in a newly fashioned regulatory scheme or possess a long line of common-law forebears. SEC (P) enforcement actions, including the one at issue here, are brought under the anti-fraud provisions of the federal securities laws and provide civil penalties that can only be enforced in courts of law. They target the same basic conduct as common-law fraud, employ the same terms of art, and operate pursuant to similar legal principles. In short, this action involves a matter of private rather than public right, so that Congress may not withdraw it from judicial cognizance under Article III. The principal case on which the SEC (P) and the dissent rely is *Atlas Roofing Co. v. Occupational Safety and Health Review Commission*, 430 U.S. 442 (1977). Because the public rights exception as construed in *Atlas Roofing* does not extend to the SEC's (P) civil penalty suits for fraud, that case does not control. The litigation in that case arose under the Occupational Health and Safety Act (OSH Act). Facing agency enforcement actions, two employers alleged that the agency's adjudicatory authority violated the Seventh Amendment. The Court concluded that Congress could assign the OSH Act adjudications to an agency because the claims involved a new cause of action, and remedies therefor, unknown to the common law. The cases *Atlas Roofing* relied on applied the "public rights" exception to actions that were not suits at common law or in the nature of such suits. Thus, *Atlas Roofing* is inapplicable here, where the statutory claim is in the nature of a common-law suit. Moreover, the Court's later precedents clarified that the Seventh Amendment does apply to novel statutory regimes, so long as the statutory claims are akin to common-law claims, and that the public rights exception does not apply automatically whenever Congress assigns a matter to an agency for adjudication. Affirmed.

DISSENT: (Sotomayor, J.) Not only does the majority's decision commit numerous legal errors, it also upends longstanding precedent and the established practice of its coequal branches of government, thereby threatening the Constitution's separation of powers balance. With its decision, the majority, for the very first time in the Court's history, holds that Congress violated the Constitution by authorizing a federal agency to adjudicate a statutory right that inheres in the government in its sovereign capacity, also known as a public right. That is plainly wrong, because until this decision, the Court has held, without exception, that Congress has broad latitude to create statutory obligations that entitle the government to civil penalties, and then to assign their enforcement outside the regular courts of law where there are no juries. Although this case involves a Seventh Amendment challenge, the principal question at issue is one rooted in Article III and the separation of powers, because the Seventh Amendment's jury-trial right "applies" only in an Article III court. Whether a defendant is entitled to a jury under the Seventh Amendment depends on both the forum and the cause of action. If the claim is in an Article III proceeding, then the right to a jury attaches if the claim is "legal in nature" and the amount in controversy exceeds 20 dollars. Yet, when as here, the claim proceeds in a non-Article III forum, the relevant question becomes whether Congress properly assigned the matter for decision to that forum consistent with Article III and the separation of powers. According to the Court's precedents going back more than a century and a half, public rights always can be assigned outside of Article III forums, notwithstanding that had those same public rights been assigned to an Article III forum, a jury trial would have been required. The pros and cons of adjudicatory schemes such as the one Congress assigned to the SEC (P) are debatable, but it is not the Court's job to decide who wins the debate. Instead, these policy choices must be made by Congress. Thus, the majority's decision is a power grab, because the majority arrogates Congress's policymaking role to itself. The majority prescribes artificial constraints on what modern-day adaptable governance must look like, and, in telling Congress that it cannot entrust certain public-rights matters to the Executive because it must bring them first into the Judiciary's province, the majority oversteps its role and encroaches on Congress's constitutional authority. Its decision offends the Framers' constitutional design so

Continued on next page.

critical to the preservation of individual liberty: the division of our government into three coordinate branches to avoid the concentration of power in the same hands.

ANALYSIS

Certain categories that have been recognized as falling within the "public rights" exception to the Seventh Amendment's right to a jury trial include matters concerning: the collection of revenue, tariffs, aspects of customs law, immigration law, relations with American Indian tribes, the administration of public lands, and the granting of public benefits. Although the Court's opinions governing this exception have not always spoken in precise terms, it is clear that even with respect to matters that arguably fall within the scope of the public rights doctrine, the presumption is in favor of adjudication in Article III courts.

Quicknotes

ARTICLE III, U.S. CONSTITUTION Limits federal judicial power to cases and controversies.

EQUITABLE REMEDY A remedy that is based upon principles of fairness as opposed to rules of law; a remedy involving specific performance rather than money damages.

LEGAL REMEDY Compensation for violation of a right or injuries sustained that is available in a court of law, as opposed to in equity.

MONETARY DAMAGES Monetary compensation sought by or awarded to a party who incurred loss as a result of a breach of contract or tortious conduct on behalf of another party.

PUBLIC RIGHTS DOCTRINE The principle that certain rights, which are vested in the government and not in private individuals, can be adjudicated by non-Article III courts, enabling Congress to assign the resolution of public rights cases to administrative agencies or specialized courts rather than traditional federal courts.

SEPARATION OF POWERS The division of government into the legislative, executive, and judicial branches, with each branch having specific duties upon with the other branches may not encroach.

SEPARATION OF POWERS DOCTRINE Each branch of government is precluded from interfering with the authority of another.

SEVENTH AMENDMENT Provides for trial by jury in "suits at common law," and that no fact tried by a jury shall be otherwise re-examined in any court of the United States, other than according to the rules of the common law.

CHAPTER 7

Preventing Harm Without Coercion: Declaratory Remedies

Quick Reference Rules of Law

Nashville, Chattanooga, & St. Louis Railway v. Wallace

Corporation (P) v. State (D)

288 U.S. 249 (1933)

NATURE OF CASE: Appeal of declaratory relief action challenging state tax.

FACT SUMMARY: Nashville, Chattanooga, & St. Louis Railway (the Railway) (P) sought a judicial declaration that a state gasoline tax was unconstitutional.

RULE OF LAW

Federal courts may issue declaratory judgments when an actual controversy exists.

FACTS: Tennessee (D) instituted a gasoline storage tax. The Nashville, Chattanooga & St. Louis Railway (the Railway) (P) brought an action for a judicial declaration that the tax was an unconstitutional burden on interstate commerce. No additional legal or equitable relief was requested. The state trial court found the tax constitutional, and the state Supreme Court affirmed. The Railway (P) appealed to the United States Supreme Court.

ISSUE: May federal courts issue declaratory judgments when an actual controversy exists?

HOLDING AND DECISION: (Stone, J.) Yes. Federal courts may issue declaratory judgments when an actual controversy exists. Federal courts may decide cases or controversies, irrespective of the judicial labels given them. While declaratory relief may be in the form of an advisory opinion, it need not be, and the fact that no relief other than the declaration is sought does not necessarily make an opinion merely advisory. Here, the respective rights of the parties are in controversy, and the holding of this Court will decide this controversy. Thus, jurisdiction is proper in this Court. Affirmed.

ANALYSIS

Federal courts may only decide cases or controversies, per Article III, § 2 of the Constitution. Advisory opinions are not permitted; adjudication of actual rights must be made. However, as the Court here points out, adjudication of rights in and of itself may be all that a case requires.

Quicknotes

DECLARATORY JUDGMENT A judgment of the court establishing the rights of the parties.

Cardinal Chemical Co. v. Morton International, Inc.

Corporation (D) v. Corporation (P)

508 U.S. 83 (1993)

NATURE OF CASE: Appeal from vacation of declaratory judgment regarding patent validity.

FACT SUMMARY: The court of appeals refused to decide a counterclaim by Cardinal Chemical Co. (Cardinal) (D) seeking a declaration that Morton International, Inc.'s (Morton's) (P) patent was invalid after Cardinal (D) prevailed in Morton's (P) infringement suit.

RULE OF LAW

Courts may not refrain from deciding a counterclaim for declaratory judgment regarding the validity of a patent in a patent infringement case.

FACTS: Morton International, Inc. (Morton) (P) owned two patents on chemical compounds used in polyvinyl chloride. In 1983, Morton (P) filed a suit alleging that Cardinal Chemical Co. (Cardinal) (D) had infringed those patents. Cardinal (D) counterclaimed for a declaratory judgment that the patents were invalid. The trial court found that Cardinal (D) had proved that the patents were invalid and gave two judgments in favor of Cardinal (D), dismissing the action for infringement and declaring the patents invalid. Morton (P) appealed, and the court of appeals vacated the declaration of invalidity on basis of a rule that courts should refrain on mootness grounds from deciding the merits of a patent validity claim when infringement action is dismissed. Cardinal (D) appealed from this ruling.

ISSUE: May a court refrain from deciding a counterclaim for declaratory judgment regarding the validity of a patent where no infringement is proved?

HOLDING AND DECISION: (Stevens, J.) No. Courts may not refrain from deciding a counterclaim for declaratory judgment regarding the validity of a patent in a patent infringement case. A party seeking a declaratory judgment has the burden of establishing the existence of an actual case or controversy. In patent litigation, a party may satisfy that burden even if there is no infringement claim. Merely the desire to avoid the threat of an infringement action is sufficient to establish a controversy under the Declaratory Judgment Act. An actual charge of infringement necessarily indicates a controversy adequate to support jurisdiction. A counter-claim for declaratory judgment of invalidity is an independent claim that must be decided unless the other party proves that subsequent events have made the claim moot. Thus, a per se rule that validity declarations are vacated when the underlying infringement claim is dismissed is inappropriate. Furthermore, strong public policy concerns indicate that a counterclaim for declaratory judgment should be decided. Companies once charged with infringement will remain concerned about the risk of future charges if they develop similar products in the future. Also, relitigating the validity of patents is wasteful. The per se rule also deprives the patent holder of appellate review of the decision. Accordingly, the judgment of the court of appeals is vacated, and the case is remanded.

ANALYSIS

The decision noted that before the adoption of the Declaratory Judgment Act, patent holders often used "scarecrow patents." These patent holders would attempt to assert claims through settlements without ever actually filing suit. The alleged infringer was placed in a difficult position because he could not determine whether the patent was valid until the holder brought an infringement action.

Quicknotes

COUNTERCLAIM An independent cause of action brought by a defendant to a lawsuit in order to oppose or deduct from the plaintiff's claim.

DECLARATORY JUDGMENT A judgment of the court establishing the rights of the parties.

DECLARATORY JUDGMENT ACT Allows prospective defendants to sue for a declaration of their rights.

INFRINGEMENT Conduct in violation of a statute or contract that interferes with another's rights pursuant to law.

MOOT Judgment on the particular issue that has previously been decided or settled.

PER SE By itself; not requiring additional evidence for proof.

Steffel v. Thompson

Leaflet distributor (P) v. State official (D)

415 U.S. 452 (1974)

NATURE OF CASE: Appeal of denial of declaratory relief in civil rights action.

FACT SUMMARY: Steffel (P), threatened with prosecution for trespassing while handing out leaflets, sought declaratory relief holding the law invalid.

RULE OF LAW

Federal declaratory relief may be given when threat of enforcement of a disputed state criminal statute exists.

FACTS: Steffel (P) was threatened with prosecution under a criminal trespass law for handing out leaflets on private property. Steffel (P) then filed an action for injunctive and declaratory relief against the State (D), claiming the statute was unconstitutional. The court of appeals denied both forms of relief, and Steffel (P) appealed only as to the declaratory relief. The state court had voluntarily stayed its proceedings pending the outcome of the federal action.

ISSUE: May federal declaratory relief be given when threat of enforcement of a disputed state criminal statute exists?

HOLDING AND DECISION: (Brennan, J.) Yes. Federal declaratory relief may be given when threat of enforcement of a disputed state criminal statute exists. Declaratory relief, unlike injunctive relief, is not coercive in that the threat of contempt does not exist. For that reason, the federalism concerns underlying the limitations on federal injunctions against pending state actions do not apply. Also, the traditional requisite of irreparable injury does not apply, so the problem of showing irreparable injury in an injunctive action of this nature does not apply in a declaratory relief action. Reversed and the case remanded.

CONCURRENCE: (Stewart, J.) Today's decision does not authorize one who thinks a state criminal law is unconstitutional to invoke federal declaratory judgment jurisdiction. In the instant case, the petitioner has demonstrated a "genuine threat of enforcement of a disputed state criminal statute."

ANALYSIS

Federal declaratory relief actions present certain problems. Ripeness is a big issue, as federal courts can decide only actual cases or controversies. Declaratory relief actions border on advisory opinions, which federal courts are not allowed to issue. However, as this case shows, federal declaratory relief actions are accepted as part of federal jurisprudence.

Quicknotes

DECLARATORY JUDGMENT A judgment of the court establishing the rights of the parties.

INJUNCTIVE RELIEF A court order issued as a remedy, requiring a person to do, or prohibiting that person from doing, a specific act.

Doran v. Salem Inn, Inc.

Town (D) v. Corporation (P)

422 U.S. 922 (1975)

NATURE OF CASE: Appeal of injunction prohibiting enforcement of ordinance proscribing topless dancing.

FACT SUMMARY: M & L Restaurant (P) and two other establishments obtained an injunction against enforcement of a criminal ordinance during the pendency of a prosecution under the ordinance.

RULE OF LAW

A party cannot evade restrictions on federal injunctions against state criminal actions by joining parties not affected by the restrictions.

FACTS: The town of North Hempstead (D) passed an ordinance forbidding topless dancing. M & L Restaurant (M & L) (P) and two other establishments (Salem Inn and Tim-Rob Bar) filed suit to have the ordinance invalidated. M & L (P), unlike the other establishments, continued to feature topless dancing. M & L (P) and its principals were served with criminal summonses. The district court found the ordinance unconstitutional and enjoined its enforcement. The district court held that federal restrictions on enjoining state criminal proceedings did not apply in M & L's (P) case, since M & L's (P) co-plaintiffs were entitled to relief. North Hempstead (D) appealed. The court of appeals affirmed.

ISSUE: Can a party evade restrictions on federal injunctions against state criminal actions by joining parties not affected by the restrictions?

HOLDING AND DECISION: (Rehnquist, J.) No. A party cannot evade restrictions on federal injunctions against state criminal actions by joining parties not affected by the restrictions. It is true that deciding the validity of a statute in a state criminal action and a federal action is not an efficient use of judicial manpower. However, as important as judicial economy may be, the federalism concerns in this area are greater. The states' rights considerations that lead to the rules regarding injunctions against pending state proceedings have full force even when the subject party is joined by nonaffected parties, as is the case here. Reversed as to M & L (P) and affirmed as to Salem Inn and Tim-Rob Bar.

ANALYSIS

A sub-issue the Court dealt with was whether an injunction, as opposed to declaratory relief, was an appropriate remedy for the other plaintiffs. The Court held that injunctive relief was proper, noting that the practical effect of the two was virtually identical. This is interesting, as the Court's holding in *Steffel v. Thompson*, 415 U.S. 452 (1974), was supposedly based on the differences between the two.

Quicknotes

INJUNCTION An equitable remedy requiring a person, entity, or governmental unit to do, or prohibiting that person, entity, or governmental unit from doing, a specific act.

INJUNCTIVE RELIEF A court order issued as a remedy, requiring a person to do, or prohibiting that person from doing, a specific act.

Newman Machine Co. v. Newman

Corporation (P) v. Shareholder (D)

N.C. Sup. Ct., 166 S.E.2d 63 (1969)

NATURE OF CASE: Action to quiet title on personal property.

FACT SUMMARY: Newman (D) claimed he had been defrauded when he sold Newman Machine Co. (P) and demanded rescission.

RULE OF LAW

An action to quiet title to personalty may be brought.

FACTS: Newman (D) owned certain shares in Newman Machine Co. (P), both individually and as trustee. Newman (D) sold a sizable number of shares to the corporation. Newman (D) later sought to rescind the transaction. Newman (D) and his attorneys continued to threaten legal action against Newman Machine Co. (P). Newman Machine Co. (P) then brought an action to quiet title as to the shares. Newman (D) demurred, claiming that North Carolina statues provided only for actions to quiet title to realty.

ISSUE: May an action to quiet title to personalty be brought?

HOLDING AND DECISION: (Huskins, J.) Yes. An action to quiet title to personalty may be brought. While statutory authorization exists only for quiet title actions in realty, suits in equity to quiet title existed before the statute. Where the usual elements necessary for an action in equity concur, no reason exists for not permitting personalty quiet title actions. Here, as Newman Machine Co. (P) is in possession, it cannot bring an action at law. Newman (D) has not sued, and the claims of Newman (D) impair the marketability of the stock. As legal remedies appear inadequate, a quiet title action is proper. Reversed and remanded.

ANALYSIS

The precursor to the quiet title action was the bill to remove cloud on title. This was an equitable action to test the validity of any instrument clouding a title. It did not actually pass on ownership itself. The quiet title action actually does declare ownership rights.

Quicknotes

ACTION TO QUIET TITLE Equitable action to resolve conflicting claims to an interest in real property.

CLOUD ON TITLE A claim or encumbrance in the title record to real property that, if valid, would have the effect of impairing or defeating the owner's title.

DEMURRER The assertion that the opposing party's pleadings are insufficient and that the demurring party should not be made to answer.

PERSONALTY Personal, movable property not attached to real estate.

RESCISSION The cancellation of a contract upon certain default by the other contracting party.

Hand v. Dayton-Hudson

Employee (P) v. Employer (D)

775 F.2d 757 (6th Cir. 1985)

NATURE OF CASE: Appeal from order of reformation summary judgment dismissing an age discrimination and breach of contract action.

FACT SUMMARY: Hand (P), an attorney, altered a release that he and his employer, Dayton-Hudson (D), executed when Hand (P) was fired and accepted a payment.

RULE OF LAW

Reformation is allowed despite the lack of a mutual mistake if there is fraud by the other party.

FACTS: Hand (P) was employed as an attorney at Dayton-Hudson (D) from 1967 to 1982. In 1982, Hand (P) was fired, and Dayton-Hudson (D) agreed to pay $38,000 if Hand (P) agreed to release Dayton-Hudson (D) from any claims. Hand (P) initially refused, but a release was drafted and presented to Hand (P). Hand (P) then prepared another release that was identical in form to the original release except that it provided that Hand (P) could bring an age discrimination and breach of contract claim. Hand (P) attached the release to the other documents in the same way as the original and tricked Dayton-Hudson (D) into signing the new release and paying the $38,000. Hand (P) then brought a suit for age discrimination and breach of contract against Dayton-Hudson (D), who sought reformation of the release and a dismissal of the discrimination suit. The trial court held that Hand (P) had committed fraud, reformed the release to conform to its original meaning, and dismissed Hand's (P) action. Hand (P) appealed.

ISSUE: Is reformation allowed despite the lack of a mutual mistake if there is fraud by the other party?

HOLDING AND DECISION: (Contie, J.) Yes. Reformation is allowed despite the lack of a mutual mistake if there is fraud by the other party. Although there is a general rule that a party is responsible for contracts that it has signed, it is not applicable where the signing is induced by fraud. Hand (P) committed fraud against Dayton-Hudson (D) by not informing them of the changes that he had purposefully made to the release. Generally, reformation of a contract is only available where there is a mutual mistake of fact. To grant reformation when there is a unilateral mistake would harm one party because the reformed contract would not represent what the parties intended. However, there is an exception to this rule where there is fraud or inequitable conduct by one party to the contract. If there is clear and convincing evidence that one party knew that the contract did not reflect the other party's intent, reformation may be allowed. A meeting of minds on the content of the reformed contract is not required because the exception is designed primarily to combat the inequities of fraud. Hand (P) was aware of Dayton-Hudson's (D) intent regarding its original release and willfully acted to make Dayton-Hudson (D) believe that it was signing the original version. Thus, Hand's (P) conduct fits squarely within the exception, and reformation to conform to Dayton-Hudson's (D) understanding is allowed. Affirmed.

CONCURRENCE: (Wellford, J.) Reformation should not be allowed unless there has been a meeting of the minds on the substantive content of the reformed contract. However, Hand (P) should not be entitled to relitigate his discrimination claim because of his unconscionable conduct.

ANALYSIS

This decision goes against the usual rule that reformation should be used to change a written contract to reflect the actual agreement of the parties. In Hand's (P) case, it doesn't appear that an agreement ever existed because Hand (P) would not have signed the release if it had not specifically exempted the discrimination and breach claims. If the release had been rescinded for fraud, Dayton-Hudson (D) would have recouped the $38,000 paid to Hand (P), who then would have been allowed to pursue any claims against the company.

Quicknotes

BREACH OF CONTRACT Unlawful failure by a party to perform its obligations pursuant to contract.

FRAUD A false representation of facts with the intent that another will rely on the misrepresentation to their detriment.

REFORMATION OF CONTRACT An equitable remedy whereby the written terms of an agreement are altered in order to reflect the true intent of the parties; reformation requires a demonstration by clear and convincing evidence of mutual mistake by the parties to the contract.

CHAPTER 8

Benefit to Defendant as the Measure of Relief: Restitution

Quick Reference Rules of Law

Blue Cross Health Services, Inc. v. Sauer

Payor (P) v. Payee (D)

Mo. Ct. App., 800 S.W.2d 72 (1990)

NATURE OF CASE: Appeal from order granting new trial.

FACT SUMMARY: The twofold data entry mistake of a hospital employee preceded the erroneous payment of more than $22,000 in claims by Blue Cross Health Insurance Services, Inc. (Blue Cross) (P) to William R. Sauer (Sauer) (D). Upon discovery of the mistake, Blue Cross (P) sued Sauer (D) to recover the monies inasmuch as Sauer (D) was unjustly enriched by the payments.

RULE OF LAW

A payor who pays money to another by mistake is entitled to restitution from the unjustly enriched payee even when both the payor and the payee share in the underlying mistake.

FACTS: Upon admission to the hospital, William R. Sauer (Sauer) (D) informed the clerk that he carried Blue Cross Health Insurance but that he did not have his insurance card with him. [In fact, his coverage had been recently canceled for non-payment of premiums.] In his patient account, a hospital employee failed to transmit Sauer's (D) middle initial and wrongly entered Sauer's (D) address as the address of record for currently insured William J. Sauer. Thereafter, Blue Cross Health Services, Inc. (Blue Cross) (P) mistakenly paid Sauer (D), a resident of Missouri, more than $22,000 intended for William J. Sauer of Wisconsin. Each of the checks sent by Blue Cross (P) was endorsed either by Sauer (D), Sauer's father, R.T. Sauer (D), who had been paying Sauer's (D) premiums, or by R.T. Sauer's (D) business, whose address Sauer had provided the hospital at the time of admission. Of note, each check mailed by Blue Cross (P) was accompanied by an Explanation of Benefits informing Sauer (D) of the details of the services provided in Wisconsin. Within a month of discovering the mistaken payments, Blue Cross (P) sent a demand letter to Sauer (D) and filed suit in equity against Sauer (D) and the R.T. Sauer Agency (D), and later, Robert T. Sauer (D). Blue Cross (P) sought to impose a constructive trust upon the funds of defendants based on unjust enrichment and mistake. The trial court entered an interlocutory default judgment against Sauer (D) and granted, upon transfer of the case to the law division, Robert T. Sauer (D) and the R.T. Sauer Agency (D) a new trial.

ISSUE: Is a payor who pays money to another by mistake entitled to restitution from the unjustly enriched payee even when both the payor and the payee share in the underlying mistake?

HOLDING AND DECISION: (Gaertner, J.) Yes. A payor who pays money to another by mistake is entitled to restitution from the unjustly enriched payee even when both the payor and the payee share in the underlying mistake. It is manifest that the remedy for unjust enrichment is restitution, even if the payor demonstrates "lack of care" or "inadvertence," and even when the payee shares in the payor's mistake. Whether a payor's remedy is in law or equity depends on the circumstances of the case. In the instant matter, payor Blue Cross (P) petitioned the court to impose the equitable remedy of constructive trust. But because Blue Cross (P) did not identify specific, identifiable property or funds upon which a trust could be attached, the most appropriate remedy is an action at law for money—in short, Blue Cross (P) was entitled to no more than a simple money judgment. However, notwithstanding the failure of Blue Cross (P) to invoke equity jurisdiction, Robert T. Sauer (D) and the R.T. Sauer Agency (D) are not entitled to a new trial. The record clearly demonstrates no disputed issue of fact and, had there been a jury trial, Blue Cross (P) would have been entitled to a directed verdict at the close of evidence. Furthermore, Robert T. Sauer (D) was owner, director and president of the R.T. Sauer Agency (D). The Agency was served with Blue Cross's (P) demand for restitution in this matter less than three months after the last of the mistakenly paid monies was sent to Sauer (D) at the R.T. Sauer Agency address. Therefore, the affirmative defense that Robert T. Sauer (D) asserts—that Blue Cross's (P) failure to name him as a defendant in this action until three years after its commencement has so changed his position that it would be unjust to require restitution—is baseless. Reversed and remanded with directions to reinstate the judgment.

ANALYSIS

Under the guidance of reporter Professor Andrew Kull (now of the University of Texas at Austin, School of Law), the Restatement (Third) of Restitution and Unjust Enrichment was published in 2011 by the American Law Institute. The Restatement (Third) restates the law in the most modern and clear terms and with the most current case updates and explanations. Of note, the commentary in anticipation of the publication of the Restatement (Third) explains that the law of restitution and unjust enrichment, although in recent times is

Continued on next page.

underemployed, increases the effectiveness and precision of the litigator of claims.

Quicknotes

ACTION IN EQUITY An action that seeks equitable relief, such as an injunction or specific performance, as opposed to damages.

Somerville v. Jacobs

Innocent improver of real estate (P) v. Landowner

W. Va. Sup. Ct. App., 170 S.E.2d 805 (1969)

NATURE OF CASE: Appeal from a judgment giving restitution.

FACT SUMMARY: Somerville (P) innocently and mistakenly built an industrial building on a lot owned by Jacobs (D) rather than his own lot and sought either payment for the building or conveyance of the lot on which construction was done at the price of an unimproved lot.

RULE OF LAW

Where a party innocently and mistakenly builds improvements on the land of another who lacks knowledge of the mistake until after completion, the innocent party may have restitution to prevent the unjust enrichment of the landowner.

FACTS: Somerville (P) owned lots 44, 45, and 46 in a development. Believing that he was building a warehouse on lot 46, he actually built it on lot 47, which was owned by Jacobs (D). Upon completion of the structure, Somerville (P) leased it to the local Coca-Cola Bottling Company. Jacobs (D) did not learn of this until after the fact and, upon so learning, claimed the improvements as his by the theory of annexation. Somerville (P) brought this action for restitution, and the court gave Jacobs (D) 60 days to elect either (1) to retain the building and pay Somerville (P) $17,500 or suffer judgment for that amount or (2) to convey title to lot 47 to Somerville (P) for $2,000 cash, its unimproved value. Jacobs (D) appealed.

ISSUE: Where a person innocently and mistakenly builds improvements on the land of another, who lacks knowledge of the mistake until after completion, may the innocent party have restitution in order to prevent the unjust enrichment of the landowner?

HOLDING AND DECISION: (Haymond, J.) Yes. Where a party innocently and mistakenly builds improvements on the land of another who lacks knowledge of the mistake until after completion, the innocent party may have restitution to prevent the unjust enrichment of the landowner. Where there are two innocent parties, the solution to the question requires application of principles of fair dealing between them. It is inequitable for one to profit by another's mistake, to take all while the other takes nothing. "An improver of land owned by another, who through a reasonable mistake of fact and in good faith erects a building entirely upon the land of the owner, with reasonable belief that such land was owned by the improver, is entitled to recover the value of the improvements from the landowner and to a lien upon such property which may be sold to enforce the payment of such lien, or, in the alternative, to purchase the land so improved upon payment to the landowner of the value of the land less the improvements, and such landowner, even though free from any inequitable conduct . . . , who, however, retains but refuses to pay . . . , must, within a reasonable time, either pay the improver the amount by which the value of his land has been improved or convey such land to the improver upon payment . . . of the value of the land without the improvements." Affirmed.

DISSENT: (Caplan, J.) The majority has approved condemnation of private property by private parties for private use. The law is clear that as between two parties, the one who is mistaken must suffer the hardship.

ANALYSIS

Restatement, Restitution § 42 (1937) basically concurs with the rule above. A comment to that section states that the harshness of the common-law rule has been mitigated in certain circumstances. "Thus a court of equity requires one seeking its assistance against an improver of land to do equity by making compensation a condition to relief, and in actions at law brought to recover damages for the improver's occupation of the land, he is entitled to have deducted from the claim against him the value of his improvements."

Quicknotes

RESTITUTION The return or restoration to rightful owner to prevent unjust enrichment.

Bonina v. Sheppard

Former unmarried cohabitant (P) v. Former unmarried cohabitant (D)

Mass. App. Ct., 78 N.E.3d 128 (2017)

NATURE OF CASE: Appeal from award of restitution granted on a theory of unjust enrichment.

FACT SUMMARY: Sheppard (D), who owned the house she and Bonina (P) lived in for 16 years in a nonmarital relationship, contended that she had not been unjustly enriched by Bonina's (P) substantial contributions to improve the house, and that even if she had been unjustly enriched, the appropriate measure of restitution was the increased value of the house with the improvements, rather than Bonina's (P) costs.

RULE OF LAW

(1) An unmarried cohabitant owner of a home is unjustly enriched by the other cohabitant's substantial uncompensated contributions to the improvement of the home absent evidence that those contributions were intended to be gratuitous.

(2) A substantial, uncompensated contribution by one unmarried cohabitant to improve the home owned by the other is recoverable in restitution, as measured by the contributor's costs, rather than the increased value of the home with the improvements, where the homeowner has been unjustly enriched by the improvements.

FACTS: After being in a nonmarital relationship for three years, Sheppard (D) and Bonina (P) decided to live together in a home. Sheppard (D) purchased the home in her name only for $131,500. Bonina (P), a contractor, paid half of the mortgage payments, taxes, and living expenses during the cohabitation, which lasted 16 years. During that period, Bonina (P) made significant contributions of materials, fixtures, time, and labor to the improvement of the house through maintenance, repairs, and improvements, including three additions. The couple's intention had been to jointly purchase the home, improve and then sell it, and then purchase a bigger house. After the relationship ended, Bonina (P) brought suit against Sheppard (D) for restitution under a theory of unjust enrichment. The trial awarded Bonina (P) $156,913.07, which reflected Bonina's (P) costs after deducting his costs for maintenance of the home and for short-term benefits, such as extension cords and lightbulbs. Neither party presented evidence regarding other possible measures of unjust enrichment, such as the increased value of the home resulting from the materials and the services. The state's intermediate appellate court granted review.

ISSUE:

(1) Is an unmarried cohabitant owner of a home unjustly enriched by the other cohabitant's substantial uncompensated contributions to the improvement of the home absent evidence that those contributions were intended to be gratuitous?

(2) Is a substantial, uncompensated contribution by one unmarried cohabitant to improve the home owned by the other recoverable in restitution, as measured by the contributor's costs, rather than the increased value of the home with the improvements, where the homeowner has been unjustly enriched by the improvements?

HOLDING AND DECISION: (Kafker, C.J.)

(1) Yes. An unmarried cohabitant owner of a home is unjustly enriched by the other cohabitant's substantial uncompensated contributions to the improvement of the home absent evidence that those contributions were intended to be gratuitous. Unmarried cohabitants may be entitled to equitable relief where one of the cohabitants has been unjustly enriched by the other. The plaintiff must establish not only that the defendant received a benefit, but also that such a benefit was unjust. Whether the benefit was unjust turns on the reasonable expectations of the parties. Sheppard (D) argued that the trial judge erred in determining that she was unjustly enriched because the parties were in a romantic relationship when Bonina (P) made his contributions to the home. The argument is rejected. The parties' romantic relationship does not prevent the plaintiff from recovering from the defendant under an unjust enrichment theory, as in this state [Massachusetts], there is no presumption that a claimant's contributions during a romantic relationship are gratuitous. Here, the trial judge's factual findings demonstrated that the substantial contributions made by Bonina (P) to improve the home were not meant to be gifts to Sheppard (D). Under the Restatement (Third) of Restitution and Unjust Enrichment § 28(1), unjust enrichment in the context of a terminated relationship of unmarried cohabitants is based on the claimant's frustrated expectations, and recovery is allowed because the claimant would not have conferred the benefit, except in the expectation that the parties' subsequent relationship would be

Continued on next page.

something other than it proved to be. Here, Bonina's (P) uncompensated contributions were substantial, and his payments toward the mortgage were determined by the trial court to be more than adequate for his use and occupancy of the residence. Accordingly, Bonina (P) could seek restitution for his contributions to Sheppard's (D) home under an unjust enrichment theory. Affirmed as to this issue.

(2) Yes. A substantial, uncompensated contribution by one unmarried cohabitant to improve the home owned by the other is recoverable in restitution, as measured by the contributor's costs, rather than the increased value of the home with the improvements, where the homeowner has been unjustly enriched by the improvements. Sheppard (D) next claims that the trial judge erred by measuring Bonina's (P) restitution as the costs he incurred in improving the home, rather than the increased value of the home with the improvements. Under the particular circumstances of this case, the trial judge did not abuse his discretion in determining that Bonina's (P) costs in improving the home constituted a proper measure of unjust enrichment and restitution. Measuring restitution for unjust enrichment poses special difficulties, and, as such, trial judges need considerable discretion to fashion appropriate remedies. These difficulties are particularly pronounced in the context of unmarried cohabitants, where the parties often have built a life together over many years, and the trial judge must untangle complicated property interests that arose during the relationship. Although restitution is not measured by the claimant's losses, but only by the defendant's gains, the claimant's costs to confer the benefit may be evidence of, and relevant to, determining the value of the benefit received by the defendant. In the context of unmarried cohabitants, there are numerous reasons why a plaintiff's actual costs may be a prudent and reliable measure of the benefit conferred on a defendant. In these relationships, the parties often have made substantial, uncompensated contributions to property over many years without a business-like or market-based approach to their financial arrangements. Instead, the contributions reflect their romantic relationship, shared expenses, and expectation of continuing to live together as a couple. Additionally, the correlation of costs with benefits is especially valid where, as here, the costs that the plaintiff incurred were for construction materials and fixtures for the defendant's home. In these circumstances, there is a direct dollar-for-dollar correlation between the costs incurred by the plaintiff and the benefit conferred on the defendant. Because Bonina (P) contributed his significant skills, labor, and expertise to the renovations and improvements—and countless hours doing so—Sheppard (D) may have received a benefit greater than Bonina's (P) recovery of his costs, as he did not seek recovery of the value of his services. Thus, Sheppard (D) undoubtedly received a substantial discount in improving her home, which the trial judge aptly noted and took into consideration in measuring her unjust enrichment. As here, where the costs incurred by the plaintiff directly relate to the benefit conferred on the defendant, and neither party has presented reliable evidence of other possible measures of unjust enrichment, a trial judge does not abuse their discretion in valuing the plaintiff's restitution as the plaintiff's costs in improving the home. In other words, the trial judge performed a sound weighing of the equities based on the specific facts of this case. Affirmed as to this issue. Affirmed.

ANALYSIS

The court in this case relied on the Restatement (Third) of Restitution and Unjust Enrichment, § 28(1), which provides that "[i]f two persons have formerly lived together in a relationship resembling marriage, and if one of them owns a specific asset to which the other has made substantial, uncompensated contributions in the form of property or services, the person making such contributions has a claim in restitution against the owner as necessary to prevent unjust enrichment upon the dissolution of the relationship." Under the Restatement, § 49(3), other possible measures of enrichment are "the value of the benefit in advancing the purposes of the defendant," "the market value of the benefit," and "a price the defendant has expressed a willingness to pay."

Quicknotes

RESTITUTION The return or restoration to rightful owner to prevent unjust enrichment.

UNJUST ENRICHMENT Principle that one should not be unjustly enriched at the expense of another.

Farash v. Sykes Datatronics, Inc.

Individual (P) v. Corporation (D)

N.Y. Ct. App., 452 N.E.2d 1245 (1983)

NATURE OF CASE: Appeal from dismissal of action for quantum meruit.

FACT SUMMARY: Farash (P) sued to recover expenditures for remodeling his building made in reliance on Sykes's (D) oral agreement to lease.

RULE OF LAW

A party may recover for the expenditures made in reliance on the promise of another, even though the promisor received no benefit from such expenditures.

FACTS: Farash (P) and Sykes (D) entered into an oral agreement whereby Sykes (D) would lease Farash's (P) building, and Farash (P) would remodel it to fit Sykes's (D) needs. Sykes (D) subsequently refused to lease the building. Farash (P) sued, contending that although the lease was unenforceable under the Statute of Frauds, he was entitled to recover the expenses incurred in remodeling the building in reliance on Sykes's (D) promise to lease it. The trial court denied Sykes's (D) motion to dismiss, but the appellate court reversed on the basis that Sykes (D) was not benefited by the expenditures.

ISSUE: May a party recover for expenditures made in reliance on the promise of another even though the promisor received no benefit from the expenditures?

HOLDING AND DECISION: (Cooke, C.J.) Yes. A party may recover the expenditures made in reliance on the promise of another even though the promisor received no benefit from such expenditures. In order to recover in quasi-contract, the plaintiff need not show that the defendant physically received benefits from the performance. It is sufficient such performance was part of an agreed-upon exchange; it is deemed received by the defendant. As a result, Farash (P) did state a cause of action. Reversed.

DISSENT: (Jasen, J.) In order to recover in quasi-contract, the plaintiff must demonstrate that the defendant was unjustly enriched by their actions.

ANALYSIS

Quasi-contract is one of the common counts and is an action to enforce a contract that is implied in law. The basis for recovery is to prevent the defendant from benefiting unjustly from the plaintiff's performance. Some commentators argue that the implied receipt concept relied upon in this case is an artificial label when used in the context of unjust enrichment.

Quicknotes

QUANTUM MERUIT Equitable doctrine allowing recovery for labor and materials provided by one party, even though no contract was entered into, in order to avoid unjust enrichment by the benefited party.

QUASI-CONTRACT An implied contract created by law to prevent unjust enrichment.

STATUTE OF FRAUDS A statute that requires specified types of contracts to be in writing in order to be binding.

Olwell v. Nye & Nissen Co.

Property owner (P) v. Tortious converter of property (D)

Wash. Sup. Ct., 173 P.2d 652 (1946)

NATURE OF CASE: Action for damages for unjust enrichment.

FACT SUMMARY: Nye & Nissen Co. (D) used Olwell's (P) egg washing machine without the owner's permission or knowledge in order to make up for a manpower shortage during World War II.

RULE OF LAW

Where a wrongdoer is consciously tortious in acquiring a benefit at the expense of the injured party, the injured party may recover not only their actual losses but the tortfeasor's profits as well.

FACTS: Olwell (P) sold and transferred his one-half interest in an egg packing company to Nye & Nissen Co. (Nye) (D) with Olwell (P) to retain full ownership of an egg washing machine formerly used by the packing company. Olwell (P) arranged to have the machine stored in space adjacent to Nye (D) but not covered by its lease. After the start of World War II, there was a manpower shortage, and Nye's (D) treasurer ordered that the egg washer be taken out of storage and put into operation. This was done without Olwell's (P) knowledge or permission in May 1941. The machine was used once a week until Olwell (P) learned of it in about January or February of 1945. Olwell (P) offered to sell Nye (D) the machine for $600, half of its 1929 cost, but Nye's (D) counteroffer of $50 was refused. Olwell (P) then sought to recover $25 a month and was awarded $10 per week, or $1,560.

ISSUE: Where a wrongdoer is consciously tortious in acquiring a benefit at the expense of the injured party, may the injured party recover not only their actual losses but the tortfeasor's profits as well?

HOLDING AND DECISION: (Mallery, J.) Yes. Where a wrongdoer is consciously tortious in acquiring a benefit at the expense of the injured party, the injured party may recover not only their actual losses but the tortfeasor's profits as well. Where a defendant tortfeasor has benefited by their wrong, the plaintiff can waive the tort and bring an action in assumpsit for restitution. Nye's (D) saving of labor costs was a recoverable benefit. It is no defense that Olwell (P) was just as well off whether or not the machine was used. There is no benefit to property ownership unless the owner has a right to exclusive use. Where a defendant has tortiously received a benefit, the defendant must pay for what the other has lost, although it is more than the benefit. If the defendant was consciously tortious, they must be deprived of any profit they derived from subsequent use as well. Affirmed as modified.

ANALYSIS

Notice that the measure of damages in cases of misuse of another's property depends on the willfulness of the defendant's conduct. Where the defendant consciously misuses another's property, the defendant pays for the owner's loss and loses any profit the defendant may have made. But if the defendant is no more at fault than the plaintiff, the defendant need not pay for losses in excess of the defendant's benefit and may retain their profit. Note that the damages were reduced only because the amount awarded was greater than Olwell's (P) request. Note also that had Olwell (P) used an assumpsit theory of implied sale of the egg washer to Nye (D), he would probably have recovered even less, as the machine's inherent value was most likely much less than the amount its use saved Nye (D).

Quicknotes

ACTION IN ASSUMPSIT Action to recover damages for breach of an oral or written promise to perform or pay pursuant to a contract.

ASSUMPSIT An oral or written promise by one party to perform or pay another.

LOSS Situation where amount realized (if any) exceeds the basis upon the sale or other disposition of an asset.

PROFIT An amount gained above those monies or value paid in the form of costs.

TORTFEASOR Party that commits a tort or wrongful act.

TORTIOUS ACTS Acts that constitute legal wrongs, resulting in breach of a duty.

UNJUST ENRICHMENT Principle that one should not be unjustly enriched at the expense of another.

Maier Brewing Co. v. Fleischmann Distilling Corp.

Corporation (D) v. Corporation (P)

390 F.2d 117 (9th Cir. 1968)

NATURE OF CASE: Action for an accounting and injunction under the Lanham Trademark Act.

FACT SUMMARY: Maier Brewing Co. (D) marketed "Black & White" beer, thereby infringing on the registered trademark of Fleischmann's (P) whiskey.

RULE OF LAW

In an infringement action under the Lanham Trademark Act, the plaintiff may, if successful, recover the defendant's profits even if the defendant was not in direct competition with, and therefore not diverting any trade from, the plaintiff.

FACTS: Fleischmann Distilling Corporation's (P) "Black & White" trademark for its Scotch whiskey was registered with the patent office. Maier Brewing Co. (D) introduced onto the market a beer labeled "Black & White." In an action under the Lanham Act, the trial court ordered an injunction and an accounting not only against Maier Brewing (D), but also against Ralph's Grocery (D), which carried the beer.

ISSUE: In an infringement action under the Lanham Trademark Act, may the plaintiff, if successful, recover the defendant's profits even if the defendant was not in direct competition with, and therefore not diverting any trade from, the plaintiff?

HOLDING AND DECISION: (Byrne, J.) Yes. In an infringement action under the Lanham Trademark Act, the plaintiff may, if successful, recover the defendant's profits even if the defendant was not in direct competition with, and therefore not diverting any trade from, the plaintiff. The majority view regards an accounting of profits by the defendant as a method of shifting the burden of proof as to damages for lost or potentially lost sales from the plaintiff to the defendant. This view requires that there be competition between the parties before this recovery can be granted. The more recent trend, adopted here, is based on the equitable concepts of restitution and unjust enrichment. If Maier Brewing (D) has used Fleischmann's (P) registered trademark for its own profit, it should account for taking this property interest. Fleischmann (P) is entitled, furthermore, to protection of its good will, and the public is entitled to protection against falsely marketed goods. To mitigate the apparent harshness of this rule, which seeks to make trademark infringements unprofitable, Fleischmann (P) is not entitled to profits demonstrably not attributable to the unlawful use of the mark. Affirmed.

ANALYSIS

Apart from an accounting, the plaintiff in a Lanham Act suit is entitled to recover any actual damages sustained, court costs, trebled damages in cases of bad-faith infringement, or where they are unable to prove any personal losses or any profits to the defendant, a compensatory "in lieu" award of damages.

Quicknotes

LANHAM ACT Name of the Trademark Act of 1946 that governs federal law regarding trademarks.

RESTITUTION The return or restoration to rightful owner to prevent unjust enrichment.

UNJUST ENRICHMENT Principle that one should not be unjustly enriched at the expense of another.

Sheldon v. Metro-Goldwyn Pictures Corp.

Individual (P) v. Corporation (D)

309 U.S. 390 (1940)

NATURE OF CASE: Appeal from an award of damages for copyright infringement.

FACT SUMMARY: Sheldon (P) contended he should receive all of Metro-Goldwyn Pictures Corp.'s (D) net profits for the latter's motion picture, which was found to infringe upon Sheldon's (P) copyrighted play.

RULE OF LAW

A court may apportion profits in a suit for copyright infringement based upon the actual use of the copyrighted material in the production of the revenue.

FACTS: Sheldon (P) sued Metro-Goldwyn Pictures Corp. (Metro-Goldwyn) (D), contending the latter's motion picture infringed on Sheldon's (P) copyrighted play. The trial court adopted the findings of a special master and awarded Sheldon (P) all of Metro's (D) net profit from the movie. The court of appeals modified the award, granting recovery equal to one-fifth of the total. This was done in recognition of the fact that the play itself did not account for 100 percent of the film's profits. Sheldon (P) appealed.

ISSUE: May a court apportion profits in a suit for copyright infringement based upon the actual use of the copyrighted material in the production of the revenue?

HOLDING AND DECISION: (Hughes, C.J.) Yes. A court may apportion profits in a suit for copyright infringement based upon the actual use of the copyrighted material in the production of the revenue. There are many factors inherent in a motion picture that make a motion picture more profitable than a play using the same raw material. The drawing power of the stars, the skill of the director, and the accessibility of the performance are things clearly unrelated to the use of the play. Thus, an apportionment of the profits was necessary for a just result. Affirmed.

ANALYSIS

The Court could not articulate a concrete standard to be used in apportionment cases. It compared the compensation paid other screenwriters for their work, yet some were compensated in a lump sum while others received a percentage of the gross or net receipts. Adding to the difficulty was the problem of determining how much of the play was plagiarized. It is clearly an area of commercial activity that does not lend itself to precise calculation.

Quicknotes

APPORTIONMENT The division of property costs in proportion to the parties' respective interests therein.

COPYRIGHT INFRINGEMENT A violation of one of the exclusive rights granted to an artist pursuant to Article I, § 8, clause 8 of the United States Constitution over the reproduction, display, performance, distribution, and adaptation of their work for a period prescribed by statute.

Hamil America, Inc. v. GFI

Corporation (P) v. Corporation (D)

193 F.3d 92 (2d Cir. 1999)

NATURE OF CASE: Appeal from judgment awarding damages for copyright infringement.

FACT SUMMARY: Hamil America, Inc. (P) sought damages from GFI (D) for infringement of a copyrighted garment pattern.

RULE OF LAW

A defendant found liable for willful copyright infringement may exclude an allocation of general overhead expenses in calculating its profits on the infringed product.

FACTS: After Hamil America, Inc. (Hamil) (P) developed a floral fabric pattern, GFI (D) sold a similar pattern to a garment manufacturer. Hamil (P) sued GFI (D) for copyright infringement and was awarded damages. After Hamil (P) elected to recover actual damages and profits under the Copyright Act, GFI (D) sought to reduce its profits by deducting its general overhead expenses. The district court refused to allow this deduction, and GFI (D) appealed.

ISSUE: May a defendant found liable for willful copyright infringement exclude an allocation of general overhead expenses in calculating its profits on the infringed product?

HOLDING AND DECISION: (Oakes, J.) Yes. A defendant found liable for willful copyright infringement may exclude an allocation of general overhead expenses in calculating its profits on the infringed product. The court undertakes a two-step approach in judging the deduction of overhead expenses from an infringer's profits. This approach must be applied with particular rigor in the case of willful infringement. The infringer must demonstrate a sufficient nexus between each expense claimed and the sales of the infringed goods. The court should not provide a deduction of overhead expenses to willful infringers unless each category is directly and validly connected to the sale and production of the finished product. Next, the infringer must propose a fair and acceptable formula for allocating a portion of overhead expenses to the infringed items. Affirmed in part, reversed in part, and remanded.

ANALYSIS

It is important to distinguish between restitution of defendant's profits from recovery of plaintiff's lost profits. Here, Hamil (P) also sought recovery of its lost profits from the sale of the infringed pattern. The court rejected this request as too speculative.

Quicknotes

COPYRIGHT INFRINGEMENT A violation of one of the exclusive rights granted to an artist pursuant to Article I, § 8, clause 8 of the United States Constitution over the reproduction, display, performance, distribution, and adaptation of their work for a period prescribed by statute.

May v. Muroff

[Parties not identified.]

Fla. Dist. Ct. App., 483 So. 2d 772 (1986)

NATURE OF CASE: Appeal from order determining damages.

FACT SUMMARY: Upon the seller's (D) consciously wrongful breach of contract for the sale of real property, the purchaser (P) maintains that he is entitled to the value of the materials removed from the subject land.

RULE OF LAW

A consciously wrongful breach of contract by the seller of real property entitles the purchaser to disgorgement of the seller's illegally obtained profit.

FACTS: The purchaser (P) and the seller (D) entered into a contract for the sale of real property. Prior to closing, the seller (D) illegally sold fill (dirt, rock, or a mixture of the two used to fill low-lying land) from the subject property to a third party for $240,000. The trial court determined that the purchaser (P) had been damaged by this sale and held that the measure of damages is the difference between the value of the land before and after the injury, which amounted to a purchase price reduction to compensate the purchaser (P) for 25 lost acres. The purchaser (P) appealed, claiming that he is entitled to the entirety of the wrongfully obtained windfall profit.

ISSUE: Does a consciously wrongful breach of contract by the seller of real property entitle the purchaser to disgorgement of the seller's illegally obtained profit?

HOLDING AND DECISION: (Letts, J.) Yes. A consciously wrongful breach of contract by the seller of real property entitles the purchaser to disgorgement of the seller's illegally obtained profit. Because it is clear the purchaser (P) was damaged by the seller's (D) deliberate breach, it does not follow that the seller (D) should be permitted to profit from his wrongful act. Inasmuch as the seller (D) wrongfully obtained $240,000 from the sale of fill, the trial court's reduction in the purchaser's (P) price of the subject land permits the seller (D) to enjoy a windfall profit of $117,933. Thus, because of the facts and circumstances of this case—specifically, the consciously wrongful breach of contract by the seller (D)—the purchaser (P) is entitled to the entire value of the materials removed, readily measured as $240,000. Affirmed in part, reversed in part and remanded for entry of judgment in favor of the purchaser.

ANALYSIS

The purchaser in this case, if he had knowledge of the impending breach, could have sued to compel conveyance of the subject property prior to the seller's removal of the fill. Nonetheless, because disgorgement of profits is a remedy easily administered following the conscious wrongdoing, the purchaser sought redress after the seller's breach. And, because it is the conscious wrongdoing by the seller that supports disgorgement of profits, the purchaser prevails in recovering what would otherwise be an inadequate damages remedy.

Quicknotes

DISGORGEMENT The act of giving up something (such as profits illegally obtained) on demand or by legal compulsion.

Mobil Oil Exploration & Producing Southeast, Inc. v. United States

Oil companies (P) v. Federal government (D)

530 U.S. 604 (2000)

NATURE OF CASE: Appeal from order denying restitution.

FACT SUMMARY: The Government (D) breached its agreement with two oil companies (P) for the rights to explore for and develop oil pursuant to the terms of the Outer Continental Lands Shelf Act (OCLSA). The Government (D) argued that despite its breach, which was based on the standards of the later-enacted Outer Banks Protection Act (OBPA), the oil companies (P) could not have met the contractual requirements of the OCLSA. But because the Government (D) agreed to follow the terms of the pre-existing OCLSA, the Supreme Court determined that the Government's (D) reliance on the OBPA in repudiating its contracts with the oil companies (P) caused substantial impairment to the value of the subject contracts.

RULE OF LAW

If a party to a contract substantially impairs the value of the contract, thereby repudiating said contract, it must refund all monies paid thus far by the other party to the contract regardless of whether the underlying contract would or would not have proved beneficial to the aggrieved party.

FACTS: Two oil companies (P) contracted with the federal Government (D) to lease the rights to explore for and develop oil off the coast of North Carolina. The oil companies (P) paid the Government (D) $156 million for the leases, the contracts for which incorporated the terms of the Outer Continental Lands Shelf Act (OCLSA). Pursuant to the OCLSA, the lease rights were conditioned on the oil companies (P) obtaining further governmental permissions. In other words, the oil companies paid $156 million for rights of permission-seeking opportunities to explore for and develop oil. Thereafter, the Government (D) denied the oil companies the permissions needed to explore for and develop oil based on the standards of the newly enacted Outer Banks Protection Act (OBPA). In claiming that the Government (D) repudiated the subject contracts, the oil companies (P) sought the return of the $156 million initially paid. The Government (D) argued that repudiation of the contracts did not damage the oil companies (P) because the oil companies (P) could not have met the OCLSA requirements for permission to explore for and develop oil. In holding that the Government's (D) withholding of approvals pursuant to the OBPA was a substantial breach of contract, the court of appeals determined that the Government's (D) breach caused no damages.

ISSUE: If a party to a contract substantially impairs the value of the contract, thereby repudiating said contract, must it refund all monies paid thus far by the other party to the contract regardless of whether the underlying contract would or would not have proved beneficial to the aggrieved party?

HOLDING AND DECISION: (Breyer, J.) Yes. If a party to a contract substantially impairs the value of the contract, thereby repudiating said contract, it must refund all monies paid thus far by the other party to the contract regardless of whether the underlying contract would or would not have proved beneficial to the aggrieved party. In the instant matter, it is clear the Government (D) repudiated the subject contracts and that it must give the oil companies (P) back their money. The Government's (D) total breach materially and substantially broke an important contractual promise thereby substantially impairing the value of the contracts as to allow the oil companies (P) to recover damages based on all remaining rights to performance. It matters not, as the Government (D) claims, that the oil companies (P) could not have met the OCSLA standards for exploring and developing oil. It is significant, rather, that inasmuch as the Government (D) made contractual promises to follow the terms of the OCSLA, the Government's (D) repudiation of the contracts based on the subsequently enacted OBPA caused substantial impairment to the value of the subject contracts. And as such, regardless of whether the oil companies (P) ultimately would have obtained definite rights to explore and develop oil, the Government (D) must refund the oil companies the $156 million initially paid. Reversed and remanded for further proceedings consistent with this opinion.

DISSENT: (Stevens, J.) The Government's (D) breach should not be treated as total.

ANALYSIS

In this case, the Court uses the term "total breach" to explain the Government's (P) substantial and material impairment to the value of the underlying contracts. The Court's use of the phrase "total breach" does not mean that the Government (P) had done nothing toward the performance of the contract, only that the breach was sufficiently important to justify the oil companies in treating the contracts as at an end. Of note, despite the use of "total breach" in the Restatement of Contracts,

Continued on next page.

the Restatement (Third) of Restitution and Unjust Enrichment avoids the phrase "total breach" in favor of "material breach."

Quicknotes

RESCISSION The cancellation of a transaction and reversal of all benefits that have been exchanged pursuant to the transaction.

Paoloni v. Goldstein

Investors (P) v. Investment promoters (D)

331 F. Supp. 2d 1310 (D. Colo. 2004)

NATURE OF CASE: Motion for summary judgment.

FACT SUMMARY: Investors (P) in a viatical settlement contracts scheme sought to recover their assets fraudulently obtained and used to purchase a condominium by the scheme's architect, Richard Doggett (D). The court determined that the subject condominium should be placed in constructive trust for the benefit of the investors (P).

RULE OF LAW

A constructive trust may be used as a remedy for unjust enrichment to compel a party who holds a property interest to convey that interest to those whose money was fraudulently obtained and used to purchase the subject property.

FACTS: Richard Doggett (D) and others created the American Benefits Group Program to perpetrate fraud on investors in their viatical settlement contracts scheme. To hide the investors' fraudulently obtained money, Doggett (D) established trusts and corporations. One such entity was the Iglesias Family Trust (Trust) (D). With funds disbursed to it from the fraudulent sale of viatical settlement contracts obtained by Doggett (D), the Trust (D) purchased a condominium in Florida, where Doggett (D) established residency. The investors (P) sought summary judgment against the Trust (D) to recover their assets. Thereafter, the court placed the condominium unit in question in constructive trust for the benefit of the defrauded investors (P) and ordered that the Trust (D) act as trustee of the constructive trust. As trustee of the constructive trust, the court ordered the Trust (D) to execute a Quit Claim Deed conveying the condominium unit to the investors (P), operating as the Viatical Administrators, Inc., and ordered that the investors (P) assume an equitable lien on said condominium. Additionally, the court ordered that the Trust (D) provide the investors (P) with a complete accounting of the assets of the Trust (D), and permanently enjoined the Trust's (D) trustees and those in its employ from transferring, selling, etc., the assets and property derived from or traceable to the sale of viatical settlement contracts.

ISSUE: May a constructive trust be used as a remedy for unjust enrichment to compel a party who holds a property interest to convey that interest to those whose money was fraudulently obtained and used to purchase the subject property?

HOLDING AND DECISION: (Kane, J.) Yes. A constructive trust may be used as a remedy for unjust enrichment to compel a party who holds a property interest to convey that interest to those whose money was fraudulently obtained and used to purchase the subject property. It is manifest that the holder of legal title, in the instant matter Doggett (D), acquired the subject property under circumstances such that in equity and good conscience he should not be permitted to retain beneficial interest to same. Inasmuch as the defrauded investors (P) are able to trace their lost assets to the purchase of the condominium in question, the investors (P) should be able to recover their assets as the beneficiaries of a constructive trust of the condominium. It is undisputed that the subject property was purchased with funds obtained by Doggett (D) in his role in the scheme to defraud the investors. Thus, under these circumstances, placing the condominium in question in constructive trust prevents Doggett (D) from being unjustly enriched at the expense of the investors (P). Furthermore, to determine whether the Trust (D) holds any other property or assets traceable to Doggett's (D) fraud of the investors (P), the Trust (D) must provide an accounting to the investors (P) and is permanently enjoined from disposing of any property or assets traceable to this source.

ANALYSIS

The constructive trust is a remedy for unjust enrichment; the court declares the party who has unjustly acquired legal ownership of assets a trustee for the aggrieved party and requires the trustee to account for the assets and ultimately turn trust assets over to the aggrieved party as beneficiary of same. But most importantly, the constructive trust, as in the instant matter, treats the defrauded investors not as creditors but as equitable owners of the property. The defrauder's other creditors thus have no claim to the condominium because it belongs not to the defrauder but to the defrauded investors, who are more likely to recover their assets not as creditors but as equitable owners of the condominium.

Quicknotes

VIATICAL SETTLEMENT A transaction in which a seriously ill person sells their life insurance policy to an investor at a discount to face value for a lump-sum cash payment.

Ruffin v. Ruffin

Wife (P) v. Husband (D)

Va. Ct. App., 2000 WL 198078 (2000)

NATURE OF CASE: Appeal from order denying petition to create constructive trust.

FACT SUMMARY: Following entry of a support order for the wife (P) and the parties' children, the husband (D) missed two payments prior to winning the lottery. Thereafter, arguing that the husband (D) used money he owed her for support to buy the winning lottery ticket, the wife (P) sought to impose a constructive trust on the lottery earnings of the husband (D).

RULE OF LAW

The imposition of a constructive trust is unwarranted when there is no evidence of fraud or unjust enrichment and when the *res* of the constructive trust sought is lottery earnings untraceable to the unpaid child support owed the party seeking imposition of the constructive trust.

FACTS: Upon the wife (P) filing for divorce, the court entered an order directing the husband (D) to pay child and spousal support. The husband (D) missed two support payments prior to winning $4.9 million in a lottery, eight days following entry of the support order. Indeed, the husband (D) did not make any support payments until three months after winning the lottery. Arguing that the husband's (D) lottery winnings were subject to a constructive trust for the benefit of her and the parties' children, the wife (P) contends that the husband (D) used his last available money—money the husband (D) owed the wife (P)—to purchase the winning ticket. The trial court, however, found no evidence of fraud or unjust enrichment warranting imposition of a constructive trust on the husband's (D) winnings, and the wife (P) appealed.

ISSUE: Is the imposition of a constructive trust warranted when there is no evidence of fraud or unjust enrichment and when the *res* of the constructive trust sought is lottery earnings untraceable to the unpaid child support owed the party seeking imposition of the constructive trust?

HOLDING AND DECISION: (Per curiam) No. The imposition of a constructive trust is unwarranted when there is no evidence of fraud or unjust enrichment and when the *res* of the constructive trust sought is lottery earnings untraceable to the unpaid child support owed the party seeking imposition of the constructive trust. Although it is clear the husband (D) was remiss in paying child and spousal support at the time he won the lottery, it cannot be said that the husband (D) unjustly enriched himself with the wife's (P) money. Specifically, the $2 with which the husband (D) purchased the winning lottery ticket is untraceable as the wife (P) and children's money. Inasmuch as the wife (P) contends that a constructive trust arose on the date of entry of the support order, it is obvious that, because the husband (D) did not win the lottery until eight days following entry of said order, no fund existed on the date of entry on which to impose a constructive trust. Moreover, the wife (P) concedes that, at the time of the husband's (D) win and his default on support payments, the husband's (D) ability to pay support was limited by his recent purchase of a car. Thus, because the husband's (D) car payments were a greater drain on his ability to pay support than the $2 he used to purchase the winning lottery ticket, it is clear the money the husband (D) used to purchase said ticket cannot be traced solely to the funds obligated for support. Notwithstanding the husband's (D) reprehensible failure to meet his support obligation, the record does not support the conclusion that the husband's (D) good fortune was fraudulently acquired or that he was unjustly enriched at the wife's (P) expense and with her specifically identifiable property. Affirmed.

ANALYSIS

The point of the constructive trust is to prefer rights to real property over lesser rights arising from contract rights and other sources of obligations to pay—recall *Paoloni v. Goldstein*, 331 F. Supp. 2d 1310 (D. Colo. 2004). Indeed, the constructive trust is frequently used to restore ownership of property in disputes within families—among blood relatives who make promises to perform services in return for ownership; who exert undue influence to acquire ownership; who seek to defraud siblings of ownership. In the *Ruffin* case, however, the wife simply does not have sufficient grounds to impose a constructive trust on the husband's money assets. Perhaps the wife's best recourse is to the Family Court under a variety of claims.

Quicknotes

CONSTRUCTIVE TRUST A trust that arises by operation of law whereby the court imposes a trust upon property lawfully held by one party for the benefit of another, as a result of some wrongdoing by the party in possession so as to avoid unjust enrichment.

In re Leitner

Debtor

236 B.R. 420 (Bankr. D. Kan. 1999)

NATURE OF CASE: Motion for summary judgment in bankruptcy proceeding.

FACT SUMMARY: Debtor Gary D. Leitner (D) embezzled a large sum of money from his employer, Leo G. Wetherill (P), and used a portion of the funds to purchase a home. Prior to the state court's entry of judgment that a constructive trust of the home existed for the benefit of Wetherill (P), Leitner (D) filed for bankruptcy. Upon the lifting of the stay of proceedings in state court and prior to the bankruptcy court's determination of the bankruptcy trustee's motion for summary judgment contesting the existence of a constructive trust, the state court entered judgment that Leitner (D) held the residence in constructive trust for Wetherill (P).

RULE OF LAW

When a debtor admits to misappropriating another's money and when that money is traceable to the purchase of the debtor's home, a constructive trust of the subject property becomes effective at the time of inception of events underlying the fraud.

FACTS: Leo G. Wetherill (P), owner of L.G.W. Energy Resources, Inc., hired Gary D. Leitner (D) to perform legal and accounting services for his business. Thereafter, Leitner (D) embezzled nearly $1,000,000 from Wetherill (P) and used a portion of the embezzled funds to purchase a home. Upon discovery of the fraud, Wetherill (P) sued Leitner (D) in state court, seeking a constructive trust of Leitner's (D) home. Leitner (D) admitted his fraud, and the state court granted prejudgment attachment of the home to Wetherill (P). But before the state court could enter judgment that Leitner (D) held the residence in constructive trust for Wetherill (P), Leitner (D) filed for bankruptcy, which automatically stayed the proceedings in state court. Following the bankruptcy court's lifting of the stay, the bankruptcy trustee, who agreed with Wetherill (P) and other creditors to sell the residence, brought a motion for summary judgment contesting the existence of the constructive trust. And before the bankruptcy court could address said motion, which it ultimately denied, the state court entered judgment in favor of the existence of a constructive trust.

ISSUE: When a debtor admits to misappropriating another's money and when that money is traceable to the purchase of the debtor's home, does a constructive trust of the subject property become effective at the time of inception of events underlying the fraud?

HOLDING AND DECISION: (Flannagan, J.) Yes. When a debtor admits to misappropriating another's money and when that money is traceable to the purchase of the debtor's home, a constructive trust of the subject property becomes effective at the time of inception of events underlying the fraud. The majority state law rule establishes that even when the property of a debtor has not been placed in constructive trust prior to the debtor's (D) filing a petition in bankruptcy, the existence of the constructive trust arises at the time of the occurrence of the events underlying the creditor's right to a constructive trust, and not at the date of entry of judgment declaring the existence of the trust. Notwithstanding the Sixth Circuit's decision in *In re Omegas Group Inc.*, 16 F.3d 1443 (6th Cir. 1994), which held that if a debtor files for bankruptcy prior to the imposition of a constructive trust on specific property, no constructive trust exists to prevent that property from becoming a party of the bankruptcy estate, it is manifest that the Bankruptcy Act does not authorize the distribution of other people's property among a debtor's creditors. In the instant matter, where the debtor has admitted their fraud, and where the bankruptcy trustee has stipulated that the misappropriated money is traceable to the residence at issue, it is likely that the state will follow the majority rule—the "relation back" rule—that a constructive trust is effective from the "inception of the transaction," rather than from the date of entry of a final judgment declaring the trust. Thus, inasmuch as the equitable interest in the subject property was not Leitner's (D) at the time he filed for bankruptcy, the residence did not become part of the bankruptcy estate, and Leitner (D) must convey legal title to Wetherill (P). The motion for summary judgment is denied and the trustee is ordered to convey legal title to Wetherill (P).

ANALYSIS

The much-criticized *Omegas* decision involved an ordinary creditor who sought a constructive trust on the basis simply that the debtor had not disclosed their precarious financial situation. *In re Omegas Group Inc.*, 16 F.3d 1443 (6th Cir. 1994). There was no attempt to identify the creditor's funds commingled with the debtor's, and, as such, there were multiple grounds upon which to deny the existence of a constructive trust. *Id.* But even following the Sixth Circuit's strong opinion contra the

Continued on next page.

"relation back" rule, a clear case of embezzlement—to the tune of $755,000—caused this Circuit to retreat from its rule in *Omegas*. In *In re Newpower*, 233 F.3d 922 (6th Cir. 2000), the Sixth Circuit, in a divided opinion, held that if the state court awarded a constructive trust as of a time before the bankruptcy filing, this would be a constructive trust imposed by judicial decree and the bankruptcy court should honor it even under *Omegas*.

Quicknotes

CONSTRUCTIVE TRUST A trust that arises by operation of law whereby the court imposes a trust upon property lawfully held by one party for the benefit of another, as a result of some wrongdoing by the party in possession so as to avoid unjust enrichment.

In re Erie Trust Co.

Debtor

Pa. Sup. Ct., 191 A. 613 (1937)

NATURE OF CASE: Appeal of adjudication determining possession of funds.

FACT SUMMARY: Erie Trust Co., before bankruptcy, converted funds from Gingrich, to which Gingrich's beneficiaries laid claim.

RULE OF LAW

Wrongfully converted funds may be traced into commingled accounts without precise identification.

FACTS: Erie Trust Co. converted certain funds belonging to Gingrich. Upon Gingrich's death, a receiver attempted to recover the funds from the estate of Erie, which had gone bankrupt. Finding that the funds had been commingled in various deposit accounts and that the receiver could not trace which specific funds went to which specific account, the trial court refused to give the receiver preference over general creditors. The receiver appealed.

ISSUE: May wrongfully converted funds be traced into commingled accounts without precise identification?

HOLDING AND DECISION: (Stern, J.) Yes. Wrongfully converted funds may be traced into commingled accounts without precise identification. Given the complexities of modern banking, the burden of precise identification of funds in commingled accounts would be virtually impossible to meet. It is sufficient that the accounts into which the funds have been deposited be identified. Once this is done, the presumption arises that all withdrawals are of other funds, and the converted funds remain in the various accounts. This is the presumption that should have been applied here. Reversed and remanded.

ANALYSIS

The basic rule in bankruptcy is that, after the government gets its share, senior creditors get priority. An exception exists where, as here, defrauded parties can prove which funds were theirs. In this instance, the law presumes that the bankrupt never had the property. The victims thereby leapfrog over the general creditors.

Quicknotes

BANKRUPTCY A legal proceeding whereby a debtor, who is unable to pay their debts as they become due, is relieved of their obligation to pay their creditors either by liquidation and distribution of their remaining assets or through reorganization and payment from future income.

COMMINGLED ASSETS The combining of money or property into a joint account or asset.

In re JD Services, Inc.

Debtor

284 B.R. 292 (Bankr. D. Utah 2002)

NATURE OF CASE: Motion for summary judgment in bankruptcy proceeding.

FACT SUMMARY: Following the miscoding and crediting of a check deposited by the debtor, JD Services, Inc. (D), into an account at the Bank of America (BOA) (P), the debtor (D) mistakenly wire transferred a substantial sum of money from the BOA (P) account to another account owned by the debtor (D) at the First Security Bank. The funds transferred by the debtor (D) were largely those of BOA (P) but were commingled in the First Security Bank account with the funds of other creditors. In the debtor's (D) bankruptcy action, BOA (P) sought the return of its monies.

RULE OF LAW

First, upon a debtor's honest mistake giving rise to a constructive trust, the beneficiary of the constructive trust must trace its funds to identifiable property held by the debtor when the funds of the constructive trust have been commingled. And second, said beneficiary must, using the lowest intermediate balance rule, trace its funds by the available balance approach.

FACTS: The debtor, JD Services, Inc. (D), filed a petition for bankruptcy. Shortly thereafter, a subsidiary of JD Services (D) deposited a check for $7,250 into an account at the Bank of America (BOA) (P). An employee of BOA (P) miscoded this check as $725,000 and gave JD Services (D) immediate credit for same. A few days later, JD Services (D) wired transferred $800,000 from the BOA (P) account to an account at First Security Bank. Of the $800,000 wired, the parties agreed that $717,750 was the property of BOA (P). At the request of BOA (P), the debtor (D) and First Security Bank placed a hold on the First Security account in the amount of $717,750. The court determined that JD Services (D) was unjustly enriched by the mistake—and it was mistake inasmuch as no one claimed that JD Services (D) had acted in bad faith—and ordered that the subject funds be held in constructive trust for BOA (P) for so long as they could be identified. JD Services (D) continued in its business operations and, in the two weeks following the order for constructive trust, approximately $6.5 million passed through the First Security account before First Security Bank began placing significant holds on the deposits made by JD Services (D). In the underlying bankruptcy action, BOA (P) sought the return of its monies.

ISSUE: First, upon a debtor's honest mistake giving rise to a constructive trust, must the beneficiary of the constructive trust trace its funds to identifiable property held by the debtor when the funds of the constructive trust have been commingled? And second, must said beneficiary, using the lowest intermediate balance rule, trace its funds by the available balance approach?

HOLDING AND DECISION: (Clark, C.J.) Yes. First, upon a debtor's honest mistake giving rise to a constructive trust, the beneficiary of the constructive trust must trace its funds to identifiable property held by the debtor when the funds of the constructive trust have been commingled. And second, said beneficiary must, using the lowest intermediate balance rule, trace its funds by the available balance approach. In a bankruptcy proceeding, the beneficiary of a constructive trust must trace the funds to identify the trust *res* in the same manner as if there were no bankruptcy. It is manifest that the tracing requirement balances a beneficiary's rights with the demands of equality of distribution among creditors of equal rank. Thus, upon the successful tracing of its funds, the Bank of America (BOA) (P) would receive its own money in trust and not the funds of the debtor JD Services Inc.'s (D) bankruptcy estate. The commingling of funds—those of BOA (P) with those of the debtor's (D) other creditors—in the First Security Bank account following the underlying order for constructive trust requires that, pursuant to the lowest intermediate balance rule, BOA (P) must trace its funds by the available balance approach. Applying the lowest intermediate balance rule—whereby, it is generally held, funds removed from or added to a commingled account are considered those of the debtor (to the extent the funds exceed the equitable interest of the constructive trust beneficiary)—BOA (P) may retrieve the lowest balance recorded in the First Security account after the funds were commingled. The Collected Balance approach to tracing funds ignores the hold imposed upon new deposits into the First Security account and relies only on the dates of deposit and withdrawal of funds. The Available Balance approach, however, takes into account the afore-referenced hold, partially rebutting the presumption that withdrawals subsequent to a new deposit were drawn first on the new deposit. As such, the Available Balance approach permits a more accurate tracing of funds and

Continued on next page.

minimizes the commingling of constructive trust funds with those of new deposits. Accordingly, upon application of the Available Balance approach to the tracing of BOA's (P) funds held in constructive trust entitles BOA (P) to the return of $394,460.47. [BOA (P) has an unsecured claim for the difference represented by the amount mistakenly wire transferred by debtor (D). And because the claim for constructive trust arose after the bankruptcy petition, the Bankruptcy Code permits said claim priority status.] And finally, because the funds held in constructive trust for BOA (P) have been BOA (P) funds all along, it is clear BOA (P) is entitled to the interest earned on its monies in trust.

ANALYSIS

The result in this case may seem arbitrary. The creditors of JD Services will be paid with Bank of America's money because said money was appropriated only by mistake. Furthermore, Bank of America's recovery depends on the history of the First Security account subsequent to the mistake. And inasmuch as the Available Balance approach to tracing recognizes the hold at First Security—checks were subtracted immediately but deposits not added for a week or more—the court's choice of tracing methods determines that Bank of America's recovery will be significantly lower than if the Collected Balance approach were applied.

Quicknotes

CONSTRUCTIVE TRUST A trust that arises by operation of law whereby the court imposes a trust upon property lawfully held by one party for the benefit of another, as a result of some wrongdoing by the party in possession so as to avoid unjust enrichment.

In re Mesa

Debtor

232 B.R. 508 (Bankr. S.D. Fla. 1999)

NATURE OF CASE: Objection to homestead exemption in bankruptcy proceeding.

FACT SUMMARY: Debtor, Alberto V. Mesa (D), participated in fraudulently obtaining funds from creditor Travelers Indemnity Company (Travelers) (P). Mesa (D) used the funds exclusively to make improvements to his home. In bankruptcy, Travelers (P) sought to prevent Mesa (D) from exerting the homestead exemption, thereby protecting the property from Travelers' (P) equitable lien.

RULE OF LAW

When a debtor has knowledge of and assists in fraudulently obtaining funds with which they made significant home improvements, the debtor is barred from exerting the homestead exemption in a bankruptcy proceeding to prevent the debtor's unjust enrichment at the creditor's expense.

FACTS: Debtor, Alberto V. Mesa (D), and his partner purchased a residence as tenants in common and resided together in the home, which Mesa (D) scheduled in the bankruptcy documents—specifically, his one-half interest—as exempt property under the homestead exemption in a bankruptcy proceeding. At the time Mesa (D) and his partner purchased the home, the partner was employed by Travelers Indemnity Company (Travelers) (P), from whom the partner ultimately stole $378,415.61. The partner caused checks payable by Travelers (P) to be issued to Mesa (D), Mesa's mother, and to construction contractors and suppliers. The misappropriated funds, the court determined, were used entirely for the home remodeling project undertaken by Mesa (D) and his partner. The court further determined that Mesa (D) had knowledge that the funds used for the remodeling project were obtained fraudulently by his partner and that Mesa (D) knowingly assisted and participated in the fraud. Upon Mesa's (D) exertion of the homestead exemption in this bankruptcy proceeding, Travelers (P) filed an objection on the basis that Mesa's (D) participation in fraudulently obtaining funds from Travelers (P) and using said funds for homestead improvements would unjustly enrich him at their expense, should the court not impose an equitable lien on the home in favor of Travelers (P).

ISSUE: When a debtor has knowledge of and assists in fraudulently obtaining funds with which they made significant home improvements, may the debtor exert the homestead exemption in a bankruptcy proceeding thus being unjustly enriched at the creditor's expense?

HOLDING AND DECISION: (Ray, J.) No. When a debtor has knowledge of and assists in fraudulently obtaining funds with which they made significant home improvements, the debtor is barred from exerting the homestead exemption in a bankruptcy proceeding to prevent the debtor's unjust enrichment at the creditor's expense. In the instant matter, the record demonstrates that debtor, Alberto V. Mesa (D), knowingly assisted in and benefitted from the scheme to defraud creditor Travelers (P). Although the law permits the exemption from forced sale of a homestead in a bankruptcy proceeding, the homestead exemption is, under certain circumstances, subject to equitable liens and can never be used as an instrumentality of fraud. Thus, because it is clear that Mesa (D) knew about and assisted in the fraudulent obtaining of funds from Travelers (P), which he used to make extensive home improvements, it is necessary to grant Travelers (P) an equitable lien on the subject homestead to prevent Mesa (D) from using said home as an instrument of fraud and to prevent Mesa's (D) unjust enrichment at Travelers' (P) expense. The amount of the equitable lien should reflect the amount of misappropriated funds that were invested in the remodeling of Mesa's (D) home, the total of which is $378,415.61. Accordingly, because the total amount paid by Mesa (D) to contractors and suppliers alone far exceeds the equity in the home, which is approximately $25,000, the court grants Travelers (P) an equitable lien in the amount of $378,415.61, the amount representing the total funds embezzled and used for homestead remodeling. Travelers' (P) objection to the homestead exemption is sustained; and Mesa (D) shall not use the homestead exemption as a defense to any action by Travelers (P).

ANALYSIS

In *Mesa*, the creditor will foreclose its lien and receive the cash proceeds of the sale, with an unsecured judgment for the remainder of the embezzled money. The Restatement (Third) of Restitution and Unjust Enrichment explains that the strongest remedy a court can award a creditor, who is the victim of conscious wrongdoing, is the choice between constructive trust and equitable lien. If the subject property is worth more than the creditor lost, the creditor will elect a constructive trust; if the property is worth less than the creditor lost, the creditor will seek a money judgment for the

Continued on next page.

full amount of loss, secured by an equitable lien on the traceable property.

Quicknotes

CONSTRUCTIVE TRUST A trust that arises by operation of law whereby the court imposes a trust upon property lawfully held by one party for the benefit of another, as a result of some wrongdoing by the party in possession so as to avoid unjust enrichment.

EQUITABLE LIEN An equitable right to have specified property applied to payment of a debt.

RESTITUTION The return or restoration to rightful owner to prevent unjust enrichment.

Mort v. United States

Assignee (P) v. Federal government (D)

86 F.3d 890 (9th Cir. 1996)

NATURE OF CASE: Appeal from dismissal of complaint seeking injunctive relief and declaratory judgment.

FACT SUMMARY: Prior to the filing of a federal tax lien by the Internal Revenue Service (IRS) (D), Cathryn Myers signed a promissory note in favor of the Kerns, secured by a deed of trust in real property in Nevada. Following the filing of the tax lien, the Belmonts loaned Myers and her husband money, secured by a deed of trust in the subject property. Thereafter, Myers and her husband paid off the Kerns loan and the Belmonts recorded their deed of trust. Later, the Belmonts conveyed their interest in the promissory note and deed of trust upon payment of consideration to them by the Morts (P). Upon seizure of the property by the IRS (D), the Morts (P) sought injunctive relief and a declaratory judgment claiming equitable subrogation.

RULE OF LAW

When there is a valid assignment of a mortgage, the assignee assumes the assignor's rights to equitable subrogation.

FACTS: In December 1990, Cathryn Myers signed a promissory note, secured by a deed of trust in real property in Nevada, in the amount of $30,000 in favor of the Kerns. In August 1992, the Internal Revenue Service (IRS) (D) filed a federal tax lien in Nevada to collect the unpaid income tax liabilities of Myers and her husband, Sol DeLee. In November 1992, the Belmonts loaned Myers and DeLee $38,000, secured by a deed of trust in the afore-referenced real property in Nevada. With the Belmonts' money, Myers and DeLee paid off the Kerns' loan. Thereafter, the Belmonts purchased title insurance on the subject property, but the title company failed to discover the federal tax lien and insured clear title. Shortly after making the loan to Myers and DeLee and following purchase of title insurance, the Belmonts recorded their deed of trust. In December 1992, the Belmonts conveyed their interest in the promissory note and the deed of trust (as well as the title insurance policy) to the Morts (P) upon payment to them by the Morts (P) in the amount of $38,000. In June or July 1993, the Morts (P) learned of the underlying tax lien, and in August 1993 the IRS (D) seized the property. The Morts (P) then filed a complaint in federal district court seeking injunctive relief and a declaratory judgment that their trust deed interest was superior to the tax lien. The district court dismissed the Morts' (P) complaint inasmuch as it concluded that the Morts (P) could not assert their claim for equitable subrogation without first pursuing legal remedy against the title insurer.

ISSUE: When there is a valid assignment of a mortgage, does the assignee assume the assignor's rights to equitable subrogation?

HOLDING AND DECISION: (Zilly, J.) Yes. When there is a valid assignment of a mortgage, the assignee assumes the assignor's rights to equitable subrogation. As an initial matter, equitable relief should not be denied unless the available legal remedy is against the same person from whom equitable relief is sought. In the instant case, the Morts (P) have a legal remedy against the third-party title company, not the Internal Revenue Service (IRS) (D), and, as such, the district court abused its discretion in refusing to exercise equitable jurisdiction. Furthermore, inasmuch as tax liens are subject to subrogation rights, and because the doctrine of equitable subrogation grants the person who pays off an encumbrance the same priority position as the holder of the previous encumbrance, the Morts (P) should enjoy the same rights to equitable subrogation as the Belmonts. The record clearly establishes that the Morts (P) purchased the note and deed of trust, with assignment of rights, from the Belmonts, who made a loan to Myers and DeLee to pay off the senior Kerns note. If the Belmonts had retained their interest, they would be equitably subrogated to the Kerns' priority position. Accordingly, the Morts (P) assume all the rights of the Belmonts in the Myers and DeLee note and deed of trust. The argument of the IRS (D) that the Morts (P) are volunteers, or persons who have no interest of their own to protect, and therefore not entitled to subrogation, is without merit. The record demonstrates that the Morts (P) loaned money to pay off an encumbrance on the subject property and secured the loan with a deed of trust on that property. And although the Nevada courts have yet to consider whether an assignee assumes the assignor's equitable subrogation rights, the general rule is that where a valid assignment of a mortgage has been consummated with proper consideration, the assignee assumes the rights of the assignor. And finally, the IRS (D) is not prejudiced by the Morts' (P) assertion of the Belmonts' rights to equitable subrogation because the IRS (D) tax lien was subordinate to the Kern mortgage in the first instance. The position of the IRS (D) does not change if the Morts (P) are equitably subrogated to the

Continued on next page.

priority position of the Kerns mortgage. Reversed and remanded for entry of judgment in favor of the Morts (P).

ANALYSIS

In *Mort*, the two refinancing transactions appear to be identical. The Belmont loan refinanced the Kern loan, and the Mort loan refinanced the Belmont loan. However, the Morts (P) took an assignment from the Belmonts; whereas, the Belmonts did not take an assignment from the Kerns (the Belmonts merely loaned money to Myers and DeLee to pay off the Kerns' mortgage). If the Belmonts had taken an assignment from the Kerns, the Morts (P) could have relied on the chain of assignments instead of the equitable doctrine of subrogation. But in fashioning a conclusion, the Ninth Circuit desired to leave the IRS in its initial position, with a second lien junior to that of the Kerns. Without equitable subrogation, the IRS would be unjustly enriched. Importantly, the IRS should not receive a windfall in this matter simply because the Kerns were paid: the subrogation plaintiffs (the Morts) are entitled to the subrogors' (the Kerns') rights as they existed just before the subrogors (the Kerns) were paid.

Quicknotes

DECLARATORY JUDGMENT A judgment of the court establishing the rights of the parties.

EQUITABLE SUBROGATION Doctrine that holds that one who assumes and pays a debt for another assumes the same position as the holder of the previous encumbrance and is subrogated to all the holder's rights and remedies.

INJUNCTIVE RELIEF A court order issued as a remedy, requiring a person to do, or prohibiting that person from doing, a specific act.

Newton v. Porter

Theft victim (P) v. Attorney for thief (D)

N.Y. Ct. App., 69 N.Y. 133 (1877)

NATURE OF CASE: Equitable action brought to establish rights of theft victim to stolen property and to compel thieves' counsel to account therefor.

FACT SUMMARY: Upon stealing government bonds negotiable by delivery from Newton (P), the thieves, William Warner and George Warner, sold the bonds and divided the proceeds. To secure legal representation at their criminal and civil trials related to the theft, the Warners paid attorneys Miner, Warren, and Porter (D) with the avails and proceeds of the stolen bonds. The judge at Special Term directed judgment against the attorneys for the value of the securities received by them as payment for representation of the instant thieves.

RULE OF LAW

When a thief conveys negotiable bonds transferable by delivery to bona fide purchasers, and when the thief invests in securities with the proceeds of the stolen bonds, the owner of the bonds—the theft victim—has the right to compel the assignees with notice of the subject securities to transfer the securities to the bonds owner as the equitable owner of same.

FACTS: Newton (P) owned $13,000 of government bonds negotiable by delivery. The bonds were stolen and sold, and the proceeds divided between the thieves. Thief William Warner loaned a part of his share in separate loans and took the promissory notes of the borrowers. Thief George Warner invested $2,000 of his share in the purchase of a bond and mortgage, which was assigned to his wife without consideration. Upon the Warners' arrest, including that of George Warner's wife, the Warners employed attorneys Miner, Warren, and Porter (D) in their defense, both in the criminal proceedings and in the resulting civil suits. William Warner paid attorneys Miner and Warren by transferring to them the promissory notes taken on loans made by him from the proceeds of the stolen bonds. George Warner's wife, as payment to attorney Porter (D), assigned to him the afore-referenced bond and mortgage. The court determined that the attorneys had notice at the time they received the securities as payment that said securities were the avails and proceeds of the bonds stolen from Newton (P). Accordingly, the judge at Special Term directed judgment against the attorneys for the value of the securities received by them as payment for representation of the instant thieves.

ISSUE: When a thief conveys negotiable bonds transferable by delivery to bona fide purchasers, and when the thief invests in securities with the proceeds of the stolen bonds, does the owner of the bonds—the theft victim—have the right to compel the assignees with notice of the subject securities to transfer the securities to the bonds owner as the equitable owner of same?

HOLDING AND DECISION: (Andrews, J.) Yes. When a thief conveys negotiable bonds transferable by delivery to bona fide purchasers, and when the thief invests in securities with the proceeds of the stolen bonds, the owner of the bonds—the theft victim—has the right to compel the assignees with notice of the subject securities to transfer the securities to the bonds owner as the equitable owner of same. In the instant matter, unless Newton (P) can elect to regard the securities in which the bonds were invested as a substitute for the bonds, she has no remedy. It is manifest that a thief cannot convey good title to stolen property except in the case of money or negotiable securities transferable by delivery, which have been put into circulation and have come to the hands of bona fide holders. As such, Newton (P) had no right to reclaim the stolen bonds from those who had in good faith purchased them from the thieves. But because the record establishes that the thieves used the proceeds from the sale of the stolen bonds to invest in securities that were traceable and identifiable as the assignments made to defense counsel Miner, Warren, and Porter (D), and because it is clear that Porter (D) and co-counsel had notice at the time they received the securities that the same were acquired with the avails and proceeds of the stolen bonds, Newton (D) has the right to compel the assignees with notice of the subject securities to transfer the securities to her as the equitable owner of the securities. And finally, as with the doctrine of wrongfully diverted trust funds and the court's pursuit of such funds into the property into which the funds have been converted, equity requires that an owner who has been deprived of their property by theft should not be less favorably situated than one who has been injured by the wrongful act of a trustee. Affirmed.

ANALYSIS

A bona fide purchaser for value–in other words, a good faith purchaser for money–can get good title to cash or its equivalent, such as securities payable to the bearer, without exception. A bona fide purchaser for value of other property can get good title and is generally protected, unless title is derived from a thief

Continued on next page.

or by wrongdoing the law treats as a theft. In *Newton*, the attorneys had notice that the bond, mortgage, and promissory notes assigned to them as payment for legal services were acquired with the proceeds of stolen government bonds. As such, and because the thieves were insolvent, the court found that equity required substitution, upon traceability, of the securities in the hands of the attorneys for the direct proceeds of the sale of the stolen bonds.

Quicknotes

BONA FIDE PURCHASER A party who purchases property in good faith and for valuable consideration without notice of a defect in title.

Banque Worms v. BankAmerica International

Beneficiary bank (P) v. Receiving bank (D)

N.Y. Ct. App., 570 N.E.2d 189 (1991)

NATURE OF CASE: Certified question of law to state high court from federal court of appeals.

FACT SUMMARY: The transferor Security Pacific International Bank (Security Pacific) (D) mistakenly executed an electronic funds wire transaction into the account of Banque Worms (P). In applying the "discharge for value" rule, the federal district court permitted Banque Worms (P) to retain the mistakenly transferred funds without demonstrating detrimental reliance. Security Pacific (D) appealed to the Second Circuit, arguing that under the instant circumstances, New York law required application of the "mistake of fact" rule, whereby it would be entitled to recover the mistakenly transferred funds, unless Banque Worms (P) demonstrated detrimental reliance. The Second Circuit Court of Appeals thus directed a certified question of law to the New York Court of Appeals, the state's high court, for a determination as to the applicable rule.

RULE OF LAW

When a beneficiary bank receives money to which it is entitled via electronic funds wire transaction, and when the beneficiary bank receives such money in good faith and for value without notice of the sender's mistaken transfer, the beneficiary bank should be able to retain the funds transferred without demonstrating detrimental reliance.

FACTS: Debtor Spedley Securities (Spedley) instructed Security Pacific International Bank (Security Pacific) (D) to wire $1,974,267.97 to the account of creditor Banque Worms (P) maintained by BankAmerica International (BankAmerica) in New York. By a second telex, a few hours following the first, Spedley instructed Security Pacific (D) not to wire money to BankAmerica, but instead to wire the same amount to National Westminster Bank USA (Natwest USA). Security Pacific (D) did not transfer funds until after receipt of the second telex and then mistakenly wired $1,974,267.97 to both Banque Worms's (P) account at BankAmerica and to Natwest USA. Inasmuch as Spedley had entered into involuntary liquidation, Security Pacific (D) failed in its attempt to recover funds from Spedley. [All of the banks sued each other in federal court, and Security Pacific (D) ultimately settled with BankAmerica. The remaining dispute was between Banque Worms (P) and Security Pacific (D).] The district court applied the "discharge for value" rule in favor of Banque Worms (P), whereby the district court permitted Banque Worms (P) to retain the mistakenly transferred funds without demonstrating detrimental reliance. Thereafter, Security Pacific (D) appealed to the Second Circuit Court of Appeals, arguing that under the instant circumstances, New York law required application of the "mistake of fact" rule, and as such, it would be entitled to recover the mistakenly transferred funds, unless Banque Worms (P) demonstrated detrimental reliance. The Second Circuit directed a certified question of law to the New York Court of Appeals, the state's high court, for a determination as to the applicable rule.

ISSUE: When a beneficiary bank receives money to which it is entitled via electronic funds wire transaction, and when the beneficiary bank receives such money in good faith and for value without notice of the sender's mistaken transfer, should the beneficiary bank be able to retain the funds transferred without demonstrating detrimental reliance?

HOLDING AND DECISION: (Alexander, J.) Yes. When a beneficiary bank receives money to which it is entitled via electronic funds wire transaction, and when the beneficiary bank receives such money in good faith and for value without notice of the sender's mistaken transfer, the beneficiary bank should be able to retain the funds transferred without demonstrating detrimental reliance. Under the instant circumstances, because the case law does not satisfactorily address the unique problems of electronic funds transfer technology, and because establishing finality in electronic funds wire transactions is singularly important, this court determines that the "discharge for value" rule applies to permit Banque Worms (P) to retain funds wired it upon the mistake of the transferor bank, without demonstrating detrimental reliance. In other words, it is not necessary for Banque Worms (P) to show that it has changed its position to its detriment in reliance upon the mistake so that requiring it to refund the money mistakenly transferred would be unjust—the sum and substance of the "mistake of fact" rule. Instead, because it is clear that UCC article 4A establishes that payments made by electronic funds transfers are the equivalent of cash payments, and because possession of money vests title in the holder when the holder receives payment in good faith and for a valuable consideration, despite the mistake of the transferor, the undisputed facts of the instant record require application of the "discharge for value" rule. Importantly, creditor Banque Worms (P) received money on behalf of debtor Spedley Securities to which it was entitled, without knowledge of

Continued on next page.

the mistake by Security Pacific (D). Accordingly, Banque Worms (P) should be able to consider this transfer of funds as a final and complete transaction not subject to revocation. And in conclusion, in answer to the certified question, the "discharge for value" rule should be applied upon the circumstances set forth here.

ANALYSIS

In answering the certified question, the New York Court of Appeals determined that antecedent debt owed Banque Worms (P) satisfied the value requirement. The bona fide purchaser rule, however, addresses the circumstances of the purchaser who gives present value in reliance on the validity of the transaction undertaken—the purchaser who gives present value would be worse off for returning property to a true owner when the intermediary has committed a wrongdoing. Whether Banque Worms (P) would be worse off if it had to return the $1.97 million is doubtful inasmuch as it had a claim against debtor Spedley both prior to and following the mistaken transfer. In agreeing to loan Spedley money, Banque Worms (P) agreed to the risk of Spedley's insolvency. Security Pacific (D), on the other hand, did not extend credit of its own to Spedley. Thus, it appears that a debtor—here, Spedley—is able to pay its debts with another party's property.

Quicknotes

BONA FIDE PURCHASER A party who purchases property in good faith and for valuable consideration without notice of a defect in title.

CHAPTER 9

Ancillary Remedies: Enforcing the Judgment

Quick Reference Rules of Law

Town of West Lakeland v. Auleciems

Municipality (P) v. Property owner (D)

Minn. Ct. App., 2021 WL 79789 (2021)

NATURE OF CASE: Appeal from order imposing criminal sanctions for civil contempt of court.

FACT SUMMARY: Despite being permanently enjoined from renting out their house, the Auleciemses (D) continued to rent it out, and, based on this conduct, the trial court held them in civil contempt of court. The court imposed three primary sanctions for the Auleciemses' (D) contempt: (1) a fine of almost $82,000; (2) payment of the costs and attorney fees incurred by the Town of West Lakeland ("township") (P) in enforcing the injunction; and (3) a jail term of 180 days, unless they fully paid the first two sanctions and a previously ordered $118,890 fine. The Auleciemses (D) contended that the district court erred by finding them in civil contempt of court but imposing criminal punishment.

RULE OF LAW

A court errs by finding a party in civil contempt of court but imposing criminal punishment based on findings that the party had violated court orders in the past, not a finding that they were in ongoing noncompliance with court orders.

FACTS: The Auleciemses (D), who lived in a house that had seven bedrooms, nine bathrooms, and 14,000 square feet of space, which was located in the Town of West Lakeland (the "township") (P), started to rent the house in 2017 to persons hosting special events with large numbers of guests, such as weddings and family reunions. A township ordinance prohibited short-term rentals of homes without a permit, and the Auleciemses' (D) neighbors frequently complained to the township (P) about large numbers of people on the property and on the roads leading to and from the property. The township (P) brought suit, and, after a trial in May 2019, the Auleciemses (D) were permanently enjoined from renting out their house without a permit. Not long after, however, the township (P) was back in court after receiving reports of continued rentals. The district court (trial court) held show-cause hearings in August and September 2019, and in October 2019, the court issued an order in which it found the Auleciemses (D) in civil contempt of court. The court found that the Auleciemses (D) had rented out their home on 13 weekends between the conclusion of trial in May 2019 and September 2019. Based on this finding, the district court imposed three primary sanctions. First, the court ordered the Auleciemses (D) to pay a fine of $81,870. The court calculated the amount of the fine by finding that the Auleciemses (D) had received at least $21,870 in income from three rentals and by estimating that they had received an additional $60,000 from the other ten rentals. Second, the court ordered the Auleciemses (D) to pay the township's costs and attorney fees related to the show-cause hearings. Third, the court ordered the Auleciemses (D) to serve a jail term of 180 days, unless they fully paid the $81,870 fine, the township's (P) attorney fees and costs related to the show-cause order, and a previously ordered $118,890 fine for violating the preliminary injunction. The Auleciemses (D) appealed, contending that the district court erred by finding them in civil contempt of court but imposing criminal punishment. The state's intermediate appellate court granted review.

ISSUE: Does a court err by finding a party in civil contempt of court but imposing criminal punishment based on findings that the party had violated court orders in the past, not a finding that they were in ongoing noncompliance with court orders?

HOLDING AND DECISION: (Johnson, J.) Yes. A court errs by finding a party in civil contempt of court but imposing criminal punishment based on findings that the party had violated court orders in the past, not a finding that they were in ongoing noncompliance with court orders. By statute, there are two forms of contempt in the state: direct and constructive. A finding of contempt is direct in nature if it occurs in the immediate view and presence of the court and arises from either disorderly, contemptuous, or insolent behavior toward the judge while holding court, tending to interrupt the due course of a trial or other judicial proceedings or a breach of the peace, boisterous conduct, or violent disturbance, tending to interrupt the business of the court. A direct contempt may be punished summarily. On the other hand, a finding of contempt is constructive in nature if it is not committed in the immediate presence of the court, so the court has no personal knowledge of it. Moreover, constructive contempt must arise from any one of 11 specified acts or omissions, the third of which is "disobedience of any lawful judgment, order, or process of the court." There is also a case law dichotomy based on the purpose of a contempt order: civil contempt and criminal contempt. A finding of contempt is civil in nature if it imposes a sanction that will be removed upon compliance with a court order that has been defied, because civil contempt proceedings are designed to induce future performance of a valid court order, not to punish for past

Continued on next page.

failure to perform; the sanction ends when the contemnor complies. Thus, civil contempt is remedial, not punitive, because its purpose is to coerce compliance with a court order, rather than to vindicate the court's authority. Criminal contempt, conversely, is intended to be punitive and to punish the contemnor for past behavior and is an offense against the state's dignity. It is a criminal matter that should be prosecuted by attorneys representing the state, where the person charged is entitled to the protections ordinarily due a criminal defendant, such as a written complaint stating the allegations of criminal conduct and a jury trial. As in other criminal cases, the charged person has a right to give testimony in their defense, and the state must prove the elements of contempt beyond a reasonable doubt. Upon a finding of guilt of constructive criminal contempt, punishment, set forth by statute, may not be a fine of more than $250, or imprisonment in the county jail, workhouse, or work farm for more than six months, or by both. If the contempt has caused actual loss or injury to a party in an action or special proceeding, the district court may, in addition to ordering a fine or imprisonment, order the guilty person to pay the party aggrieved a sum of money sufficient to indemnify the party and satisfy the party's costs and expenses, including a reasonable attorney's fee incurred in the prosecution of such contempt. Here, the district court found the Auleciemses (D) were in civil contempt but did not correspondingly find that they were in ongoing noncompliance with its prior orders. In fact, the district court specifically found that the Auleciemses (D) had complied with the order that they remove all advertisements for rentals. Rather, the conduct for which the district court found the Auleciemses (D) in civil contempt had occurred in the past. Specifically, the district court found that they had, on 13 occasions, violated court orders by renting out their home without a permit. Although the district court ordered the Auleciemses (D) to comply with the injunctions the court had issued—which is consistent with the remedial purpose of civil contempt—the court imposed sanctions that were criminal in nature. However, the court did not follow the procedures required for either a finding of constructive criminal contempt or for criminal penalties, beginning with the initiation of contempt proceedings. Such a proceeding must be prosecuted by an attorney representing the state with authority to prosecute crimes. Although the township's (P) attorney was the de facto prosecutor at all times, under state law, an attorney representing a township is not authorized to prosecute a misdemeanor offense; rather, such an offense must be prosecuted by a county attorney. Therefore, if the district court was inclined to consider allegations of constructive criminal contempt and to consider the corresponding penalties, the district court should have referred the matter to the county attorney, should have empaneled a jury (unless the Auleciemses (D) waived their right to a jury trial), and should have followed the rules and procedures that apply to criminal prosecutions. Because the sanctions that the district court ordered were constructive and criminal in nature, the sanctions were incompatible with a finding of civil contempt and incompatible with the procedures utilized during the contempt proceeding. Thus, the district court erred by imposing contempt sanctions that were criminal in nature based on a finding of civil contempt. Reversed and remanded.

ANALYSIS

As this case illustrates, because the use of fines and jail time can be sanctions imposed for both coercive civil contempt and criminal contempt, there has been a fair amount of confusion about the distinction between these two types of contempt. Here, the trial judge imposed punishment for the Auleciemses' (D) past violations, which, as the appellate court pointed out, is a defining characteristic of criminal contempt, and used civil, rather than criminal, procedure. In *Hicks on Behalf of Feiock v. Feiock*, 485 U.S. 624 (1988), the United States Supreme Court, observing that in the codified laws of contempt, the "civil" and "criminal" labels of the law have become increasingly blurred, set forth a fairly mechanical test to distinguish between civil and criminal contempt. Under that test, in the words of the Court, "the critical features are the substance of the proceeding and the character of the relief that the proceeding will afford." Thus, if the relief provided is a sentence of imprisonment, it is remedial if the defendant stands committed unless and until the defendant performs the affirmative act required by the court's order, and it is punitive if the sentence is limited to imprisonment for a definite period. If the relief provided is a fine, it is remedial when it is paid to the complainant, and punitive when it is paid to the court, though a fine that would be payable to the court is also remedial when the defendant can avoid paying the fine simply by performing the affirmative act required by the court's order. In other words, the conditional nature of the punishment renders the relief civil in nature because the contemnor can end the sentence and discharge themself at any moment by doing what they had previously refused to do, whereas, the unconditional nature of the punishment renders the relief criminal in nature because the relief cannot undo or remedy what has been done nor afford any compensation, and the contemnor cannot shorten the term by promising not to repeat the offense. In sum, under *Hicks*, an unconditional penalty is criminal, and a conditional penalty is civil.

Continued on next page.

Quicknotes

CIVIL CONTEMPT Willful disobedience of a court order, judgement, decree, direction, command, or other process, or the willful breach of an undertaking given to a court, that can result in fines or jail time unless or until the contemnor comes into compliance with their judicially mandated duty or obligation.

COERCIVE CIVIL CONTEMPT Remedial judicial sanction that will be removed upon a contemnor's compliance with a court order or process that has been defied, designed to coerce or induce the future performance of such order or process, rather than to vindicate the court's authority or to punish for a past failure to perform.

CONSTRUCTIVE CONTEMPT Conduct not committed in the immediate presence of a court, and of which the court has no personal knowledge, that arises from specified acts or omissions, such as disobedience of any lawful judgment, order, or process of the court.

CONTEMPT Willful conduct that interferes with the proper administration of justice by a court or legislature.

CONTEMPT OF COURT Willful conduct that is intended to obstruct the court's effective administration of justice or that otherwise disrespects its authority.

CRIMINAL CONTEMPT Criminal punishment for past behavior constituting an offense against a court's authority or the dignity of the state as a whole, entitling the contemnor to all the protections owed to a criminal defendant.

DIRECT CONTEMPT Conduct occurring in the immediate view and presence of a court, that arises from either disorderly, contemptuous, or insolent behavior toward the judge while holding court, tending to interrupt the due course of a trial or other judicial proceedings, or a breach of the peace, boisterous conduct, or violent disturbance, tending to interrupt the business of the court.

SHOW CAUSE Generally referred to as an "order to show cause" or a "show cause order," directing a party to appear and persuade the court why a certain order should not be enforced or confirmed, or why the court should take or not take a proposed action.

Anyanwu v. Anyanwu

Wife (P) v. Husband (D)

N.J. Super. Ct. App. Div., 771 A.2d 672 (2001)

NATURE OF CASE: Appeal from order for release from confinement for civil contempt.

FACT SUMMARY: Mr. Anyanwu (D) challenged his incarceration for failure to comply with a family court order to produce his children, who were residing in a foreign country.

RULE OF LAW

A party cannot be held in civil contempt when commitment for that purpose has lost its coercive power.

FACTS: After failing to comply with a family court order to produce his two children, who were residing in Nigeria, Mr. Anyanwu (D) was incarcerated. Mr. Anyanwu (D) made a series of appeals over a three-year period, each of which was denied. In 2001, Mr. Anyanwu (D) again moved for release and submitted two documents supporting his position that it was not possible for him to comply with the order to produce his children. After the district court granted his motion for release, Mrs. Anyanwu (P) appealed.

ISSUE: May a party be held in civil contempt when commitment for that purpose has lost its coercive power?

HOLDING AND DECISION: (Collester, J.) No. A party cannot be held in civil contempt when commitment for that purpose has lost its coercive power. Since the legal justification for incarceration for civil contempt is to force compliance, such commitment obviously loses its coercive power when the party committed is unable to comply with the court order the party is charged with violating. Here, the review hearing fell short of the requirements that the contemnor prove that continued confinement had no coercive effect and had become punitive. The district court erred in confining its review to Mr. Anyanwu's (D) refusal to comply. A contemnor's mere refusal to comply does not transform a coercive order into a punitive one. Reversed and remanded.

ANALYSIS

Courts strike a balance between the notions that coercive imprisonment requires incarceration until compliance and the reality that some defendants will forever refuse compliance. The standard for review is often whether there is a substantial likelihood that continued incarceration would accomplish the purpose of causing the confined person to comply with the required order.

Quicknotes

CIVIL CONTEMPT CITATION One party's failure to comply with a court order requiring that party to undertake an action for the benefit of another party to the action.

COERCION The overcoming of a person's free will as a result of threats, promises, or undue influence.

Griffin v. County School Board

Individual (P) v. Local school board (D)

363 F.2d 206 (4th Cir. 1966)

NATURE OF CASE: Contempt hearing based on disbursement of funds subject to judicial control.

FACT SUMMARY: The School Board of Prince Edward County (D) disbursed certain funds before the court of appeals could issue an order preventing it from doing so.

RULE OF LAW

When a certain matter is under judicial scrutiny, removal of that matter for court jurisdiction constitutes contempt.

FACTS: The School Board of Prince Edward County (Board) (D) had been making certain tuition grants to segregated private schools. This was ordered stopped by a court. However, an issue remained as to whether certain disbursements for the previous year could still be made. The trial court did not prohibit the disbursements; an immediate appeal followed. Before the court of appeals could issue a decision, the disbursements were made. The Board (D) had reason to believe the appellate court would prohibit disbursements.

ISSUE: When a certain matter is under judicial scrutiny, does removal of that matter from court jurisdiction constitute contempt?

HOLDING AND DECISION: (Bryan, J.) Yes. When a certain matter is under judicial scrutiny removal of that matter from court jurisdiction constitutes contempt. Contempt is any action which tends to defeat a decree a court might make; it does not have to be an action contrary to a presently existing order. To take a matter away from court scrutiny is to challenge court authority. Here, the Board (D) divested itself of certain funds so that they would be beyond court reach, and this was with the intent of defeating court authority. The members of the Board (D) are in contempt.

DISSENT: (Haynesworth, C.J.) 18 U.S.C. § 401 limits contempt to disobedience of lawful writs or orders of a federal court. The statute does not mention the sort of situation found here. Since the statute limited rather than created the contempt power, a court should not go farther in finding contempt.

ANALYSIS

The instant ruling was appealed, but the Supreme Court denied certiorari. A split in the circuits exists regarding the rule announced in *Griffin*. The Fifth Circuit, for instance, has held that an actual order must be disobeyed for contempt to exist. *In re Stewart*, 571 F.2d 958 (5th Cir. 1978).

Quicknotes

CONTEMPT OF COURT Conduct that is intended to obstruct the court's effective administration of justice or to otherwise disrespect its authority.

SEGREGATION The use of separate institutions and facilities for persons of different races, nationalities, religions, etc.

Walker v. City of Birmingham

Individuals (D) v. City (P)

388 U.S. 307 (1967)

NATURE OF CASE: Appeal of contempt order issued pursuant to disobedience of a temporary restraining order (TRO)

FACT SUMMARY: Walker (D) and others disobeyed an anti-assembly TRO obtained by the City of Birmingham (P), which then obtained a contempt citation.

RULE OF LAW

Disobedience of a court order is punishable by contempt even if the order is unconstitutional, unless the order has been vacated or reversed.

FACTS: The City of Birmingham (City) (P) obtained an ex parte TRO prohibiting marches or assemblies. Walker (D) and others disobeyed the order. The City (P) then obtained a contempt citation against the marchers. Walker (D) appealed, contending that the order was unconstitutional and that, therefore, they were not bound to follow it. The Alabama Supreme Court rejected this and upheld the contempt citation. Walker (D) appealed to the United States Supreme Court.

ISSUE: Is disobedience of a court order punishable by contempt even if the order is unconstitutional, unless the order has been vacated or reversed?

HOLDING AND DECISION: (Stewart, J.) Yes. Disobedience of a court order is punishable by contempt even if the order is unconstitutional, unless the order has been vacated or reversed. Respect for rule of law demands that any order issued by a court of competent jurisdiction, however invalid, be obeyed. If an order is unconstitutional, the proper avenue of redress is to attack the order on appeal. A collateral attack upon a contempt citation is not the proper way to attack an invalid order. Here, the court issuing the order was of competent jurisdiction, and the order should have been obeyed until and unless it was reversed. Affirmed.

DISSENT: (Warren, C.J.) Constitutional protections cannot be evaded by turning an unconstitutional ordinance into an ex parte order. An unconstitutional order should not be given greater weight than an unconstitutional statute, which can be disobeyed and attacked.

DISSENT: (Douglas, J.) An order given by a court without jurisdiction need not be obeyed, and a court does not have jurisdiction to issue unconstitutional orders.

DISSENT: (Brennan, J.) The Court's opinion elevates arbitrary local judicial actions above constitutionally guaranteed rights, and this should not be so.

ANALYSIS

As stated in the Court's opinion, a judicial order must be obeyed until reversed. The main exception to this is when the court lacks jurisdiction to issue the order. This is only true when the lack of jurisdiction is obvious; doubts are to be resolved in favor of jurisdiction. Justice Douglas's view of jurisdiction as stated in his dissent has not been adopted.

Quicknotes

CIVIL CONTEMPT CITATION One party's failure to comply with a court order requiring that party to undertake an action for the benefit of another party to the action.

EX PARTE A proceeding commenced by one party.

TEMPORARY RESTRAINING ORDER A court order preserving the status quo pending a hearing regarding injunctive relief.

Planned Parenthood Golden Gate v. Garibaldi

Health clinic (P) v. Protestors (D)

Cal. Ct. App., 132 Cal. Rptr. 2d 46 (2003)

NATURE OF CASE: Appeal from the extension of an injunction against the defendants.

FACT SUMMARY: In 1995, Planned Parenthood (P) obtained a permanent injunction against two entities that were protesting outside of the abortion clinic. Planned Parenthood (P) now seeks to extend the injunction to other protestors.

RULE OF LAW

A person not named individually in an injunction or who is not a member of a class covered by an injunction cannot be subject to it based solely on the person's actual knowledge of its existence unless the person aids or abets another who is properly covered by the injunction.

FACTS: In 1995, Planned Parenthood (P) obtained an injunction against Operation Rescue. The injunction, among other things, prohibited Operation Rescue from demonstrating within 15 feet of Planned Parenthood's (P) clinic. The 1995 injunction applied to "Defendants and their agents, employees, representatives and all persons acting in concert or participation with them, or either of them, and all persons with actual notice of this judgment." In 2001, Planned Parenthood (P) sought to extend the injunction against three other individuals, including Garibaldi (D), based on their actual notice of the injunction. The trial court granted summary judgment to Planned Parenthood (P). Garibaldi (D) appeals on the grounds the actual notice provision of the injunction is unconstitutional and invalid.

ISSUE: Can a person not named individually in an injunction or who is not a member of a class covered by an injunction be subject to it based solely on the person's actual knowledge of its existence unless the person aids or abets another who is properly covered by the injunction?

HOLDING AND DECISION: (Haerle, J.) No. A person not named individually in an injunction or who is not a member of a class covered by an injunction cannot be subject to it based solely on the person's actual knowledge of its existence unless the person aids or abets another who is properly covered by the injunction. Injunctions operate only against those named in the injunction. They are not effective against the world at large. They do apply to those acting in concert with parties specifically named in an injunction but notice and jurisdiction alone over a person are not enough. Because the injunction here enjoins all demonstrators and not just the parties covered in the injunction, the injunction is overbroad on its face. Garibaldi's (D) mutuality of interest with the parties named in the original injunction does not mean Garibaldi (D) was acting in concert with them. There must be evidence of an actual relationship between Garibaldi (D) and those named in the injunction. In addition, Planned Parenthood's (P) argument that the Supreme Court has upheld a Colorado statute prohibiting demonstrations within one hundred feet of a clinic does not help them. Judicial decrees, unlike statutes, can only have effect on the parties to the litigation and those properly named in the injunction. Summary judgment in favor of Planned Parenthood (P) is reversed.

ANALYSIS

This case provides a good example of the scope of judicial decrees. As the case holds, they can only apply to parties properly covered by the injunction. Note the decision did not need to apply a constitutional analysis, as the court was able to resolve the matter on the basic principles of the scope of judicial authority.

Quicknotes

INJUNCTION An equitable remedy requiring a person, entity, or governmental unit to do, or prohibiting that person, entity, or governmental unit from doing, a specific act.

Credit Bureau, Inc. v. Moninger

Bank (P) v. Individual (D)

Neb. Sup. Ct., 284 N.W.2d 855 (1979)

NATURE OF CASE: Appeal from judgment affirming order awarding proceeds of sheriff's sale.

FACT SUMMARY: Credit Bureau of Broken Bow (P) appealed from a judgment affirming an order awarding proceeds of a sheriff's sale to the Broken Bow State Bank (Bank) (P), contending that as a lien creditor without knowledge of the Bank's (P) security interest it was entitled to the proceeds.

RULE OF LAW

Notice by a debtor to a sheriff when the sheriff is proceeding to attach or levy upon property is not notice to the creditor for whom the levy is made.

FACTS: Credit Bureau of Broken Bow (Bureau) (P) obtained a default judgment against Moninger (D). After this, Moninger (D) renewed his prior note with the Broken Bow State Bank (Bank) (P), which was to be secured by a security agreement, in part on Moninger's (D) pickup truck. The security agreement was not entered at the time the loan was renewed. On June 28, 1978, at the Bureau's (P) request, a writ of execution was entered on the balance due on the default judgment. On July 7, 1978, the sheriff proceeded to execute on the pickup. Moninger (D) informed the sheriff that money had been borrowed from the Bank (D) against the pickup, but the sheriff proceeded, executing on the pickup, even though he did not take possession of the vehicle or take the keys. On July 10, 1978, the Bank (P) and Moninger (D) executed a security agreement on the pickup. An action was brought for a determination of the division of the proceeds obtained from the sale of the pickup. From a decision in favor of the Bank (P), the Bureau (P) appealed, contending that it had a superior interest in the proceeds of the sheriff's sale.

ISSUE: Is notice by a debtor to a sheriff when the sheriff is proceeding to attach or levy upon property notice to the creditor for whom the levy is made?

HOLDING AND DECISION: (Brodkey, J.) No. Notice by a debtor to a sheriff when the sheriff is proceeding to attach or levy upon property is not notice to the creditor for whom the levy is made. (The court first determined the sheriff had validly executed the levy by expressly asserting his dominion over the pickup, despite the fact he did not take possession of the vehicle at the time of the levy.) The general rule is that an unperfected security interest is subordinate to the rights of a person who becomes a lien creditor without knowledge of the security interest. Peace officers are the agents of the law and are not ordinarily agents of the parties. To impute the knowledge of the sheriff to the Bureau (P) in this situation would result in unnecessary delays and place an undue burden on sheriffs. Since there was a valid levy, and the Bureau (P) had no knowledge of the Bank's (P) interest in the pickup, and that interest was unperfected at the time of the levy, the Bureau (P) had prior rights to the proceeds of the sheriff's sale. Reversed and remanded.

ANALYSIS

The Uniform Commercial Code (the UCC) provides the general rules of priority that apply in the present case, making the Bureau (P) the holder of the superior interest. The UCC does not contain a provision that determines when a person obtains an execution lien. The states disagree over this point, and depending on the jurisdiction, a different result may be dictated.

Quicknotes

ATTACHMENT The seizing of the property of one party in anticipation of, or in order to satisfy, a favorable judgment obtained by another party.

LEVY The collection or assessment of a tax; the legal process pursuant to which property is seized and sold in order to satisfy a debt.

Dixie National Bank v. Chase

Bank (D) v. Individual (P)

Fla. Dist. Ct. App., 485 So. 2d 1353 (1986)

NATURE OF CASE: Appeal from an award of damages under a writ of garnishment.

FACT SUMMARY: Stephen W. Chase, II (P) had the court issue a writ of garnishment to Dixie National Bank (Dixie) (D) against a debtor, Gore, but Dixie (D) failed to discover an account held by Gore.

RULE OF LAW

Garnishees are liable to garnishor creditors for all debts that the garnishee owes to the debtor at the time a writ of garnishment is filed.

FACTS: In 1983, Stephen W. Chase, II (P) received a final judgment against Gore for $48,473 and shortly thereafter filed a writ of garnishment directed to Dixie National Bank (Dixie) (D). The court issued the writ and directed the garnishee, Dixie (D), to file an answer stating whether they were indebted to Gore at the time of writ. Dixie (D) responded that Gore had one account that contained only $32. However, Gore actually had another account at Dixie (D) that contained $13,870 at the time of the writ. Months later Dixie (D) filed an amended answer that disclosed the other account; but in the meantime, Gore had withdrawn nearly all the money. Chase (P) brought suit against Dixie (D), and the trial court awarded Chase (P) $13,870 from Dixie (D), which appealed.

ISSUE: Are garnishees liable to garnishor creditors for all debts that the garnishee owes to the debtor at the time a writ of garnishment is filed?

HOLDING AND DECISION: (Hubbart, J.) Yes. Garnishees are liable to garnishor creditors for all debts that the garnishee owes to the debtor at the time a writ of garnishment is filed. Florida statute § 77.06(1) states that the service of a writ of garnishment makes the garnishee liable for all debts due by the garnishee to the defendant. Upon filing its answer, the garnishee is required to hold any moneys owed to the debtor. The garnishee is protected from any suit by the defendant debtor for garnishing funds where there is a good-faith doubt as to whether funds should be reported. This statute contemplates full disclosure by the garnishee so as to fully protect the creditor garnishor. If incomplete answers were permissible, there would be little incentive for full disclosure, and funds could be spirited away by a debtor. This would be contrary to the purpose of the law. Therefore, the garnishee is liable to the garnishor creditor for all debts that the garnishee owed to the debtor at the time of the writ. Accordingly, garnishee Dixie (D) was liable to Chase (P), a garnishor creditor, because Dixie (D) owed Gore $13,870 at the time of the writ. Affirmed.

ANALYSIS

Typically, garnishees are banks or employers. The garnishee is permitted to defend this type of suit based upon the fact that it did not owe the debtor but cannot litigate the underlying judgment which the garnishee won. In some states, a garnishee who fails to answer a writ may be liable for the entire amount of the judgment, regardless of its actual liability to the debtor.

Quicknotes

GARNISHEE A party against whom a garnishment has been ordered; party holding the property of a judgment creditor who is directed to hold the property until a court determination of the proper disposition thereof.

GARNISHMENT Satisfaction of a debt by deducting payments directly from the debtor's wages before the wages are paid to the debtor by their employer; due process requires that the debtor be first given notice and an opportunity to be heard.

In re Marriage of Logston

Wife (P) v. Husband (D)

Ill. Sup. Ct., 469 N.E.2d 167 (1984)

NATURE OF CASE: Appeal of a contempt order.

FACT SUMMARY: Eugene Logston (D) contended that his Social Security, pension, and disability income were exempt from a contempt order to pay alimony arrearages to his ex-wife.

RULE OF LAW

Social Security, disability, and pension benefits are not exempt from contempt and judgment proceedings for failure to pay child support or alimony.

FACTS: Eugene Logston (D) was married to Kate Logston from 1966 to 1981. Eugene (D) was ordered to pay Kate $221.50 per month for maintenance as part of the property settlement. Eugene (D) was retired due to a disability and received Social Security, pension, and disability payments for his income. Eugene (D) failed to make any payments through May 1983. Part of these arrearages was paid through judgment and garnishment proceedings, but Eugene (D) still owed $4,707 in May 1983. Kate instituted an action for the arrearages, and a contempt order was issued against Eugene (D). Eugene (D) responded that his income was exempt from contempt proceedings under Illinois law and appealed.

ISSUE: Are Social Security, disability, and pension benefits exempt from contempt and judgment proceedings for failure to pay child support or alimony?

HOLDING AND DECISION: (Ryan, C.J.) No. Social Security, disability, and pension benefits are not exempt from contempt and judgment proceedings for failure to pay child support or alimony. Illinois law does exempt Social Security, pension, and disability payments from judgment and attachment to satisfy debts. This law was enacted based on the policy that a creditor should not wholly deprive a person from supporting their family. However, the exemption statute is ambiguous as to whether it was designed to cover contempt proceedings. Illinois law has long recognized contempt as an appropriate sanction for willful failure to pay alimony or child support. Additionally, new legislation allows courts to garnish the income of a nonpaying former spouse regardless of the source of the income and exemption provisions. Therefore, the exemption statute is not a defense to a contempt order to pay alimony arrearages. The fact that a court enters a "judgment" for the amount should not alter this result. Thus, Eugene Logston (D) does not have a valid exemption from the contempt order. Affirmed and remanded.

ANALYSIS

This decision also rejected Eugene's (D) argument that his failure to pay was not willful since he was unable to make the payments. The court noted that Eugene (D) had failed to prove that his income was spent on only bare living expenses. Under the contempt order in this case, Eugene (D) was to be imprisoned if he did not make the arrearages payment in thirty days. Most states would permit installment payments in circumstances like Eugene's (D).

Quicknotes

ALIMONY Allowances (usually monetary) that a spouse by court order pays to the other spouse for maintenance while they are separated, or after they are divorced (permanent alimony), or temporarily, pending a suit for divorce (pendente lite).

CONTEMPT OF COURT Conduct that is intended to obstruct the court's effective administration of justice or to otherwise disrespect its authority.

In re Hypnotic Taxi, LLC

[Parties not identified.]

543 B.R. 365 (Bankr. E.D.N.Y. 2016)

NATURE OF CASE: Motion by creditor of Chapter 11 bankruptcy debtors for, *inter alia*, prejudgment order to attach assets of the guarantor of the debtors' obligations.

FACT SUMMARY: Citibank had loaned $31.5 million in three loans to corporations owned and controlled by Freidman, who had personally guaranteed the loans, which were secured by taxi medallions. The corporations sought Chapter 11 bankruptcy protection. After Freidman transferred his interests in various limited liability companies (LLCs) and corporations owning real estate estimated to be worth more than $60 million to four offshore trusts for the benefit of himself and members of his family, without consideration, Citibank moved for a prejudgment order to attach those assets.

RULE OF LAW

(1) An order for prejudgment attachment of assets of a debtor's guarantor will be granted where the creditor shows that all statutory requirements for such an order have been satisfied, including demonstrating that the defendant has intended to defraud the creditor or frustrate the enforcement of a judgment that might be rendered in the creditor's favor, and that there is a need for such an order.

(2) A creditor with an order of attachment against the guarantor of a debtor's debts may reach assets that have fraudulently been transferred by the guarantor into offshore trusts in attempt to thwart the creditor's efforts to reach the guarantor's assets.

FACTS: Citibank made three loans totaling $31.5 million to corporations owned and controlled by Freidman, who personally guaranteed the loans. The loans were secured by New York City (NYC) taxi medallions. Although such medallions can be very valuable, their value has plummeted in response to competition from rideshare companies. All three loans were in default. Citibank sued Freidman in state court on his personal guarantees in March 2015, and it obtained an order allowing it to seize the medallions. In April 2015, Freidman undertook to transfer all his real estate holdings, estimated to be valued at more than $60 million, into offshore trusts. In June 2015, Freidman's real estate assets were transferred to four trusts ("Trusts") for the benefit of himself and members of his family, without consideration. The debtor corporations filed Chapter 11 bankruptcy cases in July 2015, which automatically stayed the state court's seizure order. In bankruptcy proceedings in November 2015, Citibank moved by order to show cause for a temporary restraining order and order of attachment, seeking to restrain any transfer of assets in which Freidman had an interest and to restrain any further transfer of assets transferred by Freidman to the Trusts. The bankruptcy court entered the requested orders in Citibank's favor, but the order of attachment was stayed pending a hearing, which was subsequently held. The bankruptcy court indicated that Freidman's testimony at the hearing lacked credibility. The bankruptcy court entered its decision regarding the order of attachment.

ISSUE:

(1) Will an order for prejudgment attachment of assets of a debtor's guarantor be granted where the creditor shows that all statutory requirements for such an order have been satisfied, including demonstrating that the defendant has intended to defraud the creditor or frustrate the enforcement of a judgment that might be rendered in the creditor's favor, and that there is a need for such an order?

(2) May a creditor with an order of attachment against the guarantor of a debtor's debts reach assets that have fraudulently been transferred by the guarantor into offshore trusts in attempt to thwart the creditor's efforts to reach the guarantor's assets?

HOLDING AND DECISION: (Craig, C.J.)

(1) Yes. An order for prejudgment attachment of assets of a debtor's guarantor will be granted where the creditor shows that all statutory requirements for such an order have been satisfied, including demonstrating that the defendant has intended to defraud the creditor or frustrate the enforcement of a judgment that might be rendered in the creditor's favor, and that there is a need for such an order. Under state law, for an order of attachment to be granted or confirmed, a plaintiff is required to show (1) that there is a cause of action and that it is probable that the plaintiff will succeed on the merits; (2) that one of the statutory grounds for attachment exists; and (3) that the amount demanded from the defendant exceeds all counterclaims known to the plaintiff. Additionally, it must be shown that there is a need for the order. One of the statutory grounds for attachment is met when the defendant, with intent to defraud his creditors or frustrate the enforcement of a judgment that might be rendered in plaintiff's

Continued on next page.

favor, has assigned, disposed of, encumbered or secreted property, or removed it from the state or is about to do any of these acts. Citibank has satisfied all these requirements. First, Citibank has shown probability of success on the merits of its case. To establish such probability of success, a plaintiff must show that it is more likely than not that it will succeed on the merits of its claim. This requires proof stronger than that required to establish a prima facie case. However, in evaluating whether this standard has been met, a court must afford the plaintiff the benefit of all legitimate inferences than can be drawn in plaintiff's favor. Here, it is clear the showing of likelihood of success required for an order of attachment is met, since Freidman does not dispute that the loans were advanced and have not been repaid, and that he guaranteed the loans. Similarly, Citibank has satisfied the statutory ground for attachment that requires a showing that the defendant, with the intent to defraud his creditor or frustrate the enforcement of a judgment that might be rendered in plaintiff's favor, has assigned, disposed of, encumbered or secreted property, or removed it from the state or is about to do any of these acts. Because fraudulent intent is rarely susceptible to direct proof, courts look to "badges of fraud" to establish actual intent. A non-exhaustive list of such indicators of fraud, includes the following six telling badges of fraud: (1) the lack or inadequacy of consideration; (2) the family, friendship, or close associate relationship between the parties; (3) the retention of possession, benefit, or use of the property in question; (4) the financial condition of the party sought to be charged both before and after the transaction in question; (5) the existence or cumulative effect of a pattern or series of transactions or course of conduct after the incurring of debt, onset of financial difficulties, or pendency or threat of suits by creditors; and (6) the general chronology of the events and transactions under inquiry. Here, all six of these badges of fraud are present. The first badge is unquestionably present because Freidman's transfer of his real estate interest to the Trusts was gratuitous. Likewise, the second badge is unquestionably present since the Trusts' beneficiaries were Freidman, his children, and his parents. The third badge is also present because Freidman structured the Trusts so he could use the properties, and, in fact, did so. Moreover, he retained total control over the properties, and his assertion that he was in the process of handing over control was unconvincing. The fourth badge is present because Freidman appears to have sought to convey all his property against which a judgment creditor could readily execute. Although Freidman maintained that his Statement of Financial Condition dated June 30, 2015 ("2015 SFC"), which listed a net worth of almost $130 million, demonstrated that even after the transfers he was in robust financial shape, even a cursory analysis shows that Freidman retained few assets from which a potential judgment creditor might readily recover. Of the purported net worth, $85 million was ascribed to closely held entities owning taxi medallions. However, any decline in the market value of the NYC medallions—which were heavily encumbered and had become illiquid—would affect Freidman's equity disproportionally. The second major source of value listed on the 2015 SFC was Freidman's interest in closely held taxicab management companies, which were listed as worth $34,880,000. Here, again, it is highly doubtful that these assets would actually be a significant source of recovery to a creditor seeking to execute on a judgment. The other assets listed in Freidman's 2015 SFC were Swiss bank accounts totaling over $2 million, and two residences in France worth a total of $14 million. Such property would be difficult for a creditor seeking to enforce a New York judgment to reach. For these reasons, it appears that Freidman transferred substantially all his assets available for execution by a judgment creditor to the Trusts. Similarly, Citibank has demonstrated that the fifth and sixth badges are also present. Although fraudulent intent is rarely susceptible to direct proof, much can be inferred from the chronology of events. The timing of Freidman's transfers to the Trusts suggests that it was in response to pressure from Citibank's state action, and the rulings that issued therein. The transfers occurred against the background of a suit by Citibank to recover in excess of $40 million dollars, and a confession of judgment entered by Capital One, which resulted in a judgment of almost $8.5 million dollars. It is, therefore, impossible to conclude that the timing of the transfers was merely coincidence. Moreover, Freidman used, and retained control over, his properties, as though they had not been transferred. These, and other events, strongly support the inference that Freidman undertook the transfers to the Trusts with the aim of frustrating judgment creditors. For example, Freidman fired the Trustees located in New York in order to appoint foreign trustees in Moscow, in a transparent attempt to further insulate the assets he placed in the Trusts from the reach of his creditors. In short, the badges of fraud are numerous and glaring, and the statutory ground for attachment is satisfied. The requirement that the amount demanded exceeds all known counterclaims is satisfied, since Citibank's failure to concede the counterclaims are just is sufficient to allow Citibank to satisfy this requirement,

Continued on next page.

consistent with the fact that an order of attachment is a provisional remedy. Finally, having established that the statutory requirements for attachment are met, it is necessary to consider whether there is a need for an order of attachment. The need for attachment has been amply demonstrated by the overwhelming evidence that Freidman made transfers to the Trusts in effort to strip himself of assets on which a judgment creditor could readily execute. Accordingly, the order of attachment is granted.

(2) Yes. A creditor with an order of attachment against the guarantor of a debtor's debts may reach assets that have fraudulently been transferred by the guarantor into offshore trusts in attempt to thwart the creditor's efforts to reach the guarantor's assets. Although, as a general matter, an order of attachment may not reach property in which the defendant does not have an interest, where, as in this case, intent to hinder, delay, or defraud creditors is shown, a different rule applies: in the case of a fraudulent transfer, property can be attached in the hands of a third party (other than a bona fide purchaser, an exception not relevant here). There is no need to join the Trusts to give effect to the order of attachment. If the Trustees wish to object to the order, however, they may intervene in the action. Finally, Freidman argues that an order of attachment must state with specificity what property is to be attached. However, the statute that prescribes the contents of an order of attachment contains no such requirement. Therefore, it is not necessary for the order of attachment to describe the property to be attached. Furthermore, if the order does specify certain property, the sheriff is not prohibited from levying upon any other property when it is necessary to do so to secure enough property to guarantee the availability of the amount set forth in the attachment order. Accordingly, Citibank's motion is not deficient because it seeks to attach all of Freidman's property and all the property that he transferred to the Trusts. For all these reasons, Citibank is authorized to attach the real estate assets transferred by Freidman to the Trusts. Judgment for Citibank.

ANALYSIS

Prejudgment attachment is a provisional remedy to secure a debt by preliminary levy upon the property of the debtor to conserve that property for eventual execution. Federal Rule of Civil Procedure 64, made applicable in adversary proceedings by Bankruptcy Rule 7064, permits a federal court to issue an order of attachment in the manner provided by the law of the state in which the federal court sits.

Quicknotes

CHAPTER 11 BANKRUPTCY A legal proceeding whereby a debtor, who is unable to pay their debts as they become due, is relieved of their obligation to pay their creditors through reorganization and payment from future income.

CONSIDERATION Value given by one party in exchange for performance, or a promise to perform, by another party.

FRAUDULENT TRANSFER The conveyance of title to property with the intent to defraud creditors or with the intent to deceive others.

ORDER OF ATTACHMENT An order mandating the seizing of the property of one party in anticipation of, or in order to satisfy, a favorable judgment obtained by another party.

SHOW CAUSE Generally referred to as an "order to show cause" or a "show cause order," directing a party to appear and persuade the court why a certain order should not be enforced or confirmed, or why the court should take or not take a proposed action.

W.E. Erickson Construction v. Congress-Kenilworth Corp.

Contractor (P) v. Corporation (D)

Ill. App. Ct., 445 N.E.2d 1209 (1983)

NATURE OF CASE: Interlocutory appeal from an order appointing a receiver in breach of contract action.

FACT SUMMARY: W.E. Erickson Construction (P) constructed a water slide amusement for Congress-Kenilworth Corp. (D) and then sought to appoint a receiver when Congress-Kenilworth (D) was unable to pay for the construction.

RULE OF LAW

A receiver may be appointed only where income from a special fund is in actual danger of loss from neglect, waste, misconduct, or insolvency.

FACTS: In 1981, Congress-Kenilworth Corp. (D) hired W.E. Erickson Construction (Erickson) (P), a general contractor, to construct a water slide amusement for a total cost of $535,000. When the project was 60 percent complete, Erickson (P) applied for a partial payment of $246,958, which Congress-Kenilworth (D) was unable to pay. The parties agreed that, in lieu of payment, Congress-Kenilworth (D) would deliver, to Erickson (P), the deed to the property where the water slide was located as a form of security. The project was completed and opened to the public in the summer of 1981. Congress-Kenilworth (D) paid a total of $150,000 to Erickson (P) in 1981. In August 1981, it was discovered that the Department of the Army actually owned the real property and that the water slide was an encroachment. A receiver was appointed by the court after a finding that the security deed given to Erickson (P) was worthless and that the water slide was bringing in hundreds of thousands of dollars while Congress-Kenilworth (D) was contending that it had no assets. Congress-Kenilworth (D) appealed the order appointing a receiver.

ISSUE: May a receiver be appointed only where income from a special fund is in actual danger of loss from neglect, waste, misconduct, or insolvency?

HOLDING AND DECISION: (Jiganti, J.) No. A receiver may be appointed only where income from a special fund is in actual danger of loss from neglect, waste, misconduct, or insolvency. Appointment of a receiver is a high and extraordinary remedy that deprives the legal owner of possession. It must be exercised with caution, and only when a court is satisfied there is an imminent danger of loss if it is not exercised. The general rule is that an applicant must have a clear right to the property or have some lien upon it. Secondly, the property must have been obtained by the defendant by fraud, or the income arising from the property must be in danger of loss from neglect, waste, misconduct, or insolvency. Erickson (P) was able to meet the first requirement because the property deed was given as security for the payments owed to Erickson (P), giving rise to an equitable lien because there was a mutual mistake as to the validity of the deed. However, Erickson (P) only alleged a fear of diversion of the income from the water slide. A speculative fear is not legally sufficient to support the drastic remedy of the appointment of a receiver. Thus, the second prong of the receivership requirements was not met by Erickson (P), and the appointment was improperly granted. Reversed and remanded.

ANALYSIS

On remand, a trial was held on many different issues, including construction defects and the costs of the receivership. Eventually, the court ruled that Erickson (P) was entitled to payment minus $67,000 in damages caused by the receivership. Appointment of a receiver is similar to attachment proceeding but allows an experienced businessperson to continue an operation.

Quicknotes

EQUITABLE LIEN An equitable right to have specified property applied to payment of a debt.

RECEIVER An individual who is appointed by the court to maintain the holdings of a corporation, individual or other entity involved in a legal proceeding.

RECEIVERSHIP Proceeding or condition whereby a receiver is appointed in order to maintain the holdings of a corporation, individual or other entity that is insolvent.

CHAPTER 10

More Ancillary Remedies: Attorneys' Fees and the Costs of Litigation

Quick Reference Rules of Law

City of Riverside v. Rivera

City (D) v. Individuals (P)

477 U.S. 561 (1986)

NATURE OF CASE: Appeal of an award of attorney's fees in civil rights action for damages.

FACT SUMMARY: The district court awarded attorney's fees that far exceeded the judgment for damages in a civil rights suit.

RULE OF LAW

Attorney's fees awards in civil rights actions are not required to be proportionate to the amount of damages.

FACTS: Rivera (P) and eight other Chicano individuals sued the City of Riverside (D) and individual police officers (D) who broke into their home without a search warrant and used unnecessary physical force. A jury awarded Rivera (P) and the others (P) a total of $66,000 for their constitutional claims. Rivera (P) also sought attorney's fees under § 1988 of the Civil Rights Attorney's Fees Awards Act, which authorizes attorney's fees to prevailing parties in civil rights actions. The trial court awarded Rivera's (P) attorneys $245,456 based upon 1,946 hours of work. Riverside (D) appealed the award of attorney's fees.

ISSUE: Are attorney's fees awards in civil rights actions required to be proportionate to the amount of damages?

HOLDING AND DECISION: (Brennan, J.) No. Attorney's fees awards in civil rights actions are not required to be proportionate to the amount of damages. According to the American rule, each party to a lawsuit ordinarily bears its own attorney's fees. However, under § 1988, Congress has authorized district courts to award reasonable attorney's fees to prevailing parties in civil rights action. A reasonable fee is determined by multiplying the number of hours reasonably spent by a reasonable hourly rate, a figure commonly known as the "lodestar." Congress did not intend for amount of attorney's fees to be proportionate to the amount of damages plaintiff recovers. Section 1988 was intended to serve the public interest because successful civil rights plaintiffs often secure important social benefits that are not reflected in the amount of damages. The amount awarded to Rivera's (P) attorneys was reasonable because the district court properly used the lodestar formula. Accordingly, the attorney's fees award was proper even though it was disproportionate to the amount of damages in this case. Affirmed.

CONCURRENCE: (Powell, J.) A court may consider the vindication of constitutional rights and, by extension, the public interest in addition to the amount of damages recovered.

DISSENT: (Burger, C.J.) $125 an hour is far too much to pay for the services of two attorneys like Rivera's (P) who had recently graduated from law school and only had three years of experience between them.

DISSENT: (Rehnquist, J.) The lodestar formula contemplates that only hours reasonably expended by the attorneys should be compensated. It was not reasonable for Rivera's (P) attorneys to spend 1,900 hours to recover a very small amount.

ANALYSIS

This case demonstrates one of the federal statutory exemptions to the otherwise firmly entrenched American rule that each party is responsible for its own attorney's fees. The viability of the American rule is based on the policy that litigation should not be discouraged. Moreover, as this case demonstrates, the cost and time taken up by trials to determine a fair fee would be administratively burdensome.

Quicknotes

AMERICAN RULE The rule that attorney's fees are not recoverable, unless expressly provided by law or pursuant to a contract.

In re Cabletron Systems, Inc. Securities Litigation

Class of individuals (P) v. Corporation (D)

239 F.R.D. 30 (D.N.H. 2006)

NATURE OF CASE: Trial court's determination of counsel fees in class action lawsuit.

FACT SUMMARY: After a class action for securities fraud settled for $10.5 million, counsel for the class sought $3.15 million for fees and $915,414 in costs.

RULE OF LAW

The best method to determine a fee award in common fund cases is to assess what the fee would have been had it been determined by a competitive bid process at the beginning of the case.

FACTS: A class action suit for securities fraud settled for $10.5 million. Counsel for the class petitioned the court with the class's consent for fees of $3.15 million and $915,414 in costs. Counsel asserted that they had spent 22,397 hours on the case, which would result in a fee of $8,057,300 if the typical lodestar, multifactor method for determining fees were employed.

ISSUE: Is the best method to determine a fee award in common fund cases to assess what the fee would have been had it been determined by a competitive bid process at the beginning of the case?

HOLDING AND DECISION: (Smith, J.) Yes. The best method to determine a fee award in common fund cases is to assess what the fee would have been had it been determined by a competitive bid process at the beginning of the case. There is a wide variety of methods to determine fee awards in common fund, class action suits. Some circuits apply the lodestar method, with its multiple factor approach. Recently, courts have applied a percentage of the fund (POF) method. The court simply establishes a percentage of the settlement fund or verdict amount as a reasonable fee based on a review of similar cases. Other courts use the POF method, but then also review the award under the traditional lodestar method to determine reasonableness of the POF award. This court believes a market-based approach is preferable to either the lodestar method or the POF method. This court has analyzed other class action suits where the fee amount was determined by a competitive bid process at the outset of the case. This competitive process will allow highly competent and successful attorneys to compete for the case, thus offering the class lower fees. The court has reviewed bids in other cases. This review results in an average bid amount of 17 percent for similar cases. A separate study conducted by a third party reveals a 26 percent fee amount if the class had to negotiate with their counsel alone at the start of the case. Averaging these two figures results in a 21.5 percent amount for the fee in this case, or $2,257,500.

ANALYSIS

There is currently not a great deal of decisional law at the Federal Circuit Court level regarding the use of a bid process for legal fees in class action suits. Additionally, Federal Rule of Civil Procedure 23(g)(2) states that when there is more than one applicant for counsel of a putative class, the court "must appoint the applicant best able to represent the interests of the class." While a bidding process may lead to lower fee amounts, courts should have discretion to review the bids and disqualify low bidders who are not experienced or competent enough to handle a particular case.

Quicknotes

CLASS ACTION A suit commenced by a representative on behalf of an ascertainable group that is too large to appear in court, who shares a commonality of interests, and who will benefit from a successful result.

Evans v. Jeff D.

State official (D) v. Child with disabilities (P)

475 U.S. 717 (1986)

NATURE OF CASE: Appeal of court approval of the settlement of a civil rights action.

FACT SUMMARY: The public officials (D) responsible for the education of children with disabilities (P) sought to settle a civil rights action by agreeing to virtually all the injunctive relief conditioned on a waiver of attorney's fees.

RULE OF LAW

Courts are not required to reject settlements that include a waiver of attorney's fees in civil rights litigation.

FACTS: A class of children with disabilities (P) filed a complaint based on the deficiencies in the educational and health care services provided by state public officials (D). The district court appointed Johnson, a public interest attorney, to prosecute the action. One week before the civil rights trial was scheduled to begin, the public officials (D) offered a proposal to the children (P) that included virtually all the injunctive relief that had been sought in the complaint. However, the offer included a waiver of any claim to attorney's fees for Johnson or legal costs. Johnson determined that it was his ethical obligation to accept the settlement conditioned on the district court's approval. Johnson filed a motion requesting that the court approve the settlement except for the fee waiver. The court rejected the motion and approved the settlement with the children's (P) fee waiver intact. The court of appeals, however, invalidated the fee waiver and left the remainder of the settlement standing. The public officials (D) appealed.

ISSUE: Are courts required to reject settlements that include a waiver of attorney's fees in civil rights litigation?

HOLDING AND DECISION: (Stevens, J.) No. Courts are not required to reject settlements that include a waiver of attorney's fees in civil rights litigation. In other words, courts may refuse to award fees. Under Federal Rule of Civil Procedure 23(e), courts have the power to approve or reject settlements negotiated by the parties, but courts are not authorized to require parties to accept settlements to which they have not agreed. The Civil Rights Fees Act does not require a court to disapprove a settlement that is conditioned on waiver of statutory eligibility for attorney's fees. Therefore, the district court did not abuse its discretion in approving the fee waiver. The statutory eligibility for attorney's fees for the prevailing party in civil rights litigation does not prevent a party from waiving the right. A general rule against waiver would impede vindication of civil rights because the attractiveness of settlements would be reduced. Since the potential liability for fees in this type of litigation is very great, fee awards must be allowed into the bargaining process. Parties seek to fix their liability through settlement, and many cases will not be settled if the liability for fees remains open. Accordingly, the acceptance of the settlement and its complete fee waiver for the class of children with disabilities (P) represented by Johnson was not an abuse of discretion by the district court. Reversed.

DISSENT: (Brennan, J.) Congress's purpose in allowing for attorney's fees in civil rights actions was to provide for effective public enforcement through the availability of competent counsel. Negotiated fee waivers will diminish lawyers' expectations of receiving fees and will decrease the willingness of lawyers to accept civil rights cases. Since this result is the exact opposite of what Congress sought to achieve through the Fees Act, fee waivers must be prohibited.

ANALYSIS

This decision has not had the impact that the bar expected. Many civil rights attorneys have begun to interpret their ethical obligations differently and refuse to negotiate fee waivers. Others draft contracts in which the client agrees not to accept a fee waiver. Still, it seems that there is an inherent conflict of interest between the attorney and the client where fees are negotiated at the same time as the underlying claim.

Quicknotes

INJUNCTION An equitable remedy requiring a person, entity, or governmental unit to do, or prohibiting that person, entity, or governmental unit from doing, a specific act.

INJUNCTIVE RELIEF A court order issued as a remedy, requiring a person to do, or prohibiting that person from doing, a specific act.

WAIVER The intentional or voluntary forfeiture of a recognized right.

CHAPTER 11

Remedial Defenses

Quick Reference Rules of Law

James v. National Financial, LLC

Subprime credit borrower (P) v. Subprime credit lender (D)

Del. Ct. Ch., 132 A.3d 799 (2016)

NATURE OF CASE: Action for, *inter alia*, rescission of agreement for cash advance on the grounds of unconscionability.

FACT SUMMARY: James (P), who was undereducated and financially unsophisticated, borrowed $200 from National Financial, LLC (National) (D) in a loan product that was in substance a one-year, non-amortizing, unsecured cash advance that had a cost of credit of $1,620 (Disputed Loan). After she defaulted, and National (D) rejected her request for a workout agreement, she brought suit, seeking, *inter alia*, to rescind the Disputed Loan as unconscionable.

RULE OF LAW

A loan agreement may be rescinded where it is found to be unconscionable, and where the lender has sought to use the loan to evade statutory payday loan limitations.

FACTS: James (P) borrowed $200 from National Financial, LLC (National) (D) in a loan product that in substance was a one-year, non-amortizing, unsecured cash advance that had a cost of credit of $1,620 (Disputed Loan). She needed the money for food and rent and went to National's (D) "Loan Till Payday" storefront operation, where she had previously borrowed money from National (D). National (D) had a policy of loaning borrowers up to 40 percent of their after-tax monthly income, regardless of their other expenditures, so Reilly, National's (D) general manager, initially offered James (P) a $400 loan, which represented 40 percent of James's (P) after-tax income, notwithstanding that she had requested a $200 loan. James (P) declined the $400 loan. James (P) thought she was getting a payday loan with a block rate of "$30 on $100." As James (P) understood it, this meant she would pay $60 to borrow the $200. Lenders developed the block rate concept to describe the finance charge for a traditional payday loan, which was a single-payment loan designed to be repaid on the borrower's next payday. National's (D) trade name—Loan Till Payday—embodies this concept. Because the loan was technically intended to be outstanding only for a single block of time, payday loan companies described the finance charge by identifying the dollar amount per $100 borrowed that the customer would owe at the end of the period. A block rate of "$30 on $100" meant that a customer who borrowed $100 would repay $130 on her next payday. Because the state's legislature had imposed limits on traditional payday loans (Payday Loan Law), National (D) recast its payday loans as non-amortizing installment loans that were structured to remain outstanding for seven to twelve months. The Payday Loan Law applied only to loans designed to be outstanding for sixty days or less, so by making this change, National (D) sidestepped the law. The law also provided that no consumer could receive more than five short-term loans in a single year, and that each renewal counted as a new loan. Despite shifting to longer-dated installment loans, National (D) continued to frame its finance charges using a block rate. National adhered to this practice because it made a high-cost loan product sound cheaper than it was. Although an Annual Percentage Rate (APR) was indicated on National's (D) loan agreements, National's (D) employees followed a practice of telling customers that the APR had "nothing to do with the loan" and otherwise significantly downplaying the APR's significance. When James (P) obtained the Disputed Loan, she focused on the block rate and the concept of $30 in interest per $100 borrowed, just as National (D) intended. She thought she would have to pay back $260 and indicated to Reilly that she would do so in two payments of $130 each, one each on her upcoming two paydays. The repayment schedule did not reflect either the two repayments that James wanted to make or the two repayments that Reilly entered in the Payday Loan Manager. The Loan Agreement instead contemplated 26 interest-only payments of $60 each, followed by a balloon payment comprising a twenty-seventh interest payment of $60 plus repayment of the original $200 in principal. The total amount of interest was $1,620. According to the Loan Agreement, the APR for the loan was 838.45 percent. Using Reilly's planned repayment schedule, the APR was 1,095 percent. James (P) was undereducated and financially unsophisticated, although she was hard working. She received her high school equivalency degree 10 years after dropping out of high school in 10th grade. At the time she sought the loan, she worked as a housekeeper in a hotel. She attempted to improve her skills by enrolling in a nine-month course on medical billing and coding, but family and work responsibilities forced her to drop out. James (P) thought she received a grant to attend the program, but after dropping out she learned she actually had taken out a student loan. She eventually repaid it. She did not have a savings account or a checking account, had no savings, and used a Nexis card, which is a pre-paid VISA card. The day after she signed the Loan Agreement, she broke her hand and could not work for a while. National (D) refused to give any accommodation because of her injury, and instead suggested that she increase her

Continued on next page.

bi-weekly payment. National (D) tried debiting her Nexis account, and soon left messages for her employer and sent her texts demanding payment. James (P) eventually repaid National (D) $197. James (P) brought suit, initially as a class action, alleging, *inter alia*, that the loan terms were unconscionable and that the loan, therefore, should be rescinded. The court denied class-certification, but allowed her individual action to proceed.

ISSUE: May a loan agreement be rescinded where it is found to be unconscionable, and where the lender has sought to use the loan to evade statutory payday loan limitations?

HOLDING AND DECISION: (Laster, V.C.) Yes. A loan agreement may be rescinded where it is found to be unconscionable, and where the lender has sought to use the loan to evade statutory payday loan limitations. The doctrine of unconscionability stands as a limited exception to the law's broad support for freedom of contract. An unconscionable contract is traditionally defined as a contract that no person in their senses and not under delusion would make on the one hand, and no honest or fair person would accept, on the other. The adequacy or fairness of the consideration that supports a contract is by itself insufficient for rescission of the contract, but if coupled with some circumstance that amounts to inequitable or oppressive conduct, even in the absence of actual fraud, duress or incapacity, such inadequacy or unfairness may be grounds for a court to refuse to enforce the contract. This longstanding equitable doctrine has been legislatively endorsed in the unconscionability provision contained in § 2-302 of the Uniform Commercial Code (UCC). It provides in pertinent part that if a court as a matter of law finds the contract or any clause of the contract to have been unconscionable at the time it was made the court may refuse to enforce the contract, or it may enforce the remainder of the contract without the unconscionable clause, or it may so limit the application of any unconscionable clause as to avoid any unconscionable result. Although this provision is technically limited to the sales of goods, courts have applied it more broadly. Moreover, although the doctrine is well established, it is applied sparingly. The unconscionability doctrine applies as of the time the contract was made. Broadly, the analysis of unconscionability is divided into substantive unconscionability and procedural unconscionability. Substantive unconscionability looks to a contract's terms and asks whether they are so extreme as to appear unconscionable according to the mores and business practices of the time and place. Procedural unconscionability examines the procedures that led to the contract with the goal of evaluating whether seemingly lopsided terms might have resulted from arms-length bargaining. Courts focus on the relative bargaining strength of the parties and whether the weaker party could make a meaningful choice. The concept is broadly conceived to encompass not only the employment of sharp bargaining practices and the use of fine print and convoluted language, but a lack of understanding and an inequity of bargaining power. These two facets of unconscionability do not function as separate elements of a two-prong test. Instead, the analysis is unitary, and if more of one is present, then less of the other is required. In this state, six factors relate to the concept of substantive unconscionability. The first is a significant cost-price disparity or excessive price. Although inadequacy of consideration does not of itself invalidate a bargain, gross disparity in the values exchanged may be an important factor in a determination that a contract in unconscionable. Here, there are obvious indications of unfairness. The Loan Agreement called for finance charges of $1,620 for a $200 loan, resulting in a disclosed APR of 838.45 percent. That level of pricing shocks the conscience. Additionally, the economic terms of the Disputed Loan are so extreme as to suggest fundamental unfairness. The price of the Disputed Loan is particularly egregious given its multi-period, non-amortizing structure. The finance charges incurred over the course of the loan are so high that no rational borrower would agree to pay them, unless under duress or operating under a misapprehension of fact. The first factor is, therefore, satisfied. The next four factors focus on contract provisions that can contribute to a finding of unfairness. They include provisions that deny or waive "basic rights and remedies," "penalty clauses," and "disadvantageous" clauses that are hidden or difficult to identify and understand. The sixth factor asks more generally whether the contract provisions evidence an overall imbalance in the obligations and rights imposed by the bargain. Specific provisions might not be unconscionable in isolation or under different circumstances, yet still may contribute to a finding of unconscionability in a given case. Here, these factors are also satisfied. National (D) imposed onerous financial terms and gave itself the right to collect unilaterally from James (P) any amount it wished, up to the full amount of the loan plus fees and charges. National (D) ensured that in any challenge to the Disputed Loan, James (P) would not be able to represent a class. She would have to challenge National (D) alone, based on a loan where the amount in question would make the representation economically irrational for a lawyer unless the lawyer could recover the lawyer's fees from National (D). Moreover, unless James (P) opted out of the arbitration provision within 60 days—something that no customer other than James (P) had ever done—then James (P) would have to challenge the Disputed Loan in arbitration, which was National's (D) chosen forum. Taken as a whole, for purposes of these factors, the Loan Agreement evidences an overall imbalance in the obligations and rights imposed by the bargain. The remaining four factors pertain to procedural unconscionability. These are:

Continued on next page.

inequality of bargaining or economic power; exploitation of the underprivileged, unsophisticated, uneducated, and illiterate; the use of printed form or boilerplate contracts drawn skillfully by the party in the strongest economic position, which establish industry-wide standards offered on a take it or leave it basis to the party in a weaker economic position; and the circumstances surrounding the execution of the contract, including its commercial setting, its purpose, and actual effect. These factors help a court test the degree to which a seemingly disproportionate outcome could have resulted from legitimate, arms-length bargaining. The first and second factors plumb this issue by considering the extent to which the parties to the agreement were capable of bargaining at arms-length. A court rarely will intervene when the contracting parties are both commercial entities or otherwise sophisticated. By contrast, a court may be more concerned where the contracting process involved significant inequalities of bargaining power, economic power, or sophistication, particularly between a business and a consumer. An aggravated version of this scenario arises when one of the parties is an individual who is underprivileged, uneducated, or illiterate. The third and fourth factors similarly contribute by examining the degree to which actual bargaining took place. The third factor considers whether the agreement is a contract of adhesion. The fourth factor takes into account the contracting environment, including the commercial setting and the purpose and effect of the disputed agreement. As to the first factor, National (D) specializes in providing high interest loans to underprivileged consumers who are cash-constrained and lack alternative sources of credit, and its owner and personnel are financially sophisticated and knowledgeable. On the other hand, James (P) is unsophisticated and undereducated. She did not understand how interest accrued, she did not understand what would happen upon default, and she underestimated her likelihood of repaying the Disputed Loan quickly. These attributes of the respective parties favor a finding of unconscionability. The next factor asks directly whether there was actual bargaining involved. Although a contract of adhesion is not unconscionable per se, and not all unconscionable contracts are contracts of adhesion, where a contract is one of adhesion, it is more likely that the agreement will be found to be unconscionable. Here, the Loan Agreement was a contract of adhesion. It was a form agreement, drafted by National (D), and provided to James (P) on a take-it-or-leave-it basis, with James (P) having no ability to negotiate its terms. Thus, this factor favors a finding of unconscionability. The final factor considers the circumstances surrounding the contract's execution. Here, James (P) was given standardized forms in a small storefront and was told where to sign. These conditions are not inherently oppressive. More problematic is that National's (D) employees denigrated the APR's importance while describing the interest rate in simplistic ways designed to mislead customers. Even more significant was that James (P) lacked a meaningful choice. Another critical aspect of the bargaining environment was that the purpose and effect of the Loan Agreement was to evade the Payday Loan Law. On balance, all these factors favor a finding of unconscionability, although to varying degrees. The factors that primarily suggest unconscionability are: (i) the economic terms of the Disputed Loan, (ii) the purpose and effect of the installment loan structure in circumventing the Payday Loan Law, and (iii) the exploitation of an underprivileged, undereducated, and financially vulnerable person. Secondary factors include (a) the use of a contract of adhesion, (b) the overall imbalance of rights and obligations, and (c) National's (D) practices when describing the block rate finance charge versus the APR, which presented a misleading picture of the cost of credit. In sum, and on balance, the Loan Agreement was unconscionable: no one would borrow rationally on the terms the Loan Agreement contemplated unless that person was delusional, mistaken about its terms or a material fact, or under economic duress. The proper remedy is to declare the Loan Agreement invalid and to rescind it. Invalidation of the Loan Agreement is likewise appropriate because National (D) sought to use an interest-only, non-amortizing, installment loan to evade the Payday Loan Law. In substance, the Disputed Loan was a payday loan designed to roll over 26 times, which contravened the law's five loan limit. Because James (P) repaid \$197 of the \$200 loan, James (P) owes National (D) \$3. James (P) also asked for a permanent injunction barring National (D) from collecting on similar loans it made to other customers. That relief is too broad to be granted in the current case and would embroil the court in ongoing oversight of National's (D) business. However, because James (P) also proved that National (D) violated the Truth-in-Lending Act (TILA), which provides for twice the amount of an illegal finance charge to be awarded as attorneys' fees and statutory damages, James (P) was entitled to \$3,240. Subtracting the \$3 James (P) owes to National (D) results in an award to James (P) of \$3,237, along with pre- and post-judgment interest, and attorneys' fees and costs. Judgment for James (P).

ANALYSIS

Although, as the court indicates, a contract of adhesion may signal an unconscionable contract, contracts of adhesion provide many benefits, as standardization of agreements can serve many of the same functions as standardization of goods and services; they are essential to a system of mass production and distribution. Through use of adhesion contracts, scarce and costly time and skill can be devoted to a class of transactions rather than to details of individual transactions. Legal rules that would apply in the absence of agreement can be shaped

Continued on next page.

to fit the particular type of transaction, and extra copies of the form can be used for purposes such as record-keeping, coordination, and supervision. Thus, adhesion contracts may simplify operations and reduce costs, to the advantage of all concerned. On the other hand, such contracts also carry a heightened risk of unfair terms, since standardized agreements are commonly prepared by one party, and the customer assents to a few terms, typically inserted in blanks on the printed form, and gives blanket assent to the type of transaction embodied in the standard form. The customer is commonly not represented in the drafting, and the drafter may be tempted to overdraw in the interest of the contract's provider. This dynamic creates a danger of overreaching.

Quicknotes

ADHESION CONTRACT A contract that is not negotiated and is usually prepared by the dominant party on a "take it or leave it" basis.

U.C.C. § 2-302 Provides that courts exercise their discretion to limit specific contract provisions that have unconscionable results.

UNCONSCIONABILITY Rule of law whereby a court may excuse performance of a contract, or of a particular contract term, if it determines that such terms are unduly oppressive or unfair to one party to the contract as a result of disparity in bargaining power during the formation of the contract.

Pinter v. Dahl

Seller (D) v. Buyer (P)

486 U.S. 622 (1988)

NATURE OF CASE: Appeal of a judgment allowing rescission of a securities transaction.

FACT SUMMARY: Pinter (D) sought to defend an action for rescission under federal securities laws on the basis that Dahl (P), the buyer, was equally at fault for the illegality.

RULE OF LAW

Defendants may use the *in pari delicto* defense only when the plaintiff is an active and voluntary participant in the unlawful activity that is the subject of the suit.

FACTS: Pinter (D), an oil and gas producer, met with Dahl (P), a real estate broker, about investing in oil and gas leases. Dahl (P) invested $310,000 in Pinter's (D) Black Gold Oil Company to acquire properties. Dahl (P) then solicited other purchasers to invest money in the venture but received no commission in connection with these investments. Pinter (D) subsequently sold the participating interests without registering them under the Securities Act. When the venture failed, Dahl (P) filed suit against Pinter (D) seeking rescission for selling unregistered securities. The trial court denied Pinter's (D) *in pari delicto* defense that Dahl (P) should not recover because he was equally at fault. Pinter (D) appealed.

ISSUE: May defendants use the *in pari delicto* defense only when the plaintiff is an active and voluntary participant in the unlawful activity that is the subject of the suit?

HOLDING AND DECISION: (Blackmun, J.) No. Defendants may use the *in pari delicto* defense only when the plaintiff is an active and voluntary participant in the unlawful activity that is the subject of the suit. The equitable defense of *in pari delicto*, which literally means "in equal fault," is rooted in the common law notion that a plaintiff's recovery may be barred by the plaintiff's own wrongful conduct. Traditionally, the defense was limited to situations in which the plaintiff bore at least substantially equal responsibility for the injury and where their culpability arose out of the same illegal act. Now the *in pari delicto* defense is applied to situations encompassed under the "unclean hands" doctrine. This doctrine is premised on the ground that judicial relief should be denied to wrongdoers as an effective means of deterring illegality. In order to have substantially equal responsibility, the plaintiff must be an active, voluntary participant in the unlawful activity that is the subject of the suit, and the degree of fault must be essentially indistinguishable. In the context of an action under federal securities laws against selling unregistered securities, a purchaser's knowledge that the securities are unregistered cannot, by itself, constitute equal culpability. There must be some degree of cooperation between the seller and the buyer in carrying out the scheme. Additionally, *in pari delicto* defense is not available when there would be interference with the underlying purpose of the securities laws. Precluding suits by plaintiffs who are primarily investors would interfere with enforcement of securities laws. Thus, the plaintiff's role in the offering or sale of unregistered securities must be more as a promoter than as an investor in order to invoke the *in pari delicto* defense. The record in this case does not indicate whether Dahl's (P) participation rose to the level necessary for Pinter (D) to assert the *in pari delicto* defense. Vacated and remanded.

ANALYSIS

As the decision noted, the *in pari delicto* defense is very similar to the unclean-hands maxim of equity. While the unclean-hands defense may be asserted only in equitable actions, *in pari delicto* is available as a defense in legal suits, such as the one for damages in Dahl's (P) complaint. For a discussion of unclean hands, see Zechariah Chafee, Jr., "Coming into Equity with Clean Hands," 47 *Mich. L. Rev.* 877 (1949).

Quicknotes

IN PARI DELICTO Doctrine that a court will not enforce an illegal contract in an action for losses incurred as a result of the breach of that contract; the parties are at equal fault or guilt.

UNCLEAN HANDS Equitable doctrine denying relief to a party who seeks a remedy in relation to an action in which the party did not act fairly.

Geddes v. Mill Creek Country Club, Inc.

Individual (P) v. Golf course owner (D)

Ill. Sup. Ct., 751 N.E.2d 1150 (2001)

NATURE OF CASE: Appeal from judgment in trespass and nuisance action in favor of defendant.

FACT SUMMARY: Due to the invasion of his property by golf balls from an adjacent course operated by Mill Creek Country Club, Inc. (D), Geddes (P) brought suit for trespass and nuisance.

RULE OF LAW

When a person by their statements and conduct leads a party to undertake an action the party otherwise would not, the person is equitably estopped from asserting rights that might otherwise have existed.

FACTS: Geddes (P) owned a business adjacent to Mill Creek Country Club's (Club's) (D) golf course. During the development of the golf course project, Geddes (P) and other abutters were consulted regarding the design of the project. After planners accommodated his wishes regarding placement of a fairway, Geddes (P) supported the project before a county planning committee. Later, Geddes (P) brought suit for trespass and nuisance when golf balls from the fairway began to invade his property. The trial court held that the golf course was not a nuisance and rejected Geddes's (P) request to enjoin use of the fairway. The court of appeals affirmed, and Geddes (P) appealed.

ISSUE: When a person by their statements and conduct leads a party to undertake an action the party otherwise would not, is the person equitably estopped from asserting rights that might otherwise have existed?

HOLDING AND DECISION: (Freeman, J.) Yes. When a person by their statements and conduct leads a party to undertake an action the party otherwise would not, the person is equitably estopped from asserting rights that might otherwise have existed. Here, it is not required that Geddes (P) intended to mislead or deceive the Club (D), though fraud is an essential element of an equitable estoppel claim. It is sufficient that injustice would result in allowing Geddes (P) to induce the Club (D) to make changes in the project, only later to assert claims of nuisance and trespass caused by his own inducement. Geddes (P) knowingly agreed with the developer's placement of the fairway and is thus equitably estopped from complaining about errant golf balls hit onto his property. Affirmed.

ANALYSIS

Several different formulations of the test for equitable estoppel exist, ranging from three to six elements. The tests each have in common detrimental reliance by party *A* upon an act or statement by party *B* that is inconsistent with a right subsequently asserted by party *B*.

Quicknotes

EQUITABLE ESTOPPEL An equitable doctrine that precludes a person from asserting a right to which the person was entitled, resulting from their action, conduct, or failure to act, that caused another party to justifiably rely on such action, conduct, or failure to act to their detriment.

ESTOPPEL An equitable doctrine precluding a party from asserting a right to the detriment of another who justifiably relied on the conduct.

Carr-Gottstein Foods Co. v. Wasilla, LLC

Tenant (D) v. Landlord (P)

Alaska Sup. Ct., 182 P.3d 1131 (2008)

NATURE OF CASE: Appeal from lower court decision in favor of landlord.

FACT SUMMARY: Wasilla, an affiliate of CG Properties (P), alleged Carr-Gottstein Foods Co. (D) breached its lease by subleasing a portion of a supermarket to a liquor store without CG Properties' (P) approval.

RULE OF LAW

When one party to a contract is aware of conduct by the other party that may constitute a breach but fails to protest that breach, that failure may constitute a waiver of the right to bring a claim for breach of contract.

FACTS: Carr-Gottstein Foods Co. (CG Foods) (D) operated a supermarket under a lease with Wasilla, an affiliate of CG Properties (P). The lease allowed CG Foods (D) to operate a general food supermarket. Under the lease, CG Foods (D) could not sublease any portion of the leased premises without CG Properties' consent. In 1996, CG Foods (D) brought a liquor store, Oaken Keg, into the premises. CG Properties (P) did not object but had its subsidiary perform the electrical work at the liquor store. The liquor store sales were reported to CG Properties on a monthly basis. In 2002, Safeway purchased CG Foods (D). At that time, CG Properties (P) alleged the liquor store lease constituted a breach of CG Foods' (D) lease. Litigation ensued and the trial court found that CG Properties (P) did not impliedly waive the prohibition against subleases. The trial court expressly overruled a jury sitting in an advisory capacity that found the opposite. CG Foods (D) appealed.

ISSUE: When one party to a contract is aware of conduct by the other party that may constitute a breach but fails to protest that breach, may that failure constitute a waiver of the right to bring a claim for breach of contract?

HOLDING AND DECISION: (Matthews, J.) Yes. When one party to a contract is aware of conduct by the other party that may constitute a breach but fails to protest that breach, that failure may constitute a waiver of the right to bring a claim for breach of contract. Waiver is the intentional relinquishment of a known right. It can be express or implied. Implied waiver exists where one party's conduct evidences an intention to waive the strict adherence to a contract provision. Here, CG Properties' (P) conduct constituted a waiver. It did not object to the sublease. Its own electrical subcontractor performed the work at the liquor store. CG Foods (D) submitted monthly sales amounts to CG Properties (P). Those facts, together with CG Properties' six years of acquiescence, prove as a matter of law that waiver occurred. Moreover, the non-waiver clause in the lease covered only other, future acts of the tenant. The clause only applies to future actions based on CG Properties' (P) waiver of the sublease prohibition in the past. For example, CG Foods (D) could not bring in a second liquor store onto the premises based on CG Properties' (P) failure to object to the first liquor store. However, the nonwaiver clause does not, by its terms, apply to the first liquor store. Reversed and remanded.

ANALYSIS

The court's analysis presents a generally accepted application of the law regarding waiver. However, its application of the non-waiver clause is less clear. Commercial property owners (and other parties) use non-waiver clauses in contracts to protect themselves against the factual circumstances present in this case. However, the court held the clause did not apply to this case based on the language that it only applied to other, future actions, and not all instances of waiver.

Quicknotes

BREACH OF CONTRACT Unlawful failure by a party to perform its obligations pursuant to contract.

WAIVER The intentional or voluntary forfeiture of a recognized right.

Arizona Libertarian Party v. Reagan

Political party (P) v. State official (D)

189 F. Supp. 3d 920 (D. Ariz. 2016)

NATURE OF CASE: Emergency motion for temporary restraining order and preliminary injunction to bar enforcement of certain election laws in action challenging the constitutionality of those laws.

FACT SUMMARY: The Arizona Libertarian Party (AZLP) (P) and its candidate (P), in an action challenging the constitutionality of certain election laws, filed an emergency motion for a temporary restraining order and preliminary injunction to bar the state's Secretary of State (Secretary) (D), from enforcing the challenged laws. The Secretary (D) asserted laches as defense.

RULE OF LAW

Laches will bar a request for emergency relief where the plaintiff has unreasonably delayed seeking such relief to the prejudice of the defendant and to the administration of justice.

FACTS: In 2015, Arizona amended its election laws, effective July 3, 2015, in a way that made it more difficult for the Arizona Libertarian Party (AZLP) (P) to get on the ballot. By August 2015, the AZLP (P) knew that it would be challenging the amendments, and the grounds for their challenge. On March 21, 2016, Arizona's Secretary of State (Secretary) (D)—the official responsible for administering elections—released the petition signature requirements for 2016. In 2016, the deadline for candidates to submit nomination petitions was June 1, 2016. The deadline for candidates to file as write-in candidates was July 21, 2016, and the primary election was scheduled for August 30, 2016. The AZLP (P) brought suit in federal district court on April 12, 2016, seeking to require the Secretary (D) to place their candidates on the primary election ballot if, by the June 1, 2016, deadline, they submitted nomination petitions containing the number of signatures required before the 2015 election law amendments. In its action challenging the constitutionality of the amendments, the AZLP (P) filed an emergency motion for a temporary restraining order and preliminary injunction on May 12, 2016. The Secretary (D) asserted laches as a defense, claiming that AZLP's (P) delay in bringing suit and asserting their emergency motion was prejudicial.

ISSUE: Will laches bar a request for emergency relief where the plaintiff has unreasonably delayed seeking such relief to the prejudice of the defendant and to the administration of justice?

HOLDING AND DECISION: (Campbell, J.) Yes. Laches will bar a request for emergency relief where the plaintiff has unreasonably delayed seeking such relief to the prejudice of the defendant and to the administration of justice. Laches applies when there is both unreasonable delay and prejudice. In the context of election matters, the laches doctrine seeks to prevent dilatory conduct and will bar a claim if a party's unreasonable delay prejudices the opposing party or the administration of justice. To determine whether delay was unreasonable, a court considers the justification for the delay, the extent of the plaintiff's advance knowledge of the basis for the challenge, and whether the plaintiff exercised diligence in preparing and advancing the case. To determine whether delay has prejudiced a defendant, a court considers only prejudice that stems from the plaintiff's delay in bringing suit, as defendants are entitled to reasonable time to consider and develop their case. To determine whether delay has prejudiced the administration of justice, a court considers prejudice to the courts, candidates, citizens who signed petitions, election officials, and voters. Here, the AZLP (P) knew as early as August 2015 the grounds for its challenge to the 2015 amendments. Despite this knowledge, they did not file their complaint until around eight months later; and they did not file their "emergency" motion for a temporary restraining order until less than three weeks before the deadline for nomination petitions. As a result, the court has been forced to set an expedited briefing schedule and hold a hearing on AZLP's (P) motion only eight days before the deadline. AZLP (P) argues that this delay was justified by the Secretary's (D) unreasonable delay in releasing the 2016 petition signature requirements on March 21, 2016. This argument is unconvincing. First, the Secretary (D) did not delay unreasonably. The Secretary (D) was required by statute to use March 1, 2016, voter registration data to calculate the primary election signature requirements. Second, AZLP's (P) own complaint and exhibits show that they had access to the necessary information months before the Secretary's (D) release of the signature requirements. AZLP (P) also cited the Secretary's (D) January 2016 voter registration statistics. Even a cursory examination of this data reveals that the 2015 amendments significantly increased the number of signatures AZLP (P) candidates had to obtain to secure a place on the primary ballot. This evidence fully supports the claims made by AZLP (P) in this case—that AZLP (P) members were required to obtain an unconstitutionally high percentage of signatures from AZLP (P) members, or to seek signatures from non-AZLP voters. Plaintiffs were not required

Continued on next page.

to wait for the March 21, 2016, numbers before asserting these arguments. Thus, they have not provided an adequate justification for their delay. To the contrary, the Secretary (D) argues persuasively that AZLP's (P) unreasonable delay prejudiced her ability to fully develop facts and arguments for the court's consideration in ruling on AZLP's (P) emergency motion. More importantly, AZLP's (P) delay has prejudiced the administration of justice. Their delay left the court with only 18 days before the petition-submission deadline to obtain briefing, hold a hearing, evaluate the relevant constitutional law, rule on AZLP's (P) motion, and advise the Secretary (D) and the candidates which statutory petition requirement applied. Moreover, signature gathering has been well under way, and nomination petitions were due in a week. Candidates who had been collecting signatures under the current law could be greatly disadvantaged by any injunctive relief that would change the rules at the last minute. For the foregoing reasons, the doctrine of laches will be applied. In some cases, laches requires dismissal of the entire claim, whereas in others it justifies only the denial of expedited relief. At issue is a challenge to a signature requirement that will continue to apply in future elections if it is not invalidated by a court or revised by the legislature. This is different than a challenge to a ballot proposition that will either be passed or defeated in the election. Accordingly, laches should bar only AZLP's (P) request for emergency relief, but the merits of the case may continue without the prejudice caused by the late-filed request for that relief. AZLP's (P) emergency motion for a temporary restraining order and preliminary injunction is denied. Judgment for the Secretary (D).

ANALYSIS

As the court emphasizes in this case, the hallmarks of laches are delay that is prejudicial to the opposing party and to the administration of justice, and that is unreasonable. The unreasonableness of delay is partly determined by the passing of time, as well as the reasons for the delay. In instances where a plaintiff neither knows, nor has no reason to know, they have a claim, delay is not deemed unreasonable. However, even unsophisticated plaintiffs may lose their claims if they have not been sufficiently diligent. Further, the inability to find or pay an attorney, alone, does not justify delay, although this factor may be considered if there are other legally cognizable excuses present.

Quicknotes

LACHES An equitable defense against the enforcement of rights that have been neglected for a long period of time.

TEMPORARY RESTRAINING ORDER A court order preserving the status quo pending a hearing regarding injunctive relief.

Klehr v. A.O. Smith Corp.

Individual (P) v. Corporation (D)

521 U.S. 179 (1997)

NATURE OF THE CASE: Appeal from summary judgment in favor of defendant in Racketeer Influenced and Corrupt Organizations Act (RICO) case.

FACT SUMMARY: Nearly 20 years after purchasing a feed silo from Smith (D), Klehr (P) discovered a serious design flaw and filed suit alleging mail and wire fraud and RICO violations.

RULE OF LAW

The statute of limitations does not begin to run on a claim based upon the date of the defendant's last predicate act.

FACTS: Based upon representations made by seller Smith (D), Klehr (P), a dairy farmer, purchased a feed silo in 1974. Nearly 20 years later, Klehr (P) discovered the representations that the silo would limit the intake of oxygen and that the growth of mold were untrue. Klehr (P) filed suit against Smith (D) for mail and wire fraud and violations of the Racketeer Influenced and Corrupt Organizations Act (RICO). The district court granted summary judgment in favor of Smith (D), finding the claims barred by the relevant statutes of limitation. The Eighth Circuit affirmed, and the United States Supreme Court granted review.

ISSUE: Does the statute of limitations begin to run on a claim based upon the date of the defendant's last predicate act?

HOLDING AND DECISION: (Breyer, J.) No. The statute of limitations does not begin to run on a claim based upon the date of the defendant's last predicate act. The last predicate act rule improperly creates a limitations period that is longer than legislatively intended. A series of such acts could continue indefinitely and significantly lengthen the limitations period, thereby thwarting the objective of repose. In cases of a continuing violation, each new act that causes the plaintiff a new injury recommences the statutory period, regardless of the plaintiff's earlier knowledge. Here, Klehr (P) failed to demonstrate how any new act could have caused the harm over and above the earlier acts. Affirmed.

ANALYSIS

The continuing-violation doctrine has caused a great deal of confusion in lower courts. Here, the fraudulent sale was a one-time event, making it a relatively clear case. The objective of repose is one closely guarded by judges. To allow the last predicate act rule, in the eyes of the Supreme Court, would make it possible for a plaintiff who knows of a pattern of activity to sleep on their rights until the most advantageous time to bring suit.

Quicknotes

RACKETEER INFLUENCED AND CORRUPT ORGANIZATIONS ACT (RICO) Federal and state statutes enacted for the purpose of prosecuting organized crime.

STATUTE OF LIMITATIONS A law prescribing the period in which a legal action may be commenced.

Debiec v. Cabot Corp.

Individuals (P) v. Corporation (D)

352 F.3d 117 (3d Cir. 2003)

NATURE OF CASE: Appeal from granting of summary judgment to defendant.

FACT SUMMARY: This case involves two wrongful death claims and two personal injury actions against Cabot (D) on the grounds Cabot's (D) use of beryllium caused the claimants to contract Chronic Beryllium Disease (CBD).

RULE OF LAW

In latent disease cases, the statute of limitations begins to run when a plaintiff knows or reasonably should know that they have suffered an injury and that the injury was caused by another.

FACTS: Four individuals, Debiec (P), Russo (P), Bare (P), and Branco (P), either worked at or lived near Cabot's (D) beryllium plant. They all contracted Chronic Beryllium Disease (CBD). Debiec (P) and Bare (P) died from the disease in 2000. Cabot (D) moved successfully in district court for summary judgment on the grounds the two-year statute of limitations had run on each of the four claims. Russo (P), Branco (P), and the estates of Debiec (P) and Bare (P) all appealed on the grounds that pursuant to the discovery rule, their claims accrued within the two years before the filing of their claims. [Additional facts specific to each plaintiff are discussed below.]

ISSUE: In latent disease cases, does the statute of limitations begin to run when a plaintiff knows or reasonably should know that they have suffered an injury and that the injury was caused by another?

HOLDING AND DECISION: (Becker, J.) Yes. In latent disease cases, the statute of limitations begins to run when a plaintiff knows or reasonably should know that they have suffered an injury and that the injury was caused by another. For this discovery rule to apply, a plaintiff must exercise due diligence to investigate the cause of their physical condition. In cases involving medical diagnoses, a plaintiff cannot be charged with having more information about their condition than their doctor has. Pennsylvania has a two-year statute of limitations for tort claims. Debiec's (P) doctor diagnosed her with sarcoidosis, a lung disease, in 1978. She died in 2000. The doctor never changed his diagnosis until her autopsy revealed she suffered from CBD. Cabot (D) alleges that Debiec's (P) husband and brother-in-law did significant research into a possible connection between her condition and beryllium. However, based on the fact her own doctor never wavered in 22 years that she did not have CBD, reasonable minds could differ on whether she diligently pursued the cause of her injury. The district court should not have granted summary judgment to Cabot (D) on her claim. Russo (P) filed her claim on May 24, 2001. Cabot (D) argues her claim accrued on April 12, 1999, when she read a newspaper article linking the Cabot (D) plant to CBD. However, as with Debiec (P), two doctors informed Russo (P) that she did not suffer from CBD. Based on these factual disputes, the district court should not have granted summary judgment to Cabot (D) on her claim. Bare (P) died from CBD on November 2, 2000. In the mid-1990s, Bare had asked her doctors about the possibility that her condition was CBD and that it may have been caused by the emissions from Cabot's (D) plant. There was some deposition testimony from Bare's daughter that her mother may have known about tests to confirm CBD. However, her daughter could not confirm that Bare's (P) doctor ever actually told Bare (P) about the tests. Without that evidence, there is a dispute of fact whether Bare (P) took reasonable steps to pursue her claim diligently. The district court should not have granted summary judgment to Cabot (D) on her claim. Conversely, Branco's (P) claim accrued beyond the two-year statute of limitations. Branco (P) underwent tests both in 1995 and 1997 that were negative for CBD. However, the evidence showed that his doctors informed him the tests were unreliable and that he should have undergone further testing at that time for CBD. Also, in May of 1995, Branco (P), who worked at the plant for 33 years, received a packet of information from the Department of Health and Human Services that he was under risk for CBD by virtue of his employment at the plant. These facts prove that Branco (P) has sufficient notice by 1997 that his condition was CBD. The district court properly granted summary judgment to Cabot (D) on his claim. Reversed in part, affirmed in part, and remanded.

CONCURRENCE AND DISSENT: (Ambro, J.) The Pennsylvania tolling rule regarding medical diagnosis should only apply where a doctor definitively informs a plaintiff that they do not have the illness in question and common sense would not make the plaintiff's reliance on that diagnosis unreasonable. The majority improperly reversed on Debiec's (P) claim. The efforts of her husband and brother-in-law, who wrote a research paper linking sarcoidosis to CBD, should have put her on notice well before 2001 that her condition was possibly CBD and that emissions from Cabot (D) were likely the cause of it. Moreover, there is no evidence that after her

Continued on next page.

doctor first misdiagnosed her condition in 1978 that he ever reaffirmed that diagnosis again. The majority's conclusion regarding the other three claimants was proper.

ANALYSIS

The discovery rule serves to mitigate the sometimes-harsh effects of the statute of limitations, which cuts off all recovery after a certain timeframe. Most states have three-year statutes of limitations on tort actions, but Pennsylvania's is only two years. The discovery rule therefore becomes even more important.

Quicknotes

DISCOVERY RULE A cause of action accrues when a plaintiff knows or reasonably should know that they have suffered an injury and that the injury was caused by another.

Knaysi v. A.H. Robins Co.

Individual (P) v. Corporation (D)

679 F.2d 1366 (11th Cir. 1982)

NATURE OF CASE: Appeal from summary judgment denying damages for fraud and products liability.

FACT SUMMARY: Knaysi (P) contended A.H. Robins Co. (D) was equitably estopped from asserting the statute of limitations as a defense to a suit for fraud and products liability.

RULE OF LAW

Equitable estoppel sufficient to bar the application of the statute of limitations results from fraudulent concealment of an action that is unknown to a party.

FACTS: Knaysi (P) sued A.H. Robins Co. (Robins) (D), contending the company knew of the dangers inherent in using its Dalkon Shield and intentionally suppressed such information. As a result of using such a device, Knaysi (P) had miscarried twin fetuses. Robins (D) successfully moved for summary judgment on the basis that the fraud claim could not be separated from the products liability action, and such was barred by the statute of limitations. Knaysi (P) appealed, contending Robins (D) was equitably estopped from asserting the statute of limitations as a defense.

ISSUE: Does equitable estoppel sufficient to bar the application of the statute of limitations result from fraudulent concealment of an action that is unknown to a party?

HOLDING AND DECISION: (Hill, J.) Yes. Equitable estoppel sufficient to bar the application of the statute of limitations results from fraudulent concealment of an action that is unknown to a party. In this case the medical community and the consuming public relied on Robins's (D) misrepresentations concerning the safety of the product. This misrepresentation creates a question of fact regarding the application of the doctrine of equitable estoppel. Thus, summary judgment should not have been granted. Reversed and remanded.

DISSENT: (Tjoflat, J.) The plaintiff failed to meet her burden of establishing justifiable reliance on Robins's (D) alleged misrepresentations. Thus, no question of fact was raised; Robins is entitled to summary judgment.

ANALYSIS

As can be seen by this case, equity can be used to bypass the statute of limitations on legal claims for damages. Equity will not allow the unfairness of fraudulent concealment to preclude an assertion of rights. A minority view goes farther in holding fraudulent concealment equitably estops application of a statute of limitations regardless of the plaintiff's diligence.

Quicknotes

EQUITABLE ESTOPPEL An equitable doctrine that precludes a person from asserting a right to which the person was entitled, resulting from their action, conduct, or failure to act, that caused another party to justifiably rely on such action, conduct, or failure to act to their detriment.

STATUTE OF LIMITATIONS A law prescribing the period in which a legal action may be commenced.

STRICT PRODUCT LIABILITY Liability of a manufacturer or seller of a product for injuries sustained as a result of any defects without the necessity of a showing of negligence.

SUMMARY JUDGMENT Judgment rendered by a court in response to a motion made by one of the parties, claiming that the lack of a question of material fact in respect to an issue warrants disposition of the issue without consideration by the jury.

CHAPTER 12

Fluid-Class and Cy Pres Remedies

Quick Reference Rules of Law

PAGE

1. *In re Pharmaceutical Industry Average Wholesale Price Litigation.* Courts may approve class action settlements that include the creation of a cy pres fund used for a charitable purpose related to the class plaintiffs' alleged injuries. *162*

In re Pharmaceutical Industry Average Wholesale Price Litigation

[Drug patients (P) v. Pharmaceutical company (D)]

588 F.3d 24 (1st Cir. 2009)

NATURE OF CASE: Appeal from lower court decision to approve settlement plan.

FACT SUMMARY: A drug company, AstraZeneca (D), overcharged the class of patients by allegedly inflating the average wholesale price of the drug Zoladex.

RULE OF LAW

Courts may approve class action settlements that include the creation of a cy pres fund used for a charitable purpose related to the class plaintiffs' alleged injuries.

FACTS: Insurance companies typically reimburse doctors for the average wholesale price of a drug. In the early 1990s, in order to induce doctors to prescribe their drugs, AstraZeneca (D) fraudulently inflated the wholesale price. AstraZeneca (D) then told the participating doctors that they could keep the difference between the price the doctors charged and the inflated amount the doctors received back from the insurance companies. A class of patients sued AstraZeneca (D) for fraud. Some of the plaintiffs paid four percent of the average wholesale price while others paid higher percentages based on their respective insurance plans. There was no dispute as to liability. After a long negotiation, AstraZeneca (D) agreed to pay $24 million. The court ordered that each class member would receive three times their amount of damages. The parties also agreed to create a cy pres fund for the amount that went unclaimed. The parties anticipated that roughly $6.8 million would go unclaimed and into the cy pres funds for charitable purposes. One member of the class, Howe (P), objected to the cy pres fund on the grounds all of the funds should be turned over to the claimants that could be identified. The district court approved the plan and Howe (P) appealed.

ISSUE: May courts approve class action settlements that include the creation of a cy pres fund used for a charitable purpose related to the class plaintiffs' alleged injuries?

HOLDING AND DECISION: (Lynch, C.J.) Yes. Courts may approve class action settlements that include the creation of a cy pres fund used for a charitable purpose related to the class plaintiffs' alleged injuries. Courts should approve class action settlements only if they are reasonable. The courts have wide latitude to approve such settlements and those approvals are reviewed on an abuse of discretion standard. The use of a cy pres fund comes from trusts and estates law. Cy pres means "as near as possible." Howe (P) claims use of the cy pres fund takes money away from the class members. This argument overlooks the district courts order that all claimants must receive three times their calculated damages (based on amount of drugs they purchased and amount they paid to cover the inflated average wholesale price). Affirmed.

ANALYSIS

The case law surrounding use of cy pres funds in class action lawsuits has essentially rested on consideration of practical issues. These issues include the realization that not all members of the class will collect their damages, the costs associated with finding those members, and the costs of distributing the funds. Because settlements are highly encouraged, the use of cy pres funds is almost always approved. However, such funds have yet to be challenged on constitutional grounds that they may infringe upon an individual claimant's right to a full and fair trial.

Quicknotes

CLASS ACTION A suit commenced by a representative on behalf of an ascertainable group that has the same claim as the representative (the "class") but is too large to appear in court and for whose members pursuing the claim individually might not be worthwhile, where the representative shares a commonality of interests with the group, will vigorously represent the group, and will benefit from a successful result.

CY PRES DOCTRINE Equitable doctrine applied in order to give effect to an instrument as close to the drafter's intent as possible without violating the law, which effect would be unlawful if strictly enforced.

Glossary

Common Latin Words and Phrases Encountered in the Law

A FORTIORI: Because one fact exists or has been proven, therefore a second fact that is related to the first fact must also exist.

A PRIORI: From the cause to the effect. A term of logic used to denote that when one generally accepted truth is shown to be a cause, another particular effect must necessarily follow.

AB INITIO: From the beginning; a condition that has existed throughout, as in a marriage that was void ab initio.

ACTUS REUS: The wrongful act; in criminal law, such action sufficient to trigger criminal liability.

AD VALOREM: According to value; an ad valorem tax is imposed upon an item located within the taxing jurisdiction calculated by the value of such item.

AMICUS CURIAE: Friend of the court. Its most common usage takes the form of an amicus curiae brief, filed by a person who is not a party to an action but is nonetheless allowed to offer an argument supporting their legal interests.

ARGUENDO: In arguing. A statement, possibly hypothetical, made for the purpose of argument is one made arguendo.

BILL QUIA TIMET: A bill to quiet title (establish ownership) to real property.

BONA FIDE: True, honest, or genuine. May refer to a person's legal position based on good faith or lacking notice of fraud (such as a bona fide purchaser for value) or to the authenticity of a particular document (such as a bona fide last will and testament).

CAUSA MORTIS: With approaching death in mind. A gift causa mortis is a gift given by a party who feels certain that death is imminent.

CAVEAT EMPTOR: Let the buyer beware. This maxim is reflected in the rule of law that a buyer purchases at their own risk because it is their responsibility to examine, judge, test, and otherwise inspect what they are buying.

CERTIORARI: A writ of review. Petitions for review of a case by the United States Supreme Court are most often done by means of a writ of certiorari.

CONTRA: On the other hand. Opposite. Contrary to.

CORAM NOBIS: Before us; writs of error directed to the court that originally rendered the judgment.

CORAM VOBIS: Before you; writs of error directed by an appellate court to a lower court to correct a factual error.

CORPUS DELICTI: The body of the crime; the requisite elements of a crime amounting to objective proof that a crime has been committed.

CUM TESTAMENTO ANNEXO, ADMINISTRATOR (ADMINISTRATOR C.T.A.): With will annexed; an administrator c.t.a. settles an estate pursuant to a will in which they are not appointed.

DE BONIS NON, ADMINISTRATOR (ADMINISTRATOR D.B.N.): Of goods not administered; an administrator d.b.n. settles a partially settled estate.

DE FACTO: In fact; in reality; actually. Existing in fact butnot officially approved or engendered.

DE JURE: By right; lawful. Describes a condition that is legitimate "as a matter of law," in contrast to the term "de facto," which connotes something existing in fact but not legally sanctioned or authorized. For example, de facto segregation refers to segregation brought about by housing patterns, etc., whereas de jure segregation refers to segregation created by law.

DE MINIMUS: Of minimal importance; insignificant; a trifle; not worth bothering about.

DE NOVO: Anew; a second time; afresh. A trial de novo is a new trial held at the appellate level as if the case originated there and the trial at a lower level had not taken place.

DICTA: Generally used as an abbreviated form of obiter dicta, a term describing those portions of a judicial opinion incidental or not necessary to resolution of the specific question before the court. Such nonessential statements and remarks are not considered to be binding precedent.

DUCES TECUM: Refers to a particular type of writ or subpoena requesting a party or organization to produce certain documents in their possession.

EN BANC: Full bench. Where a court sits with all justices present rather than the usual quorum.

EX PARTE: For one side or one party only. An ex parte proceeding is one undertaken for the benefit of only one party, without notice to, or an appearance by, an adverse party.

EX POST FACTO: After the fact. An ex post facto law is a law that retroactively changes the consequences of a prior act.

EX REL.: Abbreviated form of the term "ex relatione," meaning upon relation or information. When the state brings an action in which it has no interest against an individual at the instigation of one who has a private interest in the matter.

FORUM NON CONVENIENS: Inconvenient forum. Althougha court may have jurisdiction over the case, the action should be tried in a more conveniently located court, one to which parties and witnesses may more easily travel, for example.

GUARDIAN AD LITEM: A guardian appointed by the court to represent a minor or incompetent person in a legal action.

HABEAS CORPUS: You have the body. The modern writ of habeas corpus is a writ directing that a person (body) being detained (such as a prisoner) be brought before the court so that the legality of their detention can be judicially ascertained.

IN CAMERA: In private, in chambers. When a hearing is held before a judge in their chambers or when all spectators are excluded from the courtroom.

IN FORMA PAUPERIS: In the manner of a pauper. A party who proceeds in forma pauperis because of their poverty is one who is allowed to bring suit without liability for costs.

INFRA: Below, under. A word referring the reader to a later part of a book. (The opposite of supra.)

IN LOCO PARENTIS: In the place of a parent.

IN PARI DELICTO: Equally wrong; a court of equity will not grant requested relief to an applicant who is in pari delicto, or as much at fault in the transactions giving rise to the controversy as is the opponent of the applicant.

IN PARI MATERIA: On like subject matter or upon the same matter. Statutes relating to the same person or things are said to be in pari materia. It is a general rule of statutory construction that such statutes should be construed together, i.e., looked at as if they together constituted one law.

IN PERSONAM: Against the person. Jurisdiction over the person of an individual.

IN RE: In the matter of. Used to designate a proceeding involving an estate or other property.

IN REM: A term that signifies an action against the res, or thing. An action in rem is basically one that is taken directly against property, as distinguished from an action in personam, i.e., against the person.

INTER ALIA: Among other things. Used to show that the whole of a statement, pleading, list, statute, etc., has not been set forth in its entirety.

INTER PARTES: Between the parties. May refer to contracts, conveyances, or other transactions having legal significance.

INTER VIVOS: Between the living. An inter vivos gift is a gift made by a living grantor, as distinguished from bequests contained in a will, which pass upon the death of the testator.

IPSO FACTO: By the mere fact itself.

JUS: Law or the entire body of law.

LEX LOCI: The law of the place; the notion that the rights of parties to a legal proceeding are governed by the law of the place where those rights arose.

MALUM IN SE: Evil or wrong in and of itself; inherently wrong. This term describes an act that is wrong by its very nature, as opposed to one which would not be wrong but for the fact that there is a specific legal prohibition against it (malum prohibitum).

MALUM PROHIBITUM: Wrong because prohibited, butnot inherently evil. Used to describe something that is wrong because it is expressly forbidden by law but that is not in and of itself evil, e.g., speeding.

MANDAMUS: We command. A writ directing an official to take a certain action.

MENS REA: A guilty mind; a criminal intent. A term used to signify the mental state that accompanies a crime or other prohibited act. Some crimes require only a general mens rea (general intent to do the prohibited act), but others, like assault with intent to murder, require the existence of a specific mens rea.

MODUS OPERANDI: Method of operating; generally refers to the manner or style of a criminal in committing crimes, admissible in appropriate cases as evidence of the identity of a defendant.

NEXUS: A connection to.

NISI PRIUS: A court of first impression. A nisi prius court is one where issues of fact are tried before a judge or jury.

N.O.V. (NON OBSTANTE VEREDICTO): Notwithstanding the verdict. A judgment n.o.v. is a judgment given in favor of one party despite the fact that a verdict was returned in favor of the other party, the justification being that the verdict either had no reasonable support in fact or was contrary to law.

NUNC PRO TUNC: Now for then. This phrase refers to actions that may be taken and will then have full retroactive effect.

PENDENTE LITE: Pending the suit; pending litigation underway.

PER CAPITA: By head; beneficiaries of an estate, if they take in equal shares, take per capita.

PER CURIAM: By the court; signifies an opinion ostensibly written "by the whole court" and with no identified author.

PER SE: By itself, in itself; inherently.

PER STIRPES: By representation. Used primarily in the law of wills to describe the method of distribution where a person, generally because of death, is unable to take that which is left to them by the will of another, and therefore their heirs divide such property between them rather than take under the will individually.

PRIMA FACIE: On its face, at first sight. A prima facie case is one that is sufficient on its face, meaning that the evidence supporting it is adequate to establish the case until contradicted or overcome by other evidence.

PRO TANTO: For so much; as far as it goes. Often used in eminent domain cases when a property owner receives partial payment for their land without prejudice to their right to bring suit for the full amount they claim the land to be worth.

QUANTUM MERUIT: As much as one deserves. Refers to recovery based on the doctrine of unjust enrichment in those cases in which a party has rendered valuable services or furnished materials that were accepted and enjoyed by another under circumstances that would reasonably notify the recipient that the rendering party expected to be paid. In essence, the law implies a contract to pay the reasonable value of the services or materials furnished.

QUASI: Almost like; as if; nearly. This term is essentially used to signify that one subject or thing is almost analogous to another but that material differences between them do exist. For example, a quasi-criminal proceeding is one that is not strictly criminal but shares enough of the same characteristics to require some of the same safeguards (e.g., procedural due process must be followed in a parole hearing).

QUID PRO QUO: Something for something. In contract law, the consideration, something of value, passed between the parties to render the contract binding.

RES GESTAE: Things done. In evidence law, this principle justifies the admission of a statement that would otherwise be hearsay when it is made so closely to the event in question as to be said to be a part of it, or with such spontaneity as not to have the possibility of falsehood.

RES IPSA LOQUITUR: The thing speaks for itself. This doctrine gives rise to a rebuttable presumption of negligence when the instrumentality causing the injury was within the exclusive control of the defendant, and the injury was one that does not normally occur unless a person has been negligent.

RES JUDICATA: A matter adjudged. Doctrine which provides that once a court of competent jurisdiction has rendered a final judgment or decree on the merits, that judgment or decree is conclusive upon the parties to the case and prevents them from engaging in any other litigation on the points and issues determined therein.

RESPONDEAT SUPERIOR: Let the master reply. This doctrine holds the master liable for the wrongful acts of their servant (or the principal for their agent) in those cases in which the servant (or agent) was acting within the scope of the servant's authority at the time of the injury.

STARE DECISIS: To stand by or adhere to that which has been decided. The common law doctrine of stare decisis attempts to give security and certainty to the law by following the policy that once a principle of law as applicable to a certain set of facts has been set forth in a decision, it forms a precedent that will subsequently be followed, even though a different decision might be made were it the first time the question had arisen. Of course, stare decisis is not an inviolable principle and is departed from in instances where there is good cause (e.g., considerations of public policy led the Supreme Court to disregard prior decisions sanctioning segregation).

SUPRA: Above. A word referring a reader to an earlier part of a book. (The opposite of infra.)

ULTRA VIRES: Beyond the power. This phrase is most commonly used to refer to actions taken by a corporation that are beyond the power or legal authority of the corporation.

Addendum of French Derivatives

CHATTEL: Tangible personal property.

CY PRES: Doctrine permitting courts to apply trust funds to purposes not expressed in the trust but necessary to carry out the settlor's intent.

IN PAIS: Not pursuant to legal proceedings.

PER AUTRE VIE: For another's life; during another's life. In property law, an estate may be granted that will terminate upon the death of someone other than the grantee.

PROFIT A PRENDRE: A license to remove minerals or other produce from land.

VOIR DIRE: Process of questioning jurors as to their predispositions about the case or parties to a proceeding in order to identify those jurors displaying bias or prejudice.

www.ingramcontent.com/pod-product-compliance
Lightning Source LLC
LaVergne TN
LVHW082336200926
848481LV00012B/3363